中国内部控制研究中心

（辽宁省人文社会科学A类重点研究基地）

第3辑

会计与控制评论

刘永泽 主编

REVIEW OF ACCOUNTING AND CONTROL

Hiromitsu Takemi

Lessons from the Financial Crises: Corporate Governance and Inertia of Management

Toshifumi Takada

Expectations of Internal Control Reporting in Japan

田祥宇　王鹏　唐大鹏

我国行政事业单位内部控制制度特征研究

王满　姜慧琳

上市公司财务柔性对非效率投资影响的实证研究

李志斌

内部控制、股权集中度与投资者关系管理

东北财经大学出版社
Dongbei University of Finance & Economics Press
大连

图书在版编目（CIP）数据

会计与控制评论・第 3 辑 / 刘永泽主编 .—大连 ：东北财经大学出版社，2013. 11
ISBN 978-7-5654-1355-1

Ⅰ. 会… Ⅱ. 刘… Ⅲ. ①会计制度-研究 ②内部审计-研究 Ⅳ. ①F233 ②F239. 45

中国版本图书馆 CIP 数据核字（2013）第 248563 号

东北财经大学出版社出版
（大连市黑石礁尖山街 217 号 邮政编码 116025）
教学支持：（0411）84710309
营 销 部：（0411）84710711
总 编 室：（0411）84710523
网 址：http：//www. dufep. cn
读者信箱：dufep @ dufe. edu. cn

大连北方博信印刷包装有限公司印刷 东北财经大学出版社发行

幅面尺寸：180mm×255mm 字数：181 千字 印张：10 1/4 插页：1
2013 年 11 月第 1 版 2013 年 11 月第 1 次印刷

责任编辑：李 彬 王芃南 责任校对：王娟 孙萍 刘洋 毛杰
封面设计：张智波 版式设计：钟福建

ISBN 978-7-5654-1355-1
定价：30. 00 元

编委会

目　录

CONTENTS

Lessons from the Financial Crises: Corporate Governance and Inertia of Management

Hiromitsu Takemi

(Graduate School of Accounting & Finance Chiba University of Commerce Chiba Japan 272-8512)

Abstract This paper reviews the past two crises in 1997 and 2008, and tries to propose ideas for avoiding turbulence in the course of economic growth in the region.

Key Words Lessons Financial Crises Corporate Governance Inertia of Management

Introduction

Financial or economic crisis is nothing new, but it suddenly appears with a few people noticing it. Shunpei Takemori reminds us that history is a teacher for the rest of the people (Takemori, 2010). Stephen Green tells us that the effects of the financial crisis of 2008 on the world are almost comparable to or more significant to the Great Crash of 1929 (Green, 2010). Thanks to the lessons from 1929, the implemented policies by the governments seemed to be effective in preventing the global economic downward spiral.

Economic stimulus policies of Asian countries, especially of China, have been welcomed by the other countries. It is fortunate that China has reached the stage where the level of income and its corresponding population can absorb the surplus production capacity of the West. Harold James tells us that the U. S. economic miracle in the 2000 was based on the capital of the emerging Asian economies (James 2009). The tide has been reversed, the major source of global demand has apparently shifted from the West to the East since 2008, and the pattern is expected to last for a decade. Joseph E. Stiglitz tells us that developing countries were the driver of global economic growth in the early 1990s and crashed, except China, in 1997 (Stiglitz, 2010). The influx of external capital or their reliance on it to help their economic growth and, subsequently, overvalued currencies, enticed speculative transaction in their currency markets.

This paper reviews the past two crises in 1997 and 2008, and tries to propose ideas for avoiding turbulence in the course of economic growth in the region.

1997 crisis

There have been several international crises. In the fall of 1929, the flow of bond financing from the United States to Latin America suddenly stopped, and led to widespread defaults by Latin American sovereign borrowers. In August of 1982, Mexico was on the brink of a similar fate. This crisis was followed by a widespread withdrawal of credits from developing countries. It led to debt rescheduling, defaults, and renegotiation in a dozen debtor countries. Chile, Uruguay, and Argentina, following financial deregulation in the late 1970s, also experienced crises in the early 1980s. There have been, from time to time, dramatic reversals in lending to emerging countries: Mexico, Turkey, and Venezuela in 1994; Argentina in early 1995; and the East Asian countries in 1997. Common characteristics were sudden reversals in money flows (Radelet and Sachs, 1998).

Presenting the differences between the two crises, 1997 and 2008, are an appropriate approach to the first subject: assessing the impact of the global financial crises on Asian economies in general. The 1997 crisis was initiated by the influx of or reliance on external capital to keep economic growth and, subsequently, overvalued currency. It is known that there was a sudden and rapid liberalization of capital markets in tandem (Pang, 2000). Between 1990 and 1995, the stock markets of those five ASEAN countries, Singapore, Malaysia, Indonesia, Brunei and Thailand, increased their values from 40% of GDP to 120%, and the amount was almost comparable to 45% of the world's private capital. Portfolio investments in Indonesia, Korea, and Thailand were much larger than direct investments, by a factor of about two to one. Korea, Indonesia, Malaysia and Thailand, but not Singapore, also showed huge current account deficits, and few thought they could be managed. Their currencies had been stable mostly due to dollar pegging.

To reverse the trend in its current account deficit, the government raised interest rates to suppress domestic demand. The growing need to cover deficits was satisfied by short term cash, not by foreign direct investments or successfully suppressing domestic demand. There appeared economic recoveries in Latin American countries such as Mexico and Brazil. The direction of capital flows was changing its course from Asia, and capital inflows to Asia decreased from US $86 billion in 1995 to 2 billion in 1996. Besides, the confidence of foreign investors was gradually sagging due to their worries about the vulnerability of the regional economies. Most of the borrowed capital from abroad in the private sector had been known to be unhedged.

Deregulation of the markets and market-driven economy are the factors needed for a country to be integrated into global financial transactions. It is well known that the so-called impossible trinity, the combination of stable currency, autonomous monetary policy and deregulation of financial markets, is impossible to achieve. Inflows of external capital increase foreign reserve and, correspondingly, increase money supply, and usually lead to a downward pressure on currency. It is, in some cases, a politically unpopular move, because domestic consumers and investors want to buy cheaper foreign goods and services in terms of their currency. If a country chooses a stable currency and deregulated financial markets, it should abandon monetary policy. Fiscal policy is the remaining tool for controlling its economy. Observation of the continuous current account deficits in countries such as Korea, Indonesia, Malaysia and Thailand, shows that austerity measures in their fiscal policies could have been the factors not hampering the confidence of the markets.

On the other hand, substantial overvaluation of the currencies is not a plausible cause of the crisis (Chin, 2000). There remain some alternative mechanisms of the crisis. Chin showed that the Thai baht, the Malaysian ringgit, the Philippine peso, and the Hong Kong dollar were overvalued. The Singapore dollar, the Taiwan dollar, the Korean won, and the Indonesian rupiah were undervalued. Of the four overvalued currencies, three experienced the crash and of the four undervalued currencies, two faced the crash. This pattern suggests that overvaluation was not the only key to the understanding of the 1997 crisis. A new explanatory model without an exchange misalignment might be needed.

The panic of individual creditors may be understandable; each of them was trying to flee ahead of the others, even though the collective result was disastrous and the panic was unnecessary in the sense that the fundamentals could have supported a much more favorable outcome. It might mean that international financial markets are highly unstable; or to put it another way, the 1997 crisis was as much a potent crisis of Western capitalism as of Asian capitalism (Radelet and Sachs, 1998). Each of the five crisis economies had initiated, not completed, financial sector liberalization. The partial reform increased the fragility of the financial system, characterized by an increase in short term foreign borrowing, a rapid increase in bank lending, and a lack of proper regulation of financial institutions. These weaknesses left these economies vulnerable to a rapid reversal of money flows.

There are two schools of thought with regard to currency crises. One is to put more emphasis on economic fundamentals and the Russian crisis can be explained by this. The other is to emphasize the investors' expectations, and the phenomena usually observed is a combination of fragility in the domestic banking sector and an unstable currency market. It can explain the Asian crisis; negative change of expectation among investors led to exacerbated economic fundamentals. If expectation is a major factor, it will be extremely difficult to predict and a special policy response is needed.

The impact of the global financial crisis 2008 on Asian economies

The export-oriented growth model, which had begun with Japan and the newly industrialized economies, migrated to several Southeast Asian economies, and was finally adopted by the People's Republic of China, has been severely challenged by the downturn in Western demand (Dittmer, 2010). Although all of these economies were adversely affected, the region did better than most of the others. The champion was China, with a large stimulus package and attaining nearly 9% growth.

Historic dependency of the region to drive economic growth through trade is a channel of the global crisis. Those countries such as Malaysia, Singapore and Thailand are more vulnerable. Singapore, for example, showed the steepest decline of GDP, negative almost 10% from year over year in the first quarter of 2009. Indonesia and the Philippines, with less dependence on external demand, suffered less than their richer neighbors (Green, 2010). Imports of the export-driven economies in Southeast Asia adjusted faster than exports, limiting the inertia of domestic demands. This link between imports and exports shows the fact that the trade in Southeast Asia has increasingly been in processing industries. Imports are for re-exporting. Synchronization between imports and exports is a factor having little impact on the balance of payment, foreign reserves and exchange rates. By August 2008, however, all Asian currencies were depreciating and the trend was steepened in the wake of the global trade crisis. The period of the trend lasted generally until April 2009. Five currencies were stabilized and started to rebound. This rebound reflects how different the impacts of the crises of 1997 and 2008 are. The non-financial corporate sector has escaped the kind of widespread insolvency seen in 1997 and 1998, partly because they have stronger balance sheets and most countries were in good shape economically. An additional factor was the continued growth of property markets; this mitigated the negative effect on consumption.

Central banks in the region acted in an almost concerted fashion to reduce key policy rates. This helped stiffen the resolve of the region's counterparts to move to an easing monetary policy. Actions were not confined to reducing policy rates. Singapore focused on exchange rate stabilization and shifted its attention from inflation to decline in demand. Although regional banks were well connected to global capital markets, they had few bad assets linked to sub prime loans. This helped protect regional financial systems and was a cushion to lead to a smooth recovery. Overall, these actions and the condition ended the year-long slide in the stock markets.

Contrary to the concerted fashion in the monetary sector, fiscal policies have accomplished little to tackle the economic downturn. The lack of bold use of fiscal policies is puzzling. David J. Green pointed out the reasons (Green, 2010):

- Large infrastructure projects are simply not a good way to quickly add to aggregate demand.
- Spending can be bogged down in political infighting or hampered by bureaucratic procedures.
- Transferring funds to poor people can support spending on domestic goods and services, but programs must effectively target the right people.
- Spending must be financed in a fiscally sustainable fashion.

The last reason is related to experience. Spending by the central government can easily lead to a lack of fiscal discipline for years. The situation of the recent recovery from 1997 was the opposite; fiscal conservatism was pursued and considered successful. It reinforced the confidence that fiscal prudence is the way out of the crisis.

Current account and exchange rate

Two troubling features of the ongoing economy are the depressing world trade and the revival of global payment imbalances. The IMF estimates that the volume of international trade in 2010 will be 7% to 8% below that of 2008, while most countries, including industrial nations, are seeking to boost their current accounts. The world accumulated current account surpluses; accordingly, deficits must be in balance and would increase by almost 1 trillion dollars between 2009 and 2012. Export-led growth by major economies, China, Germany, Japan, and the United States, can be presented as a threat to the world economy (Ocampo, 2010). It implies that their currencies must be appreciated. It is also the case for emerging countries with current account surpluses, where disorderly appreciation would do more harm than good. In the case of China, disorderly appreciation will disrupt its export industries and will generate adverse effects on its trading partners in Asia. Rapid and disorderly appreciation of the Japanese yen has been, and is, a factor for a long term economic malaise. Past crises have also given a lesson to emerging countries of the importance of self insurance through reserve accumulation.

Currency appreciation has already taken place with massive capital inflows in emerging countries such as Brazil, and it is said to be excessive. Countries experiencing rapid appreciation can distort the upward pressure by foreign currency accumulation, such as dollar reserves. These reserves usually recycle to U. S. treasuries, and those returns are much lower than the returns required by inflowing private capital. Those countries bear the cost, not the benefit. It is very perplexing that appreciation due to free movements of capital and balancing out the current account for the sake of cost avoidance may create problems. They are, in the short term, slower economic growth, possible asset bubbles and domestic financial crisis.

Japanese corporations in the periods

With respect to the crises from the perspective of private companies, agility of management is an integral part of the survival and fitness. In the case of Japanese large corporations, they had implemented business diversification, globalization, and spinning off their operations into separate corporations in 90s (Aoki, 2009). Entropy index, an index for business diversification, was increased from 0.75 in FY 1991 to 0.89 in FY2001. There were many examples of globalization. Toyota, for example, had increased its proportion of oversea sales from 57.0% in FY 1997 to 71.4% in FY 2007. Of the top 200 large asset size companies, the number of consolidated corporations, on average, had increased from 44 in FY 1990 to 108 in FY 2005. It concurrently increased the operation costs due to information asymmetry. A solution for the problem was the delegation of authority to each business unit. It also led to requiring the strengthening of the governance for their discipline. There are two ways to enforce discipline; one is external governance and the other is internal governance. The former is enforced by equity holders and lenders. Equity holders have the liberty to hold or dispense their shares and it is called market for control, i. e., M&A. The latter is implemented by the members of the board and related stakeholders, including employees. The members of the board are appointed by major equity and/or stakeholders, and they are delegated to control the incentive of managers.

There have been significant changes in both the external and internal governance. Well-managed corporations shifted their source of funds from indirect finance, bank lending, to direct finance, equity-related issues such as CBs, in the late 80s bubble period. This trend was further propelled by the elimination of cross share holdings between banks and corporations. The banks faced a pyramid of bad debts and could no longer bear the risk of equities. Contrary to these phenomena, the proportion of foreign and institutional investors increased and the corporations were exposed to market pressure. In case of the 200 large corporations, the proportion of cross share holdings were decreased from 14.1% in FY 1991 to 7.5% in FY2005, and that of the institutional investors increased from 13.1% to 36.7% in the same period. Concerning internal governance, execution and control function of management were separated, including the introduction of outside board members and new incentive schemes, such as stock option plan, for the managers. The number of board members of corporations, on average, was dramatically decreased from 27.4 in FY 1991 to 12.2 in FY 2005, a move to make possible swift and pro-risk decision makings, e. g. concentration of the scope of the business.

Lins and Servaes (1999) showed the evidence of diversification discount for the value of Japanese corporations. Aoki (2008) also showed that high probability of business concentration was found in high performance corporations. It suggests that the performance of corporations is related to their positive responses to so-called selection and concentration. It raises the question why not to respond by the low performance corporations that essentially require more positive responses to this norm. Both activists and main banks influenced positively on the strategic decision makings, i. e. rational selection and swift concentration. It is especially true in the case of corporations which have highly competitive and high growth business segments. It suggests that besides incentive schemes, monitoring function by pro-active stakeholders is essential for the efficient use of business resources, such as capital.

Inertia of management

Common characteristics of the crisis were sudden reversals in money flows, and currency overvaluation was not the only key to the understanding of the 1997 crisis. If expectation is a key factor for the 2008 crisis, it will be extremely difficult to predict. A sure thing was that the continued growth of the property markets mitigated the negative effect on consumption in the latest crisis. These words, such as sudden and expectation, are used to imply that events are uncontrollable, and require private corporations to do considerable tasks to keep themselves afloat. Recent literatures of Econophysics have suggested that Pareto distribution, power law, appeared more commonly than Gaussian distribution, normal distribution, in many instances, such as price distribution of financial products (Pellicer-Lostao and Ropez-Ruis, 2010). If long tail phenomena are common in the economic transaction, major concern of governance should fall on pro-revolution, not mere evolution, attitude of management.

Pro-revolution attitude of management is typically required in case of restructuring of operations. Selection and concentration process, more specific, needs rigorous efforts to persuade stakeholders, except equity holders and the main bank. Barrier of exit is considered to be the major problem (Sakakibara, 2009, 2010). The barrier enhances the inertia of an organization and causes it to lose the momentum of change. There were several examples, such as Japan Airlines, Daiei, etc. They were finally overwhelmed by the lost time and were forced to accept severe restructurings in a limited time period, accompanied by painful layoffs.

Management tends to try to avoid the exit and to keep the status quo. There are several factors for management to hamper the exit incentive. They are as follows: the amount of severance pay, decrease in both sales and income in the short term, vague possession of expecting results, and repercussion from society as a whole, etc. These factors can be divided into internal and external ones. Examples of internal factors are cognition bias between management and middle and front line employees, and profit supplement for the other business segments. There is no conspicuous difference in cognition between them under normal business conditions, but at times when change is needed, it becomes apparent. Profit supplement for rooted operations gives, from time to time, good excuses for keeping money losers. Examples of external factors are assets peculiarity and the difficulties of their liquidation, and outside stakeholders. The latter is known as the theory of resource dependency (Pfeffer and Salancik, 1978). The stakes seem to be the nexus of business resource interdependencies, and the exit intention of the management faces outside resistance.

Getting rid of success experience and/or getting rid of old practices are hard for the excellent heads of management, who are Mr. T Suzuki of Seven & I Holdings, and Mr. T Yanai of First Retailing. It means that invalid cognition and following false value judgment should be replaced. It needs constant management practices to prepare for the perpetual paradigm change. To secure the process, corporate governance needs outside talents, such as consultants and outside board members. It also needs to promote information sharing among all stakeholders, and to create objective and transparent exit criteria, and to promote steady PDCA cycles, which enhance the constant changes of business structure and contents. Having outside talents widens the scope of informative sphere. Information sharing shortens the time to create the exit consensus among stakeholders. PDCA cycles in operations are like an experiment in a laboratory. Having criteria eliminates the exit hesitancy and is the most important measure, because it can tell the exit timing, i. e. eliminate inertia.

Concluding remarks

Consideration of the two crises' factors and of the recent literatures on long tail phenomena shows that the level of uncertainty in business has been increasing and can be expected to continue increasing. If it is necessary to prepare for uncertain events in a cost conscious manner, agile management is one of the answers. Proof of the agility can be shown in the exit of operations, because organization commonly tends to want to keep the status quo. Corporate governance has many facets, and they relate to each stockholder's interests. While their interests are varied, it is indispensable to keep the going-concern status of a corporation. Management inertia looks like an old rechargeable battery. A PC owner, stakeholder, notices that the time span of recharging gets shorter; he or she does not want to be bothered by changing it to a new one. An unexpected blackout occurs, and he or she will realize that there is not much remaining charge of electricity. To avoid this kind of situation in business, there should be a consensus on criteria through information sharing among stakeholders, and strict compliance with the criteria. Corporate governance should be concerned with creating proper incentives for these conducts and put more emphasis on constant monitoring to prevent management inertia.

References

[1]AOKI H. Restructuring of Business Portfolio and Corporate Governance [M]//Frontier Analysis of Corporate Governance, Nippon Hyoronsha Co. , Ltd. , 2008.

[2]AOKI H. Trend of Business Diversification of Japanese Corporations [J]. The Journal of Chiba University of Commerce, 2009, 46(4).

[3]AOKI H, MIYAJIMA, H. Governance on Business Structure of Japanese Corporations [J]. Discussion Paper, 2010, 10(57).

[4] CHIN M D. Three Measures of East Asian currency overvaluation [J]. Contemporary Economic Policy, 2000, 18(2).

[5]CLOUD D. Scientific Capitalism [OL]. http://www. project-syndicate. org/commentary/dcloud1/English, 2009.

[6]DITTMER L. Asia in 2009[J]. Asian Survey, 2010, 50(1).

[7]FILARDO A. Short-term Policy Responses to the International Financial Crisis and Risks to Sustainable Medium-term Policy Frameworks in Asia: Complications arising from enduring Global Imbalances[G]. EBER Working Paper Series,2009,59.

[8]GREEN,DAVID J. Southeast Asia's Policy Response to the Global Economic Crisis [EB]. ASEAN Economic Bulletin,2010,April.

[9]GREEN,STEPHEN K. Study on Diversity of Economic Activities in Asian Pacific region and Possible Solutions for Cooperation: Summary and Policy Recommendation[J]. Chiba University Economics Research,2010,24(1).

[10]JAMES H. The Great Depression analogy [OL]. http://www.project-syndicate.org/commentaryjames27/English,2010.

[11]KOHAMA,H. Global Economic Crisis and the future of Capitalism[J]. Discussion paper at the Japan Society of International Economics,2009.

[12]LINS K, SERVAES H. International Evidence on the Value of Corporate Diversification [J]. Journal of Finance,1999,45(6).

[13]OCAMPO J A. Exchange Rate Disorder [OL]. http://www.project-syndicate.org/commentary/ocampo6/English,2010.

[14]PANG E S. The Financial Crisis of 1997-1998 and the end of Asian developmental state [J]. Contemporary Southeast Asia,2000,22(3).

[15]PARK D,SHIN K. Savings,Investment,and Current Account Surplus in Developing Asia [G]. ADB Economics Working Paper Series,2009,158.

[16]PFEFFER J, SALANCIK G R. The external control of Organizations: A resource Dependence Perspective[M]. Stanford University Press,1978.

[17]RADELET S, SACHS J D. The East Asian Financial Crisis: Diagnosis, Remedies, Prospects[G]. Brookings Papers on Economic Activity,1998.

[18]SAKAKIBARA K. Research on Creative Exit[G]. Chuo University Graduate School Year Book,2009.

[19]SAKAKIBARA K. Creative Adaptation in case of Exit of Businesses [G]. Corporate Research Paper,2010,16.

[20]SHIRAI S. Global Financial Crisis and Economic Policy over G20 Financial Summit [OL]. MPRA Paper,2009.

[21]STIGLITZ, JOSEPH E. Freefall, Japanese translation [M]. Tokyo: Tokuma shoten Publishing Co,Ltd,2010.

[22]TAKEMORI,SHUNPEI. Central Banks fight: whether they save capitalism[M]. Tokyo: Nikkei Publishing Co,Ltd,2010.

[23]ZACHMANN G. Meltdowns and Fallouts [OL]. http://www.project-syndicate.org/commentary/zachmann1/English,2011.

金融危机的教训：公司治理与管理惯性

武见浩充

（千叶商科大学会计与财务研究院　日本千叶　272-8512）

摘　要　本文回顾了1997年和2008年发生的两次金融危机，并提出了避免发生经济波动的几点建议。

关键词　教训　金融危机　公司治理　管理惯性

Expectations of Internal Control Reporting in Japan

Toshifumi Takada

(Accounting School Tohoku University Sendai Japan 980-8576)

Abstract Based on comparing the Internal Control Reporting in Japan with similar reporting in other countries, this paper does a field study on the expectations of Internal Control Reporting by questionnaires and then empirically studies the reaction of the Tokyo Stock Exchange to the pre-legislation stage of the preparation for Internal Control Reporting.

Key Words Expectation Internal Control Reporting Questionnaires

I OBJECTIVES AND BACKGROUND

The objectives of this research are as follows.

Comparison of Internal Control Reporting in Japan with similar reporting in other countries. Internal Control Reporting in Japan started April 1, 2008. Our research is focused on the conditions before 2008.

Field study on the expectations of Internal Control Reporting by questionnaires. This was done by two methods; one was done by mail to audit firms and the other was done at seminars on internal control completed by the seminar attendees.

Empirical research on the reaction of the Tokyo Stock Exchange to the pre-legislation stage of the preparation for Internal Control Reporting. We tried to observe the change of capital cost.

After the well known Enron scandal, Internal Control Reporting and its audits was initiated in the United States based on the Sarbanes Oxley Act (SOX). Other countries, like Japan, China, and Korea have introduced and started similar systems—Korea since 2007 and China having finished preparations. Since 2001 Japan has experienced many financial reporting scandals such as Yamaichi and Kanebo, so the Financial Services Agency of the Japanese government decided to introduce

Internal Control Reporting. According to the manifests of the standards of Internal Control Reporting, the objectives of the system are (1) to strengthen internal controls of listed companies and to improve their financial structures, and (2) to strengthen the transparency of listed companies through audits of Internal Control Reports. Based on these conditions, we decided to do this research project.

Internal Control Reporting systems should report the construction of the necessary internal controls to secure the reliability of financial reporting by management and to audit the report by using an independent auditor. Before this system, Audit Standards in Japan required a check of the internal controls in the financial audit. This requirement was introduced as a risk based auditing procedure since 1991. Research on audit risk and risk based auditing has been done; for example, Takada (2002) and Takada (2003). Internal Control Reporting in Japan is a much more powerful procedure than before. In the United States we can find many research articles on SOX, for example in 2007 alone Zang (2007) on the effects of internal control audits on the market; Engel et al. (2007) on the effects of the post legislation of the system on hot issues; Ashbaugh-Skaife (2007) on field research of the pre-legislation stage of internal controls; and Doile et al. (2007) on field research of internal control auditors reports. In the present study we report on field and empirical research on the pre-legislation stage of Internal Control Reporting and its Auditing in Japan.

Ⅱ METHODS AND LIMITATIONS

Our research is divided into three parts. The first part is a comparison of Internal Control Reporting in major countries. The second part is field research of the pre-legislative stage of Internal Control Reporting in Japan. The third part is empirical research on the effects of preparations by listed companies on the market.

PART 1: COMPARATIVE STUDY

We compared Internal Control Reporting in major countries. We did this by comparing Internal Control Standards and related legal structures of each country. Some countries have already started the systems and others have finished the preparations for initiating the system. We can identify the characteristics of the Japanese system through this study. Ashbaugh-Skaife (2007) did a similar study.

PART 2: FIELD RESEARCH

Internal Control Standards is a guideline for listed companies to construct their internal controls. The Standards prescribe four objectives and six components of internal controls, but there are many variations of pragmatic internal controls in companies. Some of the listed companies that have prepared the installation of internal controls complied with the requirements of the Standards before 2008. Some of the listed companies are very sensitive to the preparations because the Internal Control Reports are to be audited by CPA firms. The field study at the pre-legislative stage is meaningful because some listed companies have already installed the required systems. In addition to this, we can select several independent variables in the empirical research by this field study.

We did the field study by using questionnaires. As the Privacy Security Act prohibits disclosing the directories of public organizations, it was impossible for us to use the directories. Instead, we asked people at several academic conferences to complete the form of questions on Internal Control Reporting. The Japanese Institute of Certified Public Accountants (JICPA) helped us to send and collect the questionnaires to CPAs and CPA firms.

PART 3: EMPIRICAL RESEARCH

Several listed companies prepared for Internal Control Reporting as mentioned above. They have installed internal controls in compliance with the requirements of the Internal Control Standards. They invested lots of resources for the installations of internal controls. The market knew the invested amounts of money through their financial statements. On the other hand, some listed companies did not prepare for it. The objective of our empirical research is to confirm the effects of preparation for Internal Control Reporting on the market. We used capital costs as a dependent variable and several independent variables based on the field study and prior research papers.

Ⅲ COMPARATIVE STUDY

1. JAPAN

The Financial Services Agency of the Japanese government (FSA) decided to introduce Internal Control Reporting in 2008 following the United States'

SOX. According to the Internal Control Standards, the Japanese system has the following unique points:

Focus on financial reporting.

Indirect auditor's reporting.

Audits of all listed companies.

The FSA has initiated the revision and relaxing of the standards for the small and medium companies since 2010. They finished the due process to revise the standards and you can download the revised standards soon from the website of the FSA.

2. KOREA

Internal Control Reporting in Korea began in December, 2003,, prescribed by the External Audit Acts Article 2 – 2. The Korean government has expanded the number of participating companies gradually. At first, it was voluntary disclosure. Large listed companies were required to report after January, 2006, the listed medium and small companies and large private companies after January, 2007, and the medium and small companies after January, 2008.

Internal Control Standards were prescribed in 2005 and the Review of Internal Control Reports by CPAs was initiated in 2005. The characteristics of the Review are the following:

Direct reporting.

Review of the all the components of internal controls.

3. CHINA

The Chinese government prescribed Internal Control Standards in June, 2008. Listed companies have to disclose Internal Control Reports, but auditing of the reports is not compulsory. Three guidelines—Evaluation Guideline, Practice Guideline and Audit Guideline—have been disclosed.

4. UNITED STATES

The United States began Internal Control Reporting by the enactment of SOX in 2002. The first reporting started after November 15, 2004 for about 20% of listed companies, totaling 3 651. It has been expanded gradually and all listed companies were required to report after November 15, 2007. However, Internal Control Audits have been exempted for small listed companies (the total value of the company's outstanding stocks is under US $75 million).

The characteristics of Internal Control Reporting and its Audits in the United States are as follows:

The Report of the Committee of Sponsoring Organization of the Treadway Commission (COSO Report) is used as a conceptual framework.

The SEC prescribes rules for the evaluation of internal controls by management.

The Public Company Accounting Oversight Board (PCAOB) prescribes Audit Standards on Internal Control Reports.

Direct reporting.

5. CANADA

Canadian Securities Administrators (CSA) disclosed an exposure draft (MI 52-111) on Internal Controls on Financial Reporting. Because of discussions of heavy costs of Internal Control Reporting in the United States, they withdrew the proposals by MI 52-313.

At present, the Canadian government requires directors of listed companies to declare the effectiveness of internal controls in quarterly and annual reports. This requirement is similar to that of the confirmation letter used in Japan. Audit or review of the declaration is not necessary.

6. FRANCE

France introduced the Internal Control Reporting system by enactment of the Financial Security Act of 2003, Article 117. According to the law, both public and private companies are required to disclose the reports after January 1, 2003, but the clause was revised and only public (listed) companies needed to submit the reports after July, 2005.

The characteristics of the Internal Control Reporting of France are the following:

In addition to the Report of the Committee of Sponsoring Organization of the Treadway Commission (COSO Report), the internal control framework designed by the Association of Corporations is used as a conceptual framework.

Management evaluation of internal controls guidelines was disclosed by the French government in December, 2006.

Internal Control Reports cover all the components and they are reported at the annual meeting of a company by the president of the board of directors.

The main contents of the report are explanations of internal controls. Therefore, the related law does not include any sanctions or penalties on the companies.

CPAs are required to review the reports.

Independent auditors are needed to make a clear observation report on whether or not the Internal Control Report reflects the state of the internal controls of a company or has misleading content.

7. ENGLAND

The Combined Code D. 2. 1, revised in July, 2003, prescribed Internal Control Reporting. Internal Control Standards in England were disclosed as Turnbull Guidance of 1999 (revised in 2005). Directors of listed companies have been required to disclose compliance with the Turnbull Guidance since 1999. Auditors of

Financial Statements must report any irregularities of the internal controls.

In England, discussions on whether or not the UK should introduce Internal Control Reporting like SOX were done in the Parliament when the United States enacted SOX and started the Internal Control Reporting and its Review, but officials decided that they would not introduce such a system. The main reason was that they already had Turnbull Guidance, which covered a much wider coverage of internal controls than the COSO framework. In addition to this, such a new reporting system might have become a heavy burden of costs for listed companies.

8. GERMANY

The revised Commercial Acts Article 289-5 in March, 2009 prescribed Internal Control Reporting after January, 2010. This article requires directors to explain Internal Control Report on accounting processes, but it does not require the evaluation of the effectiveness of internal controls.

The Stock Acts Article 92 - 2 requires independent auditors to report their judgments on the compliance of directors with legal requirements on the risk managements of the company and the effectiveness of monitoring functions by the directors.

9. EU

The European Commission with the authority to prescribe economic systems within the European Union disclosed a discussion paper on Internal Control and Risk Management in March, 2005. Based on comments letters submitted to the paper, the Commission expressed conclusions on Internal Control Reporting in May, 2006. The decision reached was not to introduce a system like SOX Article 404 into the EU, and that as the Turnbull Guidance and COSO framework were applicable to companies in the EU, it was not necessary for them to have new internal control standards.

As they admitted the necessity of a legal requirement for listed companies in the EU to accord with effective internal controls, each member country initiated preparation for constructing legal structures for internal controls. The discussion paper stimulated the actions in France and Germany.

SUMMARY

The followings are our observations.

Internal Control Reporting is required in the following countries:

Japan, Korea, England, Canada, France, China and Germany.

Audits of reporting is required by the United States and Japan.

Review of reporting is required by Korea, England and France.

Internal Control Reporting and its Audit in Japan is complete and thorough for listed companies. The Japanese system is very visible from the viewpoint of other countries. SOX Article 404 is not a de facto standard of Internal Control Reporting. The international trend of the discussion is that countries prefer total legitimacy of companies' activities—that is, corporate governance, risk management and internal control. It is significant for us to do research on the effects of Internal Control Reporting in Japan on the market. Based on the results of the research, we can reconsider the necessity of such a rigorous system.

Ⅳ FIELD STUDY BASED ON QUESTIONNAIRES

1. RESPONDENTS AND METHOD

The field study was done for two respondents groups: personnel in companies and audit firms. These were done by using questionnaires.

The two times of study for personnel in companies were done at seminars on Internal Control Reporting on March and April, 2009. We collected 116 replies, half of these from personnel at big companies with annual sales over 100 billion yen.

The study for audit firms was done by emails from April to May, 2009. We collected 27 replies out of 164 firms, see Table 1.

TABLE 1 DESCRIPTIVE STATISTICS OF RESPONDENTS

Group 1 Personnel of Companies

Industry	Finance	Construction	Retailing	Wholesale	Service	Manufacturing	Others	Total
Number	13	11	6	9	9	49	19	116

Group 2 Audit Firms

Client Size	1-10	Over 10	Total
Number	17	10	27

2. QUESTIONS AND THE SUMMARY OF REPLIES

The following Table 2-Table 6 and comments are main questions and the summary of replies.

(1) Strengthen Management

TABLE 2 STRENGTHEN MANAGEMENT

	Positive	Negative	Unknown
Group 1	74.1%	15.2%	10.7%
Group 2	74.1%	7.4%	18.5%
	(90.0%)		(10.0%)

The numbers with parentheses are replies from big audit firms with over 10 clients.

(2) Contents of Strengthened Management

TABLE 3 CONTENTS OF STRENGTHENED MANAGEMENT

	Group 1	Group 2
Job Flow Management	85. 5%	63. 0% (80. 0%)
New Organization of IC	56. 6%	40. 7% (70. 0%)
Strengthen Internal Audit	56. 6%	33. 3% (60. 0%)
Documentation	42. 2%	48. 1% (90. 0%)
Financial Reporting	36. 1%	48. 1% (80. 0%)
Compliance	34. 9%	22. 2% (40. 0%)

(3) Strengthen Subsidiary Companies Management

TABLE 4 STRENGTHEN SUBSIDIARY COMPANIES MANAGEMENT

	Positive	Negative	Unknown
Group 1	46. 2%	24. 8%	13. 7%
Group 2	51. 5%	37. 0%	18. 5%

(4) Costs and Procedural Issues

About 40% of Group 1 replied that a hundred million yen was used for Internal Control Reporting preparations. Companies with annual sales over 100 billion yen replied that over a hundred million yen was used for preparations. Many companies identified the following procedural issues:

Increase of Audit Fee	76. 5%
Increase of Documents	67. 3%
Increase of Management Costs	43. 9%
Increase of Authorization Procedure	41. 8%

(5) Problems and Issues to Solve

TABLE 5 PROBLEMS

	Group 1	Group 2
Execution of the Schedule	61. 9%	70. 4% (100. 0%)
Time Consuming for RCM	71. 4%	66. 7% (90. 0%)
Internal Audit Knowledge	39. 7%	51. 9% (80. 0%)

TABLE 6 ISSUES TO BE SOLVED

	Group 1	Group 2
Strengthen Internal Audit	45.7%	48.1% (70.0%)
IT Controls	44.8%	18.5% (30.0%)
Subsidiary Companies' IC	37.1%	44.4% (40.0%)
Organization of IC Department	35.2%	51.9% (60.0%)
IC for Job Flow	32.4%	7.4% (10.0%)
Understanding of Top	31.4%	25.9% (30.0%)
IC for Financial Reporting	23.8%	33.3% (40.0%)

V EMPIRICAL RESEARCH

1. OBJECTIVE

We did empirical research. The objective of our research here is to identify the effects on capital costs of investment in preparations for Internal Control Reporting by listed companies. Some listed companies spent large sums for consulting services for installment of internal controls that satisfy the requirements of Internal Control Standards. The cost for consulting services was listed in the financial statements. Our research objective is to identify relationships between capital costs and consulting costs.

2. PRIOR RESEARCH

Lambert et al. (2007) gave us an important idea. Their objective was to identify the effects of the level of accounting information quality on the cash flows of companies. They divided the effects into two: direct and indirect. Direct effect means cash flow distributions. Their conclusion was that high quality accounting information did not have a direct effect on present cash flow distribution, but it did have a direct effect on the value of the companies and future cash flow distribution. According to their theoretical model, we can infer that high quality accounting information has effect on capital costs. If capital costs of a company are affected by low quality accounting information, improving accounting information quality will bring benefit to the company. That means that investment in internal controls is beneficial to the company.

Ogneva et al. (2007) demonstrated that material weakness of internal controls did not have statistically significant effect on capital costs. However, Ashbaugh-Skaife et al. (2009) demonstrated the opposite conclusion; that is, they indicated that material weakness had effect on the increase of capital costs. This complete opposite conclusion might have been caused by the method of the difference of the capital cost calculation. For example, the Ogneva et al. method might have had some kind of bias on the calculation of capital costs.

We used a regression model based on Ashbaugh-Skaife (2009). They used data on material weakness of internal controls, whereas we used consulting costs as one of the independent variables. As a result, our research focused on the pre-legislative stage of Internal Control Reporting.

3. RESEARCH DESIGN

Hypothesis

The hypothesis is that consulting services for the installment of internal controls has an effect on lowering capital costs of a company.

Efficient internal controls for financial reporting generate high quality accounting information. According to Lambert et al. (2007), high quality accounting information had an effect on capital costs. As investors prefer companies with high quality accounting information, the capital costs of such companies become lower. The above hypothesis implies this logical inference.

Sample Selection

The sample selection standards are as follows. The period of sample was 2007 and 2008.

Companies issuing new equity stocks during 2007 and 2008.

Accounting period: April 1 to March 31. Consolidated Financial Statements.

Companies without Bank, Stock, Insurance and other Financial Companies.

Data from Nikkei Needs Financial Quest database.

Sample companies numbered 1 051 in 2007 and 627 in 2008, totaling 1 678. The number of companies that disclosed consulting service costs for internal controls were 288. 1 390 companies did not disclose the costs.

Model

The regression model is as follows:

$$C_0F_{i,t} = \alpha_{i,t} + \beta_1 AIID_{i,t} + \beta_2 Ch\_Sales_{i,t} + \beta_3 Establish_{i,t} + \beta_4 Inventory_{i,t} + \beta_5 Receivables_{i,t} + \beta_6 Leverage_{i,t} + \beta_7 Loss_{i,t} + \beta_8 M\&A_{i,t} + \beta_9 ROA_{i,t} + \beta_{10} TSE_{i,t} + \beta_{11} IC_{i,t} + \varepsilon$$

The definitions of variables are as follows:

CoE as capital costs calculated by the method of Easton [2004].

AUD as big 4 (Azusa, Arata, Shinnihon, Tohmatsu) as 1, others as 0.

Ch_ Sales as an average variable rate of the change rates of sales amount in the past five years.

Establish as a square root of the years after the establishment of a company.

Inventory as an average of the percentages of the inventory to the total assets in the past three years.

Receivables as an average of the percentage of the receivables to the total assets in the past three years.

Leverage as the total liabilities divided by the total assets.

Loss as the company with loss as 1, others as 0.

M&A as the company with M&A as 1, others as 0.

ROA as the profit divided by the total assets.

TSE as the listed companies on the Tokyo Stock Exchange I as 1, others as 0.

IC as companies that disclosed consulting costs for internal controls as 1, others 0.

Table 7 shows the descriptive statistics.

TABLE 7 DESCRIPTIVE STATISTICS OF VARIABLES

Variable	Average	Standard Deviation	Q1	Q2	Q3	Q4
CoE	0.214	0.280	0.011	0.121	0.185	0.251
AUD	0.584	0.493				
Ch_Sales	1.815	17.085	-0.297	-0.055	0.113	0.532
Establish	7.239	1.548	2.000	6.245	7.616	8.062
Inventory	0.101	0.101	0.000	0.039	0.078	0.124
Receivables	0.227	0.151	0.000	0.116	0.217	0.315
Leverage	0.481	0.198	0.043	0.320	0.491	0.635
Loss	0.017	0.129				
M&A	0.006	0.075				
ROA	0.075	0.062	-0.096	0.035	0.059	0.099
TSE	0.618	0.486				
IC	0.086	0.279				

4. RESULTS

The results of regression analysis are as follows:

The independent variables that are statistically significant are Establish, Inventory, Receivables, Leverage and ROA.

IC is not statistically significant but it had a general tendency to decrease capital costs in 2007.

Disclosure of consulting costs for internal controls might not have been known to investors.

Table 8 shows the results of regression analysis.

TABLE 8 RESULTS OF REGRESSION ANALYSIS

Panel A 2007 Sample = 1 051			Panel B 2008 Sample = 627		
Variable	Coefficient	t-value	Variable	Coefficient	t-value
Constant	0. 392	6. 962 ***	Constant	0. 104	2. 633 **
AUD	0. 006	0. 355	AUD	0. 001	0. 122
Ch_Sales	0. 000	−1. 319	Ch_Sales	−0. 109	−1. 680
Establish	−0. 021	−3. 454 ***	Establish	0. 000	0. 074
Inventory	−0. 093	−1. 042	Inventory	0. 134	2. 073 *
Receivables	−0. 021	−2. 096 *	Receivables	0. 065	1. 640
Leverage	0. 097	2. 012 *	Leverage	0. 061	1. 904
Loss	−0. 040	−0. 607	Loss	−0. 031	−0. 628
M&A	−0. 006	−0. 057	M&A	−0. 008	−0. 176
ROA	−0. 224	−1. 464	ROA	0. 424	3. 982 ***
TSE	−0. 032	0. 075	TSE	−0. 018	−1. 481
IC	−0. 028	−0. 926	IC	0. 019	1. 577

Significance level: *** 0. 1% , ** 1% , * 5%.

Ⅵ CONCLUSION AND IMPLICATIONS

The hypothesis that consulting services for internal controls had effects on capital costs was not supported. Precisely, the null hypothesis was not rejected because t-values of the partial regression coefficient were −0. 926 in the sample of 2007 and 1 577 in the sample of 2008. Two t-values were not significant at 0. 1% , 1% and 5% levels respectively.

Based on this conclusion, we posit three implications:

We have to continue the empirical research. Prior empirical research demonstrated that high quality accounting information had effects on future cash flow (See Lambert et al. (2007)) . Internal Control Reporting has just begun in Japan. As we did the research in a very short span of years (2007 and 2008), future cash flow might not yet have been realized.

We did not use the data on the material weakness of internal controls because we could get the data for only two years (2008 and 2009) when we wrote this paper. Empirical research using material weakness data has become popular in the

United States. Disclosure of material weakness may have effects on capital costs and cash flow in the market. We need to expand our research to include material weakness.

Internal Control Reporting in Japan is most rigorous and complete among major countries. Good internal controls on financial reporting bring high quality accounting information. If high quality accounting information has effects on future cash flow (capital costs) in the market, it is beneficial for listed companies to invest resources in internal controls. There are many variations in Internal Control Reporting among countries as revealed in the comparative study we did in Chapter 2. We need to do research on the comparative study of international investments in the stock markets.

Based on field study, we observed that although there were many issues to be solved for listed companies, they expected that Internal Control Reporting would have effects on strengthening the management controls over the companies and subsidiaries.

The contributions of this paper to research in accountancy are as follows:

The Japanese government has invested heavily in legal structures such as Internal Control Reporting in accounting and auditing. This paper concentrated on the cost benefit analysis. Although we could not support the hypothesis, we contributed to the research in accountancy in that we offered many research opportunities.

Field studies using questionnaires has been becoming more and more difficult to do because of the Privacy Security Act. We did the field study by sending emails to auditing firms as they disclosed e-mail addresses on their websites. One of the contributions of this paper was that it demonstrated the methodology of the field study. Some researchers suggested that we could not do the field study using questionnaires, but we could.

Personnel in listed companies and audit firms have strong interest in the pragmatic aspects of Internal Control Reporting, whereas researchers and educators are more interested in the theoretical foundations of internal controls. This research contributed to bridging between professionals or business people and academicians. For example, the team members of this research consists of university professors and CPAs.

References

[1] ASHBAUGH-SKAIFE, COLLINS H D, KINNEY W. The Discovery and reporting of internal control deficiencies prior to SOX—mandated audits? [J]. The Journal of Accounting and Economics, 2009, 44 (9): 166-192.

[2] ASHBAUGH-SKAIFE, COLLINS H D, KINNEY W. The Effect of SOX Internal Control Deficiencies on Firm Risk and Cost of Equity[J]. The Journal of Accounting Research, 2009, 47(3): 1-43.

[3] EASTON P. PE Ratios, PEG Ratios, and Estimating the Implied Expected Rate of Return on Equity Capital[J]. The Accounting Review, 2004, 79(1): 73-96.

[4] LAMBERT, LEUZ R C, VERRECCHIA R. Accounting information, disclosure, and the cost of capital[J]. The Journal of Accounting Research, 2007, 45: 385-420.

[5] OGNEVA, SUBRAMANYAM, RAGHUNANDAN. Internal Control Weakness and Cost of Equity: Evidence from SOX Section 404 Disclosures[J]. The Accounting Review, 2007, 82(10): 1255-1298.

[6] TAKADAT. Departure From the Past - Risk Based Auditing and Strengthening Internal Controls[J]. *The Keiri Jouhou*, 2002, 978: 12-14.

[7] TAKADAT. Quality of Auditing Standards[J]. The Kaikei, 2003, 6(163): 1-13.

[8] U. S. Securities and Exchange Commission. Internal Control Over Financial Reporting in Exchange Act Periodic Reports of Non-Accelerated Filers Agency.

[9] Zhang. Economic consequences of the Sarbanes-Oxley Act of 2002[J]. The Journal of Accounting and Economics, 2007, 44(9): 74-115.

[10] The Business Accounting Council, Financial Service Agency, the Japanese Government. On the Setting of the Standards and Practice Standards for Management Assessment and Audit concerning Internal Control over Financial Reporting (Council Opinions)[OL], http://www.fsa.go.jp/singi/singi_kigyou/tosin/20070215.pdf, 2007.

[11] http://www.fsa.go.jp/en/news/2007/20070420.html.

[12] The Business Accounting Council, Financial Service Agency, the Japanese Government. On the Setting of the Revised Standards and Practice Standards for Management Assessment and Audit concerning Internal Control Over Financial Reporting (Council Opinions)[OL], http://www.fsa.go.jp/singi/singi_kigyou/tosin/20110330/01.pdf, 2011.

日本内部控制报告的发展前景

高田敏文

（东北大学　日本仙台　980-8576）

摘　要　本文在比较日本与其他国家和地区内部控制报告的基础上，通过问卷调查实地研究了内部控制的发展前景，并实地检验了东京股票交易所对编制内部控制报告立法前期的反映。

关键词　前景　内部控制报告　调查问卷

我国行政事业单位内部控制制度特征研究

田祥宇[1]　王鹏[2]　唐大鹏[3]

（1. 山西财经大学会计学院　030006；2. 财政部会计司　100820；
3. 东北财经大学会计学院　116025）

摘　要　为了全面贯彻和落实党的十八大会议精神和要求，建立廉洁高效的行政事业单位内部控制体系，财政部于2012年11月发布了《行政事业单位内部控制规范（试行）》，并在2014年1月1日全面执行。各级行政事业单位如何建立和实施内部控制已经成为刻不容缓的重要任务，也从客观上强调了行政事业单位内部控制相关理论探讨的重要性。本文正是在这种背景下，针对行政事业单位内部控制的中国特色、行政事业单位内部控制的管理特质和行政事业单位内部控制与监督的关系特点等问题，拓展相关问题的内涵和外延，丰富了行政事业单位内部控制的理论基础，有助于行政事业单位全面实施内部控制过程中统一思想和认识。

关键词　行政事业单位　内部控制　中国特色　管理特质　监督特点

2012年11月，财政部发布了《行政事业单位内部控制规范（试行）》（以下简称《规范》），于2013年7月19日财政部组织召开“行政事业单位内部控制规范实施动员视频会”，要求全国行政事业单位从2014年1月1日起正式执行。《规范》的全面实施不但有利于推动廉洁高效、人民满意的服务型政府的建设，还有利于提高行政事业单位内部管理水平，更有利于推进财政规范化、科学化、信息化管理。习近平总书记强调，要加强对权力运行的制约和监督，把权力关进制度的笼子里，形成不敢腐的惩戒机制，不能腐的防范机制，不易腐的保障机制。行政事业单位内部控制在权力制衡方面主要能够起到制度笼子的作用，减少自由裁量权的空间和余地，用制度来限制权力的滥用。

一、行政事业单位内部控制的中国特色

《规范》的出台是根据我国国情和行政事业单位内部控制的成功经验，源自于基层实践经验的总结和提炼，并上升为顶层制度设计，构建了具有中国特色的行政事业单位内部控制标准。相对于堪称“世界政府内部控制模板”且国际影响广泛的美国《联邦政府内部控制准则》，本文主要从基本概念、控制目标、控制范围、控制标准、评价监督和实施机制等六方面对我国行政事业单位内部控制的中国特色进行分析。

（一）基本概念

根据美国《联邦政府内部控制准则》的规定，内部控制是持续的且与业务运行融为一体的业务组成部分，受人的影响，并提供合理保证，而不是绝对保证。内部控制是一个组织用来实现其任务、目的和目标的计划、方法和程序，并且处于保护资产，预防和发现错误、舞弊、浪费、滥用、管理不善的第一线。我国行政事业单位内部控制方面具有非常悠久的历史，早在西周时期，政府就开始建立相关职位对社会生产情况进行监督和控制。现阶段，作为政府提高管理水平、保证经济活动和合法合规、防范舞弊和腐败的主要手段，行政事业单位内部控制的出发点是行政事业单位“经济活动的风险”，也就是通过对单位层面与业务层面实施风险评估，系统分析经济活动风险，确定风险点，选择风险应对策略。行政事业单位进行防范和管控的主要手段是“制定制度、实施措施和执行程序”。从静态上来说，行政事业单位的内部控制体现为与行政、管理、财务和会计系统融为一体的组织管理结构、政策、程序和措施；从动态上说，内部控制是行政事业单位为履行职能、实现总体目标及应对风险的自我约束和规范的过程，使行政事业单位日常管理达到“规范化”、“科学化”和“信息化”。《规范》所称内部控制是指单位为实现控制目标，通过制定制度、实施措施和执行程序，对经济活动的风险进行防范和管控。

不难看出，联邦政府内部控制更加强调内部控制是从政府审计角度提供合理保证，以实现组织目标。相对于联邦政府内部控制，我国行政事业单位内部控制的概念总结是以提升内部管理水平，加强廉政风险防控机制建设为目标，立足于单位内部管理实际情况，重点突出了控制目标、控制制度和控制程序三大方面，既包括静态目标和制度、也包括动态控制措施，从单位具体的经济活动入手，以风险为导向，设计防范和管控措施，带有明显的中国行政事业单位的组织特色。

（二）控制目标

修订后的 OMB 通告 A-123 指出，内部控制是组织管理的一个组成部分，它为下列目标的实现提供合理的保证，其目标是保证运营的效率与效果，财务报告的可靠性和遵循有关的法律法规。《规范》规定单位内部控制的目标主要包括：合理保证单位经济活动合法合规、资产安全和使用有效、财务信息真实完整，有效防范舞弊和预防腐败，提高公共服务的效率和效果。应该说，美国联邦政府内部控制目标与 COSO 内部控制目标从形式上看没有明显区别，延续了运营目标、报告目标和合规目标，在目标解释上也没有就联邦政府部门的具体特点进行分解和细化。

我国行政事业单位内部控制目标则完全建立在我国国情和单位实践的基础

上，从公共部门使用财政资金的角度出发，从业务同质化角度对美国联邦政府内部控制目标进行分析，强调了行政事业单位必须从国际上公共部门无差异业务特点出发，保证经济活动必须遵守相关法律法规和单位财务信息真实完整。同时，《规范》充分结合我国行政事业单位的特点，从公共部门行政职能角度出发，更加关注内部控制提高公共服务的效率和效果，保证单位国有资产的安全和使用有效，要求单位在开展各项业务过程中有效防范舞弊和预防腐败，真正实现单位对公共资源、公共资金和国有资产分配和使用环节的公平、公开和公正。

（三）控制范围

我国行政事业单位内部控制的控制范围创新主要包括控制主体范围创新和控制客体范围的创新两大方面。

从控制主体范围来说，美国联邦政府内部控制要求管理层负责机构内部控制建设工作，控制主体范围包括联邦政府系统内所有使用公共资金的公共部门，但是并不包括政党、社团的社会组织。我国《规范》具有鲜明的实施特色，即党政机关联合实施，将承担政府职能的所有行政事业单位都包含在内，并主要由行政单位和事业单位两大类组成。行政单位即行政机关，指国家政权机构中的行政机关，是一个国家政权体系中依法享有行政权力的组织体系，不但包括国务院、省、市和县级的各级政府下辖的相关行政机关，还包括各级党的机关、人大机关、政协机关、审判机关、检察机关、各民主党派机关和团的机关等各种使用公共资金的行政类机构。事业单位是我国特有的一种公共组织类型，指国家为了社会公益目的，由国家机关举办或者其他组织利用国有资产举办的，从事教育、科技、文化、卫生等活动的社会服务组织。事业单位不具有社会生产职能和国家管理职能，不以盈利为主要目的，是为上层建筑和经济基础及人民生活服务的社会组织和机构。因此，我国行政事业单位内部控制主体和美国联保政府内部控制主体在范围和职能上都有着不同程度的差异。从范围上来看，政府作为国家权力的代表和执行机关，不但在纵向上包括不同行政级次的各级政府，还包括各级政府体系中的全部职能部门，更多意义上是宏观上的“大政府”概念。行政事业单位作为政府职能的责任单位和实施单位，承担各级政府下达的各项行政任务和社会职能。《规范》所指的事业单位与政府行政部门的最大区别则在于其不具有行政管理的职能，只是在特定情况下接受国家的委托，作为行政事业单位内部控制主体的重要组成部分。从职能上来看，政府内部控制主体基本在宏观政府概念上作为内部控制活动的承担主体，从财政预算的角度对各级政府进行政策规制和财政预算等宏观层次上的权力制衡和约束，而行政事业单位更加强调从单位个体出发，将每个单位作为内部控制主体，从单位内部预算角度对单位各个职能部门权力进行约束。

从控制客体的范围来说，美国联邦政府内部控制更多强调财务报告内部控制，将控制客体定位于保证财务报告真实完整的财务类经济活动。《规范》的适用对象为行政事业单位管理职能范围内的全部经济活动，将财务报告内部控制融入单位经济活动中，通过预算、收支、采购、资产、工程项目与合同业务管理实现对单位全部经济活动的管控要求。从理论上说，行政事业单位内部控制的对象应该为单位的全部活动，不仅仅是经济活动，还包括对审批权、职权等事权的控制，但考虑到我国现状，现阶段我国行政事业单位内部控制的控制范围不宜界定为全部活动，而应界定为经济活动即财权，随着内部控制思想概念和理念在行政事业单位领导和人员之间的广泛认可和接受，再逐步扩大范围。

（四）控制标准

美国联邦政府为了实现内部控制的三个目标，管理层要负责建立并维护满足下列标准的内部控制活动，其类同于 COSO 的内部控制 5 要素，即控制环境、风险评估、控制活动、信息与沟通、监督。第一，控制环境是管理层和雇员为了维持组织层面对有效的内部控制的支持而创造的组织结构和文化，要求组织清晰地界定权力和责任领域，建立适当的报告层级，支持恰当的人力资本政策，以及理解在组织内部维持有效的内部控制的重要性。第二，风险评估要求管理层应当识别可能妨碍组织实现其目标的内外部风险。在识别风险时，管理层应当考虑组织内部和外部之间的相互作用。应当分析被识别的风险，判断其对机构的潜在影响。第三，控制活动包括为了实现机构目标而设置的政策、程序和机制；第四，信息与沟通要求将信息相关、可靠、及时的传递给组织内各个层次的有关员工，并要注意与组织外部进行沟通，无论是提供信息还是接受信息。第五，监督是针对内部控制的效果，并发生在正常的运营过程中，而且定期评价应当成为管理层对内部控制进行持续监督的一部分，并且应当嵌入机构的运营当中。从控制标准的总体要求来看，我国《规范》并没有沿用这种控制标准分类，而是在对风险评估与控制活动内容总结和提炼的基础上，创新性地提出了单位层级和业务层级两大类内部控制体系，最后提出评价和监督机制。

我国《规范》是完全以行政事业单位实际情况为基础，并没有照搬《美国联邦政府内部控制准则》关于 COSO 五要素模式的复制应用。首先，《规范》对风险评估和控制活动在行政事业单位的具体应用进行本土化设计，在风险评估环节提出了单位层级和业务层级的分离评估，并在控制活动中加入预算控制、归口控制、单据控制、内部信息公开等有中国行政事业单位特色的控制方法；其次，《规范》并没有延续五要素的传统分类，摆脱了理论界对五要素逻辑关系的诟病和质疑，针对我国行政事业单位组织和业务特点，对控制标准进行梳理与整合，建立单位层级和业务层级内部控制体系；最后，《规范》按照制衡思想和三权分离机制，建立了与行政事业单位内部控制相对独立的评价与监督体系。我国行政事业单位内部控制在控制标准上的创新是建立在对单位情况深入调研、细致分析、精细归纳的基础上的，符合单位组织和业务的应用情况，具有很强的针对性和适应性。

（五）评价监督

《美国联邦政府内部控制准则》要求机构管理者应当持续地监督和改进与其项目和活动相关联的内部控制的有效性，这种持续的监督以及其他的定期评估，应当为机构负责人每年评估和报告内部控制（如FMFIA所要求的）提供基础。机构管理层应当确定支持这种评估所需要的恰当层次的文件记录，特别是应当记录高层管理评估团队对机构财务报告内部控制的理解以及财务报告内部控制的评估过程。机构负责人在对内部控制进行评估时可以运用各种来源的信息，在评估和监督控制方面承担主要责任，并且应当运用其他的来源补充而非替代其自身的判断。我国《规范》要求单位建立内部监督制度，规定相关内部监督程序和要求，建立检查和自我评价机制，设置内部审计部门和岗位，识别内部控制存在的问题并提出改进建议。单位应对内部控制的有效性出具自我评价报告。各级财政部门和审计部门要对单位内部控制建立和实施情况进行监督。

通过两者的比较，不难发现联邦政府内部控制的评价和监督更多采用程序、交易或应用层面来评估财务内部控制，以此对内部控制进行测试并评估其遵循性以支持管理层的声明，最后就财务报告内部控制设计和运作作出一个综合性的结论。而我国行政事业单位内部控制突破传统会计控制的局限，将评价和监督的范围扩大到单位的组织与业务层面，应用执行、决策和监督职责分离的控制思想，设计独立于内部控制体系的内部监督机制，针对我国政府监督的体制和组织结构，设置外部监督的责任部门和工作机制。

（六）实施机制

在美国联邦政府内部控制体系中，各部所设的部门审计机构称监察长办公室，其负责人为监察长，并由部长提名总统任命，定期向部长、总统和国会提交工作报告，是内部控制的建设与实施过程中的核心部门和岗位，负责协调内部控制实施中的相关事宜，也直接决定了内部控制能否真正建立和高效运行。

我国建立当前政治体制下的行政事业单位内部控制体系，格外需要外部推动力量，建立有中国特色的实施机制。行政事业单位内部控制要求对单位的监督实行内外结合，在内部实行内审和党内纪检监察监督，在外部实施立法监督、政府监督和社会监督，既要维护立法机构和行政部门的职能和权力，又要保持党和政府的行政方向和管理效率，由党将全国人民代表大会和政府部门衔接起来，并通过内部控制设计和实施，实现我国行政事业单位决策、执行和监督的三权分立机制创新，探索出一条符合我国国情、特色和民族文化的内向型国家治理路径。针对外部的强制要求，行政事业单位需要对各部门、机构和岗位按照不相容职位分离和授权审批原则进行组织层级内部控制架构的设计，并通过业务流程一体化将各部门、机构和岗位链接在业务层级内部控制体系中，构建组织层级的主体空间维度、业务层级的逻辑时间维度和单位具体人员参与的三维协同体系，最后通过信息化手段实现制度、组织、业务和人员在内部控制体系中的角色固化。可以说，行政事业单位内部控制是对公共权力主体在资源分配过程中的制衡型政治体制的重大协同创新，同时，其也是一个循序渐进提高政府治理水平的过程（刘玉廷、王宏，2008）。

二、行政事业单位内部控制的管理特质

企业内部控制无论从制度设计还是具体标准都领先于政府部门内部控制，并成为政府内部控制的示范对象。张庆龙、聂兴凯（2011）认为政府部门内部控制对于企业内部控制框架的借鉴也是非常明显的，并且表现出企业内部控制建设先行，政府部门内部控制适时跟进、合理吸纳的基本特征。同时，两者在管理体制和单位属性上有本质区别，有学者认为“企业是赚钱的单位，行政事业单位是花钱的单位”。本文主要从运营目标、管理核心、预算管理、绩效评价、法律约束和风险应对等方面分析行政事业单位内部控制的管理特质。

（一）运营目标要求保证公共服务的效率和效果

行政事业单位内部控制和企业内部控制的运营目标截然不同。行政事业单位运营目标是保证公共服务的效率和效果，其职能履行是实现社会公共服务目标的动态过程，并需要雇佣必要的公职人员，占有并支配一定数量的资源和物质资料，不但与企业单位、家庭个人共同构成市场经济主体，还是宏观市场环境中最大的单一产权单位主体，财政资金收支也逐步扩展到经济领域，如政府对特殊企业单位的财政补贴，政府对社保基金等民生项目的保障和政府对国有企业的直接管理等。行政事业单位虽然也有在政府职能正常运转的前提下降低运营成本的客观要求，其运营目标核心还是向社会公众提供非营利性的产品和服务。因此，行政事业单位与企业单位内部控制在运营目标上的根本区别不是提供服务或产品是否有偿，而在于有偿收益的动机是公共服务还是盈利服务。一般来说，企业单位的持续发展完全依赖于运营目标能否实现，即盈利情况是否达到预期，要求企业决策运营过程必须关注市场因素即顾客需求。而行政事业单位内部控制更加关注社会公共服务的效率和效果而不是盈利方面。这是由于行政事业单位作为公共部门，其业务活动主要以实现社会效益为目的而不是经营效益最大化。可以说，行政事业单位是通过公共服务效率的高低来评价其业务活动的绩效，强调公共服务的覆盖面和满意度，注意平等地对待公共服务

对象以及其他相关利益主体，制订科学合理的资金分配方案，有效地实现财权与事权的匹配，并发挥预算管理的引导和监督作用，提高公共服务的效率和效果。

（二）预算管理是行政事业单位内部控制的法律依据

行政事业单位内部控制和企业内部控制在预算管理方面的明显差异主要体现在预算管理的社会功能和内部功能两个方面。一方面，从社会功能角度出发，企业内部控制中的预算管理范围仅限于单位内部的经济资源优化效果，而行政事业单位预算管理虽然目前针对单位内部预算管理，但是未来将逐步扩展到通过公共财政手段实现全社会资源优化配置，降低整个市场交易费用。而且行政事业单位在社会资源稀缺情况下的分配体系会影响诸多相关集团和个人的利益，甚至可能降低社会资源配置效率。其预算管理则以节约社会资源并加快资源运转速度为出发点，通过社会资源分配的三个阶段，即事前计划的科学化分析、事中计划的执行性监督和事后计划的完成性评价，实现社会资源高效分配。另一方面，从预算管理的内部功能角度出发，其仅仅被企业作为内部财务管理工具。而预算管理相关内容已经在行政事业单位管理体制中形成相对应的法律基础，并成为国家法律法规和政策体系中的重要组成部分。预算管理作为行政事业单位加强收支的计划性的主要手段，应当作为单位内部控制的核心业务，发挥在以预算管理为主线、以财政财务收支管理为核心的行政事业单位内部控制体系中的主导作用。从预算管理的不同阶段考虑，行政事业单位应在全部经济活动实施前通过科学、充分和及时的前期论证形成预算草案，实施中成为全部经济活动和收支项目的参照和标杆，实施后则转变为预算绩效、行政效能和经济责任审计的依据和标准。

（三）绩效评价注重提高行政事业单位行政效能

根据委托代理理论，代理方契约履行情况的考量主要可以通过绩效评价来实现。企业单位绩效评估强调经济效益，形成效率型内部控制。而行政事业单位绩效评估不但要关注单位预算完成情况绩效评价，还要重视社会效益，形成效能型内部控制。具体来说，企业之所以建立效率型内部控制是由于企业内部控制体系要求以实现企业价值最大化作为运营目标，并主要体现在单位资产运营效率方面，以投入和产出的比例作为绩效评价的主要依据，即经营效率型内部控制。而行政事业单位由于其公共属性，内部控制目标也主要体现在社会公共服务和产品提供方面，在考虑投入产出比的基础上重点强调公共财政财务收支的社会功能，因此形成了行政事业单位的行政效能型内部控制。虽然理论界尚未对行政效能型内部控制形成体系完整的概念框架，但是已经形成较为稳定的理论，其内涵主要是为了在行政主体实施行政行为的过程中，保证以较小的行政资源投入来实现最佳的行政工作目标，达到资源配置的最优状态所实施的控制活动。具体而言，行政效能型内部控制质量的高低主要反映了公共部门向公众提供服务的水平和能力，它包括数量、质量、效果、影响、能力、公众满意度等多方面的要求。与企业经营效率型内部控制相比，行政事业单位行政效能型内部控制不仅仅关注投入和产出的比例，更加注重产品和服务的质量，更加强调行政管理行为的功能和效果，要建立单位内部控制对行政效能的长效约束机制。可以说，行政效能型内部控制积极响应了十八大以来我国政府管理体制改革对行政事业单位提高行政效能的政策要求，变效率至上为质量至上，从绩效达标型转向服务能力型，促进单位服务公共产品和服务职能的全面优化。

（四）法律约束限定行政事业单位内部权力的行使

由于行政事业单位和企业单位的不同性质，法律约束在内部控制体系中的表现形式差异很大，主要体现在法律约束环境对单位内部权力行使的制约程度上，其合规性内部控制特色十分显著。治理结构和管理体系如何设置、经营活动决策和执行等内部权力如何行使都要得到企业所有者的认可，其合法合规具有明显内部规制性。行政事业单位外部行为和内部权力行为都受到相关法律制度的严格约束，任何权力行使都具有强烈的外部规制的特点。具体来说，从法律的外部监管和内部控制的限制因素考虑，尽管企业内部控制体系要求经营活动必须在法律的约束条件下进行，但是企业是按照市场机制的要求去管理，只要顾客愿意购买，它就会大量地生产以求最大限度地获利，所以经济气候是企业合规合法程度的主要影响因素。法律约束无法完全实现企业内部控制目标，而仅仅作为一个保证持续经营的前提条件和外部制约因素，企业内部权力往往也是根据经营业绩的考虑进行分配和行使。而行政事业单位内部控制目标则要求单位无论外部职能还是内部权力的行使都必须受制于相关法律法规，如我国的《预算法》和《政府采购法》等。由国家立法机构和行政机构对行政事业单位的社会职能、管理权限、组织形式、治理结构、业务范围、活动方式和法律责任等方面以条文形式明确予以规定，并要求单位必须在法律规定的程序和范围内严格遵照和执行单位外部和内部权力的分配和行使。同时，行政事业单位内部控制的合规目标也导致组织机构和管理人员一般对国家法律和政治环境异常敏感。机构和人员的行政管理直接受国家法律、法规和政策的约束，甚至被外界认定为一种非市场经济行为，而仅仅当成一项政治任务。所以，行政事业单位内部控制的合规合法目标就是对单位行政职能的一种法律约束和政治限制，其相对于企业的突出特点就是保障单位运营合规合法以降低行政风险，因此更倾向于合规性内部控制。

（五）风险应对实现将风险控制在可承诺的范围内

风险应对是指在风险识别和评估之后确定决策主体运营存在的各种风险，并在分析风险概率及风险影响程度的基础上，根据风险性质和决策主体对风险的承受能力制订回避、承受、降低或者分担风险等相应的防范计划。因此，组织制定风险应对策略主要考虑四个方面的因素：可规避性、可转移性、可缓解性、可接受性。由于企业的盈利属性，只有较少的风险投资类企业为了追求高收益而接受风险，而正常情况下接受高风险的企业几乎是不存在的，一旦其发现风险无法降低和分担，往往会采用风险规避手段迅速退出该领域。根据行政事业单位的属性和业务特点，本文认为其风险应对采用无选择承担、有选择降低和无条件规避的三种策略。这是由于行政事业单位从事的工作，是对国家、对人民有承诺的，要将风险控制在可承诺的范围内，既不能从事超出可承诺风险范围的业务活动，也要杜绝低级错误。相对于企业内部控制，行政事业单位所面对的风险更为复杂和多样，同时大多数风险必须采取风险部分甚至全部承受的应对方案。例如我国社会保险基金运营体系中包括偿付能力风险和投资风险，由于历史转制成本形成的隐性负债，偿付能力不足的情况在未来很长时间内已经成为既定事实，尽管社保基金偿付不足部分绝对数金额巨大，政府不可能拒绝履行社会责任和放弃承担，而必须由政府财政无条件接受（刘永泽，唐大鹏，2012）。另一方面，在我国社保基金结余资金保有量依然庞大和CPI指数居高不下的条情况下，基金管理者要想实现保值增值就必须承担一定的投资风险，应对社会保险结余资金进行多元化投资，只要投资风险小于通货膨胀风险，那么投资就是可行甚至必须的。因此，行政事业单位要通过制衡机制、流程再造和信息化手段在日常管理中的运用，对单位业务管理活动的市场风险、操作风险、法律风险、声誉风险等进行事前的防范、事中的控制、事后的监督和纠正，及时堵塞制度漏洞、消除管理隐患，不给极个别的违法违规违纪人员以可乘之机。

（六）监督机制更强调内外监督主体的协同机制

由于企业与其利益相关者具有直接的经济关系，内部控制实施和建立的监督机制主要来源于企业股东、债权人和其他外部利益相关者等方面。出于对股东和债权人提出的管理目标和自身报酬的考虑，管理层也有动力实施内部控制，降低企业的经营风险，提高盈利能力。尽管企业外部监管部门会对内部控制提出相关要求，但是更为强烈的内部控制实施的监督动力来自于企业治理结构，还包括财务报告披露等外部监督机制的压力。而行政事业单位是以满足公共利益为目标，以追求社会公平和效率之间的均衡为价值取向。针对我国行政事业单位属性及使用公共资金的特点，资金支出有很强的财政资金管理特点，单位与所支配的资金和资产没有直接的权属关系，相关部门和领导缺乏内部控制设计和实施的监督动力，也没有积极性向利益相关者进行信息列报，且单位支出方向和重点一般是由政府职能规划而不是由单位本身来决定的，单位只是遵照预算执行，所以单位缺乏积极性监督内部控制的建立和实施。

三、行政事业单位内部控制与监督的关系特点

根据我国当前的实践情况，监督机制的不断完善将解决单位内部控制建立过程中很多实际问题。监督机制是对现场或某一特定环节、过程进行监视、督促和管理，使其结果能达到预定目标的保障制度体系。监督机制作为内部控制制衡原则的具体表现，体现在行政事业单位组织层级和业务层级内部控制中的全架构和全流程中。为了提高我国行政事业单位内部控制建立和实施效率，保证内部控制运行的有效性，单位应不断强化监督机制的制度保障功能。王美文（2011）认为公共权力的监督制衡机制都是一个二元结构模式，即外部社会监督制衡机制和内部政府系统部分间的监督制衡机制。鉴于监督对于行政事业单位内部控制的积极影响，本文从两者之间的关系特点出发，按照监督职能实施主体和范围的差异，从内部监督和外部监督两个角度阐述监督机制在行政事业单位内部控制运行过程中的实践意义、监督主体、监督客体和监督实施机制等问题。

（一）内部监督应当与内部控制的建立和实施保持相对独立

行政事业单位内部监督机制的建立具有自身的特点和重要的现实意义。内部监督与内部控制的关系正如《规范》所述，即内部监督应当与内部控制的建立和实施保持相对独立。这是行政事业单位内部控制与企业内部控制的重要区别之一，也是由于二者在单位属性和运营目标的不同造成的。党的十七大报告就已经提出建立健全决策权、执行权、监督权既相互制约又相互协调的权力结构和运行机制。这是在探索权力制约和监督机制方面的重要经验和实践成果的总结，也是对权力结构和运行机制认识的进一步深化，更是对行政事业单位内部监督机制的建立提供了方向和思路，要求内部监督必须与内部控制保持相对独立，以保障内部监督的效率和效果。同时，行政事业单位内部监督机制建设一方面可以完善权力结构并规范权力运行，防止权力滥用且从源头上防治腐败，通过加强单位内部监督可以建立制度化的权力分配和制衡机制，对权力进行约束，适当分解决策权和执行权的集中度可以促进不同性质权力之间互相制约、互相协调，形成决策科学、执行高效、监督有力的权力结构。另一方面，加强行政事业单位内部监督机制建设将促进行政事业单位组织层级体系的完善，把对权力的科学配置、组织机构建设与有效的内部监督机制结合起来。

行政事业单位内部监督机制是建立在三权分立思想的基础上的。陈国权，谷志军（2012）认为决策、执行与监督三分的内在逻辑依次是三事分工、三职分定、三责分置、三权分立，最终实现权力机构优化和运行机制完善。一般来说，行政事业单位职责是站在机构岗位个体视角定位自身在组织机构和业务流程环节中的权力和责任，而职能大多是从机构部门集体视角定位自身权力和

责任的统一。按照三权分立原则，行政事业单位决策、执行和监督之间并不是包含与被包含的关系，而是相互独立、相互制约的关系，不能按照企业内部控制体系将监督职能完全融入决策和执行机制中，通过单位机构部门职能的履行，保障单位内部监督的独立性和工作效率效果（如图1所示）。根据社会人理性假设，单位内部监督环境下的决策和执行活动比缺乏内部监督环境下更加科学和透明。内部监督机制是建立和实施行政事业单位内部控制的保障，其主要功能是保障单位内部控制、财务信息以及业务运行管理的科学、高效、有序和规范。秦荣生（2007）认为内部审计通过测量、评估、报告内部控制系统各个要素的有效性，向管理层提供服务。内部控制的监督可以包括组织层级和业务层级两部分，并通过财务信息和管理信息两种载体实现，重点对单位内部控制的有效性作出评价和判断，合理估计单位运营目标得以实现的保证程度。内部监督机制既可以通过财务信息监督单位业务的真实情况，也可以通过内部控制信息监督单位业务的合规情况，还可以通过管理信息监督单位业务的效率情况。

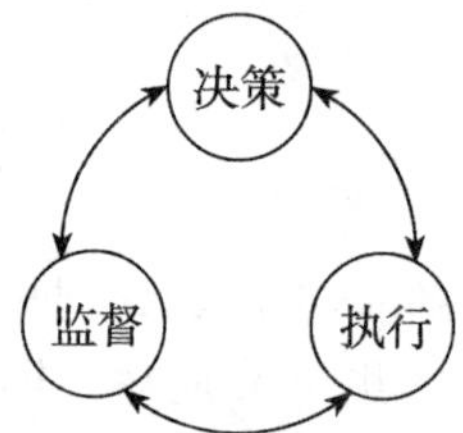

图1　决策权、执行权和监督权三者关系图

行政事业单位内部监督机制源自于西方发达国家的经验总结。早在20世纪70年代中期以后，西方发达国家为了提高行政效率、改进政府服务质量、发展政府责任和提高政府绩效，推行了新公共管理运动（即行政改革），其中一项非常重要的措施就是把内部监督机制从决策权与执行权中分离出来，设置机构、人员和资金属性都完全独立于决策机构和执行机构的监督部门，体现政府内部控制针对权力制衡的核心思想。在领域性质上，这种内部监督划分及其关系不涉及政治领域，也不涉及政治与行政之间关系领域，而只是涉及行政领域内部。西方新公共管理运动的成功经验也证明，在我国行政事业单位内部建立健全决策、执行、监督既相互制约又相互协调的权力结构和运行机制，只能依靠深化行政体制改革、提高监督角色地位和明确监督责任才能得以实现。第一，内部监督功能的实现必须依靠行政事业单位大部门制改革和行政职能优化，打破旧有部门和机构设置，科学划分决策权、执行权、监督权的机构归属，尤其是对监督权职能进行划分与配置，构建行政事业单位组织层级内部控制的监督机制。第二，内部监督功能的实现必须以科学的权力结构体系为基础，明确决策权和执行权在组织层级与业务层级各个业务阶段的表现形式，设定权力监督体系的监督对象范围和内容，并将监督权通过国家法律和单位内部制度的形式确立下来。第三，内部监督功能的实现必须建立健全单位各内设部门和下属单位之间权力运行的协同机制，明确各个业务中不同部门的监督职能，划分不同业务流程的监督环节和节点，并通过监督机制制度化对单位决策和执行过程承担规制责任。

行政事业单位内部监督机制需要明确监督主体的职责分工。根据我国行政事业单位管理体制，单位内部监督主要在领导总体监督的基础上，将内部监督职能分为业务监督和干部监督两个方面，分别由单位内部审计部门和纪检监察部门组织具体实施。第一，单位一把手应突出内部监督的核心领导地位，不但要负责设计内部监督总体规划，在内部监督过程中也要对监督工作进行实时指导，还要对内部审计结果进行审核和确认，最后严格按照结果执行干部奖惩制度。第二，内部审计部门作为单位经济业务内部监督的具体牵头部门，负责具体组织实施预算绩效审计和经济责任审计等工作，并对单位领导班子直接负责。内部审计部门应认真领会和贯彻单位领导班子的总体指导安排，开展单位全员参与的内部审计工作，严格执行国家颁布的相关制度，依法行使审查权和建议处理权，采用风险导向的审计程序和方法对内部控制相关的财务信息和管理信息进行实质性测试与分析，对审计发现内部控制缺陷并提出整改意见，并在监督过程中遵循独立性、客观性、效益性和谨慎性等基本原则。第三，单位纪律监察部门应在单位领导班子直接授权下，从干部纪律和党员作风角度加强单位内部监督。为了避免职能交叉或者责任推诿，纪检监察部门必须与内部审计部门职责权限划分明确，即侧重于对干部行政管理过程中的错误、失误甚至贪污腐败行为进行监督和检查。纪检监察部门可以加强纵向体系建设，由上级单位纪检监察部门直接领导，体现出一定的内部机构外部化特征，也对单位内部监督的结果处理进行持续跟踪。

行政事业单位内部监督机制的实施需要三个前提条件。尽管适度独立和专业化的部门职能分工有助于行政水平和行政效能的提高，但是同步增加的职能设置容易出现交叉重复和多头指挥，加大同级和上下级部门之间的沟通协调成本，造成组织资源分散与浪费、行政整体效能低下等多方面的问题。因此，行政事业单位需要加强机构职能整合、岗位职责设置和部门协同机制，作为内部监督机制实施的基础。第一，内部监督机制的发挥必须通过机构整合优化，使部门科学设置、职能分配合理。内部监督功能的发挥必须依靠行政事业单位大部制改革和行政职能优化，打破旧有部门和机构设置，科学划分决策权、执行权、监督权的部门归属，尤其是对内部监督职能进行划分与配置。第二，内部监督功能的实现必须以业务流程梳理和优化为基础，设置相对独立的内部监督业务岗位，并对岗位职责进行设计，明确决策权和执行权在业务层级内部控制中各个业务环节和节点的具体表现形式，设定内部监督体系在业务流程监督过程中的对象范围和监督内容。第三，内部监督功能的实现必须建立健全单位各部门和岗位之间的协同机制。内部监督机制实施无法依靠相互割裂的部门机构，也不能简单将职能相近的监督部门合并设立新的“超级部门”，而应当以内部控制目标为导向，建立内部监督在各相关部门的协调机制。单位应当在保证内部监督相对独立的前提下，实现监督部门的跨部门合作与协同，明确各个业务中不同部门的监督职能，划分不同业务流程的岗位监督职责，并通过监督机制制度化对单位决策和执行过程承担规制责任。这里需要说明的是，内部监督的独立性是指内部监督部门对内部各部门及下属单位独立，而对领导班子则无法做到完全独立，这是内部监督和外部监督的重要区别之一（刘永泽、张亮，2012）。

（二）外部监督应当对内部控制的建立和实施保持适度推力

行政事业单位外部监督机制的建立和实施具有自身的特点和重要意义。对于企业内部控制来说，投资者和债权人往往通过对财务状况和经营成果的持续关注，及时把握企业运营情况与战略目标的符合程度。而提供公共产品和服务的行政事业单位作为现代市场经济的一个主体，当其垄断了一部分公共职能，没有优胜劣汰的竞争机制时，单位领导干部则有可能利用公共权力谋私利，进而产生腐败行为，出现内生性行政管理失灵。而行政事业单位由于管理体制和资金属性的特点，造成内部监督在一定程度上缺位。因此，广大外部利益相关者行使外部监督职责，对于促进单位内部控制合规和高效是具有重要的现实意义的。由于行政事业单位公共服务职能与公共资金属性，内部管理活动也必须接受来自单位以外其他利益相关者的外部监督。对于企业内部控制来说，投资者和债权人往往通过对财务状况和经营成果的持续关注，及时把握企业运营情况与战略目标的符合程度。行政事业单位掌握着社会公共资源，如果没有优胜劣汰的竞争机制，个别领导干部则有可能利用公共权力谋私利，出现内生性行政管理失灵。因此，在行政事业单位存在不同程度的内部监督缺位的情况下，广大外部利益相关者行使外部监督职责，对于加强内部控制有效性具有重要意义。一方面，从管理体制角度来看，外部监督有利于克服行政事业单位内部监督的先天缺陷。当前我国采用国家、省、市、县区、乡镇等多级次的行政管理体制，在各级政府体系中还包括平行设置的行政单位和和事业单位，并由其承担具体行政职能。每个行政事业单位既要接受上级单位的领导和监督，还要接受本级政府中财政、审计和纪检监察部门的指导和检查，容易造成职责冲突或者互相推诿。审计部门和纪检监察部们分别隶属于政府部门和党委，不仅受上级业务部门的领导，而且受制于同级党委、行政机关的领导班子，监督主体的地位低于监督客体，被监督者往往是监督者的领导，削弱了监督主体的独立性和主动性，监督活动也缺乏应有的权威性。因此，外部监督是针对现有管理体制的缺点，梳理行政事业单位上级主管部门和同级监管部门的关系，建立纵横监督方向的外部监督模式。另一方面，从财政资金属性视角来看，外部监督应当成为行政事业单位建立和实施内部控制的推动力。我国行政事业单位由于使用公共属性的财政资金，产权结构不够明晰，单位领导缺乏内部控制建立和实施的主观能动性，也没有积极性向利益相关者进行信息列报，导致内部控制实施内生动力不足，实施动力主要来源应定位于单位外部监督力量。从公共财政角度来看，行政事业单位所使用的财政资金属于社会公众，而从税收角度来看则属于全体纳税人，需要引入社会公众的力量，推动公众立法和公众监督机制建设，加强外部监督的广泛参与性，扩大外部监督的社会基础。因此，根据社会要素的系统相关性，设置一个外部监督网是解决和克服外部监督力量不足的有效办法。

行政事业单位外部监督机制是建立在外部利益相关者要求社会公共资源管理公平、公开和公正的基础上。外部监督机制需要由外部监督主体依据有关财政收支、财务收支的法律、法规和国家其他有关规定进行监督和评价，在法定职权范围内提出相关管理意见。行政事业单位掌握着公共领域的强制力量和改变市场行为的能力，如果不受制约，公权力就很有可能成为个人用来谋私的工具，公权力的无限扩大无疑会导致市场其他主体权利的损害，任由其发展必然会带来腐败和专制。因此，对具有强制力量的权力进行制约就必须运用同样具有强制力量的权力（徐行，崔翔，2013）。从委托代理理论和契约理论出发，社会公众和行政事业单位形成社会资源分配与管理过程中的委托代理关系，并通过契约形式上升到国家法律和制度安排，主要体现在社会公众对政治、经济和文化权利和义务等方面。从公共财政角度出发，公共财政的目标是提供公共产品以满足公共消费需求，其产品和服务的提供也具有明显的非营利性、公众性和公平性。一旦公共财政支出偏离社会公众对公共产品和公共消费的预期，社会公众作为公共产权所有者将会要求便宜预期的公共产品与公共消费公众化，如国有企业国有股减持充实社保基金行为。行政事业单位外部监督正是建立在这些社会管理理论基础上，通过公共契约关系的梳理，将公共资源、国有资产和公共资金纳入外部监督体系中，以利于接受纳税人等社会公众的监督，防止公共属性的资源、资产和资金被浪费、损失、挪用甚至贪污。

行政事业单位外部监督机制的实施需要多元化的监督主体分工协作。行政事业单位外部监督主体主要包括立法监督、政府监督和社会监督三个方面。第一，从立法监督的角度，我国应加强全国人民代表大会、检察院、法院等机构在法律监督中的核心地位，拟定和颁布诸如《廉政法案》、《公务员财产公开法案》等针对行政事业单位组织层级规范的法律，与《预算法》、《政府采购法》等业务层级法律规范相结合，形成我国行政事业单位法律体系。检察院、法院等司法机构应加大对行政事业单位违法案件的查处力度，引入对重点单位、部门和岗位的廉政监督机制，真正构建我国行政法治化体系。第二，从政府监督角度出发，我国行政事业单位体系应明确单位外部的政府审计部门和纪检监察部门的权限和职责，明确政府审计部门的法律地位和审计监督范围。但是由于政府审计资源非常有限而审计任务却非常繁重，外部审计机制又必须依托社会审计，形成政府审计和社会审计的优势互补。纪检监察部门则应发挥在党组织建设和干部队伍建设方面的监督职能，专司监督党的机构和党员贯彻执行党的路线、方针、政策的情况，查处违纪党组织和党员，处理领导干部贪污腐败等违法行为。第三，从公众监督角度出发，我国应明确社会公众在外部监督体系中发挥的角色和监督方式。行政事业单位应利用现代信息技术做好信息交流工作，以电子政务为平台，建立和完善共享的监督信息资源网，提高监督信息的公开性和透明度，降低监督成本，利用有关的监督信息，准确、及时、全面地掌握权力运行情况，实现信息沟通畅通。我国应在现有的政务、党务新闻发言人制度的基础上，尝试建立起新闻媒体联系人制度，扩大发言人制度基础，并利用新闻媒体和舆论的监督功能，作为体制外与体制内之间监督信息输入与转换的重要桥梁，增加体制内监督与体制外监督的多元互动效应。

（三）内外监督应当对内部控制的建立和实施保持持续评价

在内部监督体系中，单位负责人应当指定专门部门或专人负责对单位内部控制的有效性进行评价并出具单位内部控制评价报告。在外部监督体系中，各外部监督主体应聘请相关评价机构或自行对单位内部控制有效性进行评价并出具内部控制评价报告。行政事业单位内部控制评价是对内部控制有效性发表意见。因此，内部控制评价的对象即内部控制的有效性。由于受内部控制固有单位限制（如评价人员的职业判断、政治关联等）的影响，内部控制评价只能为内部控制目标的实现提供合理保证，而不能提供绝对保证。内部控制评价的有效性包括单位层面和业务层面内部控制设计和执行的有效性，还包括内部控制缺陷的评价。单位内部控制设计的有效性是指为实现控制目标所必需的内部控制程序都存在并且设计恰当，能够为控制目标的实现提供合理保证。对于财务报告目标来讲，内部控制设计的有效性表现为所设计的相关内部控制能够规范会计行为，保证会计资料的正确性、可靠性，防止、发现并纠正财务报告的重大错报；对于资产安全目标而言，内部控制设计的有效性表现为所设计的内部控制能够合理保证单位财产的安全与完整，防止国有资产流失；对于合规目标来说，内部控制设计的有效性表现为所设计的内部控制能够合理保证单位遵循国家相关法律法规，确保国家相关规章制度能够得到有效贯彻和落实；对于公共服务目标而言，内部控制设计的有效性表现为所设计的内部控制能够合理保证单位经济活动的效率和效果。

评价单位层面内部控制设计的有效性，可以从以四个方面来考虑：第一，内部控制的设计的合法性，即行政事业单位在对内部控制进行设计的过程中，是否做到以内部控制的基本原理为前提，以相关法律法规作为依据。第二，内部控制的设计全面性，即内部控制的设计是否覆盖了所有关键岗位，对单位内部各相关部门人员和相关工作任务都具备约束力。第三，内部控制的设计适当性，即内部控制的设计是否与行政事业单位自身的机构属性、复杂程度以及风险管理要求相匹配。第四，内部控制的设计适应性，即内部控制的设计是否具有机构适应性，能够依外部环境和自身条件的变化适时地调整关键控制点和控制措施。

单位业务层面内部控制评价主要应包括预算控制、收支控制、政府采购控制、资产控制、建设项目控制、合同控制。单位内部控制执行的有效性是指在内部控制设计有效的前提下，内部控制能够按照设计的内部控制程序正确地执行，从而为控制目标的实现提供合理保证。内部控制执行的有效性离不开设计的有效性，如果内部控制在设计上存在漏洞，即使这些内部控制制度能够得到一贯的执行，那么也不能认为其运行是有效的。评价内部控制执行的有效性，应当着重考虑以下几个方面：一是相关控制在评价期内是如何运行的；二是相关控制是否得到了持续一致的运行；三是实施控制的人员是否具备必要的权限和能力。单位内部控制制度不是一成不变的，它需要行政事业单位不断根据外部环境和自身业务的变化作相应的调整，比如当单位开始从事经营类基金项目的管理运营业务，就需要对金融投资产品的种类、特点、风险以及对公共服务目标的影响进行评估，设计针对该业务的控制程序。此外，单位业务层面内部控制设计的动态调整性和内部控制执行的有效性应该成为内部控制评价的重点。

内部控制建立和执行情况总体评价是对单位组织层面和业务层面内部控制的建立和实施情况进行总结和评价。总结和评价主要围绕着单位内部控制制度建设的完整性和内部控制制度实施的有效性，并对内部控制实施的总体效果进行分析和总结，主要包括单位组织层面中的组织架构、工作机制、岗位职责、人员资质和信息技术，也包括业务层面中的预算控制、收支控制、政府采购控制、建设项目控制、资产控制和合同控制。内部控制效果分析是对内部控制在单位实施后，对单位组织架构和各项业务活动顺利开展的积极效果进行总结。具体可以包括单位完成各级政府交给的各项任务，公共资源、公共资金和国有资产管理的履约责任完成情况等。可以说，对行政事业单位内部控制评价是完善内部控制制度的有效途径，而内部控制评价的核心任务是找出单位内部控制在设计和实施过程中的缺陷，对缺陷的性质进行分析，进而有针对性地提出相应的整改措施并督促落实。因此，从某种意义上说，单位内部控制评价的成效在很大程度上取决于对内部控制缺陷的认定。在对缺陷分析中涉及的制度订立和执行中的具体缺陷进行分析和完善时，有针对性地设计相应的内部控制活动，调整组织机构和岗位，设置相关工作机制，消除缺陷及其不利影响。因此，内部控制评价机构应汇总各评价工作组的评价结果，对工作组现场初步认定的内部控制缺陷进行全面复核、分类汇总，对缺陷的成因、表现形式及风险程度进行定量或定性的综合分析，按照对控制目标的影响程度判定缺陷等级。内部控制评价机构以汇总的评价结果和认定的内部控制缺陷为基础，综合内部控制工作整体情况，客观、公正、完整地编制内部控制评价报告，并报送单位领导班子、内审部门和纪律监察部门，经上级主管部门最终审定、签字后报送同级财政部门。内部控制评价的结果应当作为单位内部考核的依据，对执行内部控制成效显著的内部机构和人员提出表彰，对违反内部控制的内部机构和人员提出处理意见。对于认定的内部控制缺陷，内部控制评价机构应当结合单位领导班子、内部审计部门和纪检监察部门的要求，提出整改建议，要求责任单位及时整改，并跟踪其整改落实情况。已经造成损失或负面影响的，单位应当追究相关人员的责任。另外，应明确行政事业单位内部控制评价对外报告的使用者，包括上级主管部门、有关监管部门、其他利益相关者、中介机构和研究机构等；对内报告的使用者主要是行政事业单位领导班子、内部审计部门和纪律监察部门等。

四、结论和建议

本文主要针对我国行政事业单位内部控制制度特征进行具体分析。首先，本文从历史发展、制度环境、控制范围和协同机制四个方面探讨了我国行政事业单位内部控制的中国特色。其次，本文从运营目标、管控核心、预算管理、绩效评价、法律约束和风险应对六个角度总结了我国行政事业单位内部控制区别于企业内部控制的制度特点，即运营目标。最后，本文深入阐述了行政事业单位与监督的关系特点，着重从内部监督、外部监督和评价三个方面论证了监督意义、监督机制、监督主体和监督方法等问题。行政事业单位内部控制作为“制度笼子”的具体措施，已经成为实现合理制约公共权力的机制保障，有利于我国行政事业单位科学合理地使用和分配公共资金，履行社会服务职能，严格控制“三公经费”，杜绝“假发票”和“小金库”现象。

总体来说，《规范》是对行政事业单位内部控制建设提出原则上的要求，对内部控制的标准和内容进行框架性的指导，单位应该根据自身情况的不同，按照内部控制的逻辑顺序，建立健全单位内部控制管理制度作为《规范》的实施细则和管理办法，对《规范》要求的具体内容进行落实，并针对单位的特殊业务设计有针对性的管理制度。在收支管理中，《规范》只是明确了收支的大体范围和控制方法，各个单位需要针对自身情况，对收支范围进行界定，按照收支分类的重要性设计管理制度。因此，行政事业单位内部控制建立和实施首先要从内部控制制度构建入手，根据《规范》和本单位实际情况制定内部控制相关制度，明确内部控制实施的标准及具体的实施办法，从制度角度建立本级各部门和上下级部门的协同机制。接下来，行政事业单位就要进行组织层级内部控制建设，即从内部控制的核心内容入手，构建单位内部控制的整体组织框架，为后续的内部控制具体措施的落实奠定组织基础。第三个步骤就是要构建单位标准的业务流程内部控制。行政事业单位在全面分析本单位主要业务流程各环节风险点的基础上，制定详细的业务流程内部控制措施并形成标准的流程图，并通过信息系统得以固化。此外，社会公众应该作为外部监督机制中除政治系统外的重要监督力量，单位也应该依靠广泛的民众意识和公民监督，提高行政行为的透明度。

参考文献

[1]中华人民共和国财政部.《行政事业单位内部控制规范(征求意见稿)》,2012.

[2]财政部、证监会、银监会、保监会及审计署．企业内部控制基本规范[M]．上海:立信会计出版社,2008.

[3]爱德华·卡尼等.2009.联邦政府内部控制.北京:中国时代经济出版社.

[4] COSO. 内部控制——整合框架[M]．方红星,译．大连:东北财经大学出版社,2008.

[5]卡尼．联邦政府内部控制[M]．王光远,译．北京:中国时代经济出版社,2009.

[6]科斯．企业的性质[M]．孙经纬,译．上海:上海财经大学出版社,2001.

[7]诺斯．制度、制度变迁与经济绩效[M]．刘守英,译．上海:上海三联书店,1994.

[8]阎德民．新中国的权力制约和监督:历史嬗变与经验启示[J].中共福建省委党校学报,2011(3):4-11.

[9]刘永泽,唐大鹏.关于行政事业单位内部控制的几个问题[J].会计研究,2013(1):57-62,96.

[10]刘玉廷,王宏.美国加强政府部门内部控制建设的有关情况及其启示[J].会计研究,2008(3):3-10,95.

[11]张庆龙,聂兴凯.政府部门内部控制研究述评与改革建议[J].会计研究,2011(6):50-56.

[12]刘永泽,唐大鹏．社保基金偿付能力风险理论分析与实证检验[J].审计与经济研究, 2012(1):55-63.

[13]王美文．公共权力二元监督制衡机制与效能优化[J].科学社会主义,2011 (6):53-56.

[14]刘永泽,张亮.我国政府部门内部控制框架体系的构建研究[J].会计研究,2012(1):10-19.

[15]陈国权,谷志军．决策、执行与监督三分的内在逻辑[J].浙江社会科学,2012(4):27-32.

[16]秦荣生．深化政府审计监督 完善政府治理机制[J]．审计研究,2007(1):3-9.

[17]徐行,崔翔．机制创新与多元互动:关于加强执政党自我监督和外部监督的新思考[J]．理论探讨,2013(3):107-112.

[18]TIERNEY C,KEARNEY E,FERNANDEZ R. Audit Federal Financial Controls: Sooner Rather Than Later? Would Sarbanes-Oxley Benefits Federal Financial Management? [J]Journal of Government Financial Management,2004.

The Research on the System Characteristics of Internal Control in Administrative Institutions of China

Abstract In order to implement the spirit and requirements in the eighteen meeting of the party, establish internal control system in administrative institutions efficiently, MOF China? published the? "internal control of administrative institutions(on trial)"? in 2012 November, which will fully implement on January 1 of 2014. How to establish and implement internal control in the all administrative institutions at all levels has become an important task in crunch time. At the same time how to establish theoretical basis of internal control of administrative institutions also has become a very difficult task. In this context, this article is in view of the Chinese characteristics, management characteristics and supervision characteristics of internal control in administrative institutions to expand the intension and extension of the related problems, enrich the theory of internal control of administrative institutions. Finally it will be useful for the administrative institution in the process of the full implementation of the internal control with the unified thought and cognition.

key words administrative institutions internal control Chinese characteristics management characteristics supervision characteristics

内部控制、股权集中度与投资者关系管理
——来自A股上市公司投资者关系调查的证据①

李志斌[1,2]

（1. 扬州大学商学院，扬州 225009；2. 南京大学工程管理学院，南京 210093）

摘 要 投资者关系管理是公司自主性治理机制，而内部控制作为具体落实公司治理的制度基础自然影响投资者关系管理，股权集中度是影响内部控制对投资者关系管理的作用强弱的重要因素之一。本文在理论分析的基础上进行了实证检验，研究发现：①内部控制对IRM的状态水平、质量指标、组织指标和总体水平均有显著的正向影响；②股权集中度除了对管理指标存在显著负向作用，对IRM其他指标的作用均不显著；③相对于股权集中度低的公司，内部控制对股权集中度较高公司的IRM的状态水平、管理指标和总体水平的正向作用更强，而对质量指标无显著差异。

关键词 内部控制 投资者关系管理 股权集中度 Chow检验

一、问题的提出

投资者关系管理（IRM）是指公司为获得资本而开展的战略营销活动，其目标包括公司价值最大化、投资者保护和企业声誉提升等，核心内容是强化公司与投资者的信息沟通和交流，被称为上市公司的“救生圈”。马连福等（2007）将IRM定位由管理层次上升到治理层面，将其认定为公司自主性治理机制之一。我国上市公司在IPO之前一般非常重视投资者关系管理，而公司一旦上市成功，则往往忽略投资者关系管理，投资者关系管理缺乏制度化和规范化已经严重影响了公司股价和持续融资，本文认为通过建设和完善企业内部控制能够解决这一问题。

内部控制经过了长期发展，已经从最初的内部牵制发展至今天的整体框架，其作用边界在不断拓展，内控目标从单一的遏制舞弊到COSO报告提出的财务报告的可靠性、合规合法性和经营效率效果性的三目标；我国财政部等五部委在2008年颁布的《内部控制基本规范》在COSO报告的基础上又增加了内部控制的资产安全目标和战略目标，目标的演进说明内部控制的内涵和功能

① 基金项目：财政部全国会计领军（后备）人才培养计划；国家自然科学基金重点资助项目（70932003）；教育部人文社科青年基金项目（10YJC790157）；中国博士后科学基金（2012M511257）。

在不断深化和拓展。杨雄胜（2011）对内部控制的定义范畴进行了有益的探索，超越了COSO报告的定义，认为内部控制是运用专门手段工具及方法，防范与遏制非我与损我，保护与促进自我与益我的系统化制度。内部控制的内涵由此扩展为企业制度体系和自律系统，超越传统意义上的消极性防弊纠错，还发挥着积极的建设性作用。内部控制的系统性和嵌入性特征决定了其对包括投资者关系管理在内的公司治理和管理存在广泛而深入的影响。

本研究的基本理论基础是内部控制的作用范围已经超越了COSO报告所规定的三大范畴，即财务报告、合规合法和经营效率与效果，存在溢出效应。对于上市公司而言，保护投资者权益是内部控制最为重要的溢出效应之一，而IRM是投资者权益保护的基础工作之一。本文研究的主题是内部控制是否影响IRM水平，并讨论在不同股权集中度公司，内部控制对IRM的作用强度是否存在差异，以期发现内部控制与IRM之间关系的经验证据，论证内部控制溢出效应的存在。

二、理论分析与假设提出

（一）内部控制与投资者关系管理

已有的研究表明公司治理和公司管理是影响IRM的两大重要因素。第一，公司治理因素包括外部治理环境因素和公司治理结构。外部治理环境越好的地区，上市公司投资者关系管理水平越高（马连福等，2008；张慧敏等，2009）。公司股权性质与结构对投资者关系管理水平有着显著的影响，流通股比重与投资者关系管理正相关（林斌，2005）；机构投资者持股、外部股权比例的提高能有效促进公司提升投资者关系管理水平，管理层持股与投资者关系管理呈U型关系（肖斌卿等，2007），但也有研究认为管理层持股比例与投资者关系管理线性正相关（赵颖，2011）。董事会结构也是影响投资者关系管理的重要因素之一，独立董事比例及设置审计委员会等6个因素会对上市公司的投资者关系管理水平有着显著的正向影响，董事长与CEO分离与投资者关系管理呈弱正相关关系（赵颖，2009）。第二，公司管理因素。研究认为，公司财务杠杆与投资者关系管理水平负相关，再融资计划、盈利能力、公司规模与投资者关系管理水平正相关（林斌等，2005；肖斌卿等，2007；赵颖，2009）。

内部控制作为公司治理的制度基础和公司管理的制度体系能够更直接地影响投资者关系管理水平。内部控制经历了内部牵制、内部会计和管理控制、内部控制结构与内部控制框架等阶段，从萌芽到不断成熟，COSO报告的出台更是将内部控制的理论研究和实践总结推向了新的高峰，内部控制发展为包含控制环境、风险评估、控制活动、信息与沟通、监控等五要素的系统架构，涵盖了员工、管理层和董事会等不同层次的控制活动，对企业的影响范围不断拓展，早已不再仅仅规制会计和审计工作，成为企业运营、战略执行和公司治理的制度体系。正是基于这种对内部控制内涵的充分挖掘，内部控制的投资者保护的功能逐步进入研究者的视野。实证研究的结论基本支持内部控制对于投资者保护的价值存在，张先治等（2004）较早关注投资者需求对内部控制的影响，通过实证研究证明了投资者对上市公司内部控制有着较强的需求。杨德明等（2010）认为，内部控制有利于投资者保护，对于投资者保护较弱的地区，内部控制可能成为补偿弱投资者保护负面影响的一种替代机制。杨有红、毛新述（2011）的研究结论是内部控制能够在一定程度上改善财务报告的质量，并强化对投资者利益的保护。杜海霞（2012）从理论视角归纳了内部控制对投资者保护的直接路径和间接路径：一方面，内部控制通过内部控制运行、信息披露和外部监督三个层面直接实现对投资者的保护。另一方面，内部控制通过保障会计信息质量，间接实现对投资者的保护。投资者关系管理的主要任务是将公司信息及时准确地与投资者沟通，回答投资者有关公司发展的疑问，是投资者保护体系中的基础性工作，内部控制的制度控制和价值引领功能能够提高公司信息披露质量，以及与投资者沟通的质量和时效性，有效提高投资者关系管理水平。

从更高层次看，投资者关系管理体现了公司的社会责任意识。内部控制是“虚实结合”的系统，既有具体的可操作的风险评估、控制活动和内部监控等，也包括形而上的价值观、企业文化、管理哲学的控制环境。内部控制已然发展成为企业内部“兴利除弊、惩恶扬善”的系统，通过控制制度的建立和实施杜绝“恶”，同时在控制环境部分倡导企业应该向“善”。哈佛大学罗伯特·西蒙斯（2004）提出控制的“阴阳体系”，信念系统和交互式控制系统产生的是积极和鼓动力量，代表太阳、温暖和光明，即为“阳”，其功能更多的是引导“善”，边界系统和诊断控制系统产生的是约束和确保服从命令，即为“阴”，代表阴暗和寒冷，更多的作用是制约“恶”。投资者关系管理除了信息披露功能外，同时还具有公共关系、资本营销和承担社会责任的性质，内部控制作为公司制度体系和自律系统，毫无疑问从制度上规范了企业行为的道德底线——合规合法性，而在控制环境中则提出了通过适当的价值观、管理哲学和企业文化将企业引领到更高层次的道德水准上，促进公司诚信、向善、承担社会责任。内部控制从制度和道德的视角促进了企业社会责任的履行，当然也提升了投资者关系管理的水平。

总之，内部控制已然成为企业制度性体系和自律系统，能够全面提升投资者关系管理水平，包括完善投资者关系机构设置、管理制度和流程规范化程度。因此，良好的内部控制能够全面提升投资者关系管理的水平。无论从投资者关系管理影响因素的研究视角还是从内部控制的投资者保护功能视角切入分析，结论均为内部控制能够提高公司投资者关系管理水平。据此，本文提出如下研究假设：

H1：内部控制对投资者关系管理水平存在正向影响。

（二）内部控制与投资者关系管理：股权集中度的影响

股权集中度是决定公司治理模式和机制的重要因素，其经济后果非常显著，对公司经营绩效（安烨，钟廷勇，2011）、公司价值（杨汉明，2008）和社会责任的履行（冯丽丽等，2011）均有正向的作用。股权集中度对公司投资者关系管理同样存在影响，股权集中度与公司投资者关系管理水平显著负相关，股权制衡度与投资者关系管理呈正向关系（马连福等，2008）。但赵颖（2011）认为适当的股权集中度对促进上市公司开展投资者关系管理有显著的积极效果，但股权过于集中对提升上市公司的投资者关系水平来说也存在着所谓的“壕沟效应”。本文认为，较高的股权集中度将降低公司IRM水平，这是因为股权过度集中会导致公司治理的过度强化（吴淑琨，2002），影响公司在治理方面的创新和主动作为；另一方面，股权集中使控股股东剥削中小股东的可能性增加，控股股东为实现这一掠夺，倾向于降低信息披露与沟通质量，从事较少的投资者关系管理活动。据此，提出如下假设：

H2：股权集中度对投资者关系管理水平存在负向影响。

在“法与金融”理论视野下，股权集中度与投资者法律保护之间存在替代关系（LLSV，1998），许年行和吴世农（2006）认为LLSV的研究巧妙地将公司治理的外部机制（投资者法律保护）与内部机制（股权结构）有机地联系起来，投资者关系管理作为投资者保护的重要机制，自然同时受到外部机制和内部机制的作用，但由于公司股权集中度的差异，内外部机制发挥作用的程度并不平衡，股权集中作为投资者法律保护的替代机制，实质上是强调在股权集中度高的公司，内部治理机制将起到主导作用，在提升投资者关系管理中发挥的作用更大。于建霞（2007）分析了股权集中度对公司治理模式选择的影响，认为在股权分散条件下，小股东参与治理的积极性普遍不高的，完善外部治理环境，偏重外部治理机制的作用是明智之举；股权集中条件下的大股东往往偏好于对公司谋求直接监督与战略控制，内部控制成为大股东行使控制权的系统，是实现大股东意志的重要工具，这类股权集中公司更强调通过强化内部控制完善包括投资者关系管理在内的公司治理机制。因此，在股权集中公司中，内部控制对投资者关系管理的作用更强。据此，本文提出如下研究假设：

H3：相对于股权分散的公司，股权集中度较高的公司的内部控制对投资者关系管理水平的提升作用更强。

三、研究设计

（一）变量定义

1. 投资者关系管理水平

本文运用李心丹等构建的南京大学投资者关系管理指数（$CIRI^{nju}$）作为衡量投资者关系管理水平的指标，该指标由三个一级指标构成：分别为状态水平指标（股价波动率、股东忠诚度和分析报告数量）、质量指标（沟通关系质量和信息披露质量）、管理指标（高层参与、IRM 组织机构和 IR 人员素质）。为了保证评价体系的合理性和投资者关系管理指数的有效性，李心丹等继续利用结构化方程模型验证评价体系的内在运行机理，采用 Botosan（1997）提出的信息披露指数有效性检验方法对投资者关系管理指数进行了检验，实证结果表明该评价体系和投资者关系管理指数是合理、有效的。指数构建所需数据来源于对公司的问卷调查和公司公开的数据，本文利用 2009 年度的 $CIRI^{nju}$ 数据作为 IRM 水平的衡量指标。

2. 内部控制有效性

本文运用王宏等主持开发的 2009 年度的“中国上市公司内部控制指数”[24]作为公司内部控制有效性的评价指标。该指数的构建是以 COSO 报告中对内部控制有效性的定义作为理论依据的，即内控的有效性是用内控目标的实现程度衡量的。计量该指数的变量有两个层次：一是我国《内部控制基本规范》规定的五大目标，内部控制指数包括战略指数、经营指数、报告指数、合规指数和资产安全指数；二是各类目标下的分类变量。在基本评估的基础上，还增加了内部控制修正指数变量，即对内部控制存在重大缺陷的予以扣分，该指数较为全面和准确地反映了上市公司内部控制的有效性。根据评价的结果，上市公司内部控制指数的取值范围为［0，1 000］。考虑到量纲的统一性，在实证分析时取其自然对数。

3. 控制变量

根据已有的研究，本文选择股权集中度、董事会独立性、财务杠杆、盈利能力、成长性、规模和行业等因素作为控制变量。具体变量内涵及定义见表 1。

表 1 变量定义表

变量性质	变量含义	符号	定义
被解释变量	投资者关系管理的状态水平	IRL	用以下 3 个指标进行度量：股价波动率、前十大股东变化率、分析师报告的数量
	投资者关系管理的质量指标	IRQ	用以下 2 个指标进行度量：沟通关系质量、信息披露质量

续表

变量性质	变量含义	符号	定义
	投资者关系管理的管理指标	IRS	用以下3个指标进行度量：高层参与程度、组织设置情况、人员素质情况
	投资者关系管理总体水平	IRMI	由IRL、IRQ和IRS指标构成，即南京大学投资者关系指数$CIRI^{nju}$
解释变量	内部控制有效性	ICI	中国上市公司内部控制指数（2009）
控制变量	股权集中度	HHI	赫芬达尔—赫希曼指数，计算前三大股东持股比例的平方和
	董事会独立性	IBD	独立董事数占全体董事成员的比例
	财务杠杆	LEV	资产负债率，负债总额与资产总额的比值
	成长性	GROW	营业收入增长率，营业收入的增长额与上年营业收入的比值
	盈利能力	ROE	净资产报酬率，净利润与平均净资产的比值
	规模	SIZE	资产总额自然对数
	行业	IND	行业哑变量，12个行业（不含金融、保险类），设置11个哑变量①

（二）研究模型

根据上文分析，本文构建如下基本检验模型：

$$IRMI=\alpha+\beta_1 ICI+\beta_2 HHI+\beta_3 IBD+\beta_4 LEV+\beta_5 GROW+\beta_6 ROE+\beta_7 SIZE+\beta_8 IND+\varepsilon$$

（三）样本选择

本文以南京大学2009年为构建和发布投资者关系管理指数而选为问卷调查对象的上市公司作为研究样本，剔除被谴责、处罚和数据不全的上市公司，最后获取的有效样本为371个。为了控制极端值对研究结论的影

① 证监会2001年颁布的《上市公司行业分类指引》中将上市公司分为13个行业，剔除金融类公司后，样本公司的行业类型共计12类，以综合类上市公司为参照系，设置11个行业虚拟变量。

响，对回归模型中存在极端值的变量在样本 1% 和 99% 分位数处做了 Winsorize 处理。

四、实证研究结果

（一）描述性统计

从表 2 可以看出，上市公司投资者关系管理总体指数的最小值为 23.74，最大值为 83.82，均值为 49.5337，说明我国上市公司在投资者关系管理方面存在较大差距；内部控制指数的最小值为 440.96，最大值为 990.42，均值为 715.80，表明我国上市公司之间的内部控制质量差异悬殊；公司股权集中度用赫芬达尔—赫希曼指数 HHI 衡量的最小值为 0.0045，最大值为 0.7560。描述性分析表明我国上市公司在投资者关系管理水平、内部控制有效性和股权集中度等方面差异较大，为研究提供了良好的契机。

表 2 **相关变量的描述性统计结果**

变量	N	最小值	最大值	均值	标准差
IRL	371	1.58	84.94	46.2200	18.1000
IRQ	371	26.10	90.44	60.8602	12.5566
IRS	371	11.38	99.53	40.0172	22.0336
IRMI	371	23.74	83.82	49.5337	13.6063
ICI	371	440.96	990.42	715.80	98.2040
HHI	371	0.0045	0.7560	0.1908	0.1290

（二）相关分析

为了检验内部控制与投资者关系管理水平之间的关系，本文对主要变量进行了相关系数分析。表 3 中的左下部分为 Pearson 系数，而右上部分为 Spearman 系数。两种相关系数均显示，上市公司内部控制有效性与投资者关系管理的状态水平、质量指标、组织指标和综合水平之间均存在显著的正相关关系；股权集中度与投资者关系管理状态水平 Pearson 系数表明两者呈弱正相关，而 Spearman 系数则显示两者不显著相关，股权集中度与投资者关系管理其他方面的相关性均不显著。

表3 主要变量相关系数

	IRL	IRQ	IRS	IRMI	ICI	HHI
IRL	1.000	.498 *** (.000)	.238 *** (.000)	.720 *** (.000)	.502 *** (.000)	.060 (.252)
IRQ	.510 *** (.000)	1.000	.482 *** (.000)	.813 *** (.000)	.396 *** (.000)	-.016 (.763)
IRS	.300 *** (.000)	.480 *** (.000)	1.000	.760 *** (.000)	.259 *** .000	-.073 (.162)
IRMI	.754 *** (.000)	.798 *** (.000)	.801 *** (.000)	1.000	.470 *** .000	-.006 (.913)
ICI	.504 *** (.000)	.433 *** (.000)	.348 *** (.000)	.539 *** (.000)	1.000	.126 ** (.015)
HHI	.090 * (.084)	-.022 (.666)	-.043 (.414)	.009 (.859)	.128 ** (.014)	1.000

注：括号内标注的是显著性水平；*** 表示在1%水平下显著；** 表示在5%水平下显著；* 表示在10%水平下显著。

（三）回归分析

1. 全样本回归

表4显示的是全样本回归结果。内部控制有效性对投资者关系管理的总体水平、状态水平、质量指标和管理指标的回归系数分别为0.074、0.093、0.098和0.080，且均在1%水平下显著，说明公司内部控制对投资者关系管理水平存在显著的正向促进作用，支持了上文的假设1；而股权集中度除了对管理指标有显著的负向作用，其他均不显著，假设2基本未能得到支持。此外，董事会独立性、财务杠杆、盈利能力、成长性和规模等控制变量对投资者关系管理水平的影响均不显著，这与已有文献的结论不一致。

表4 全样本回归结果

	总体水平（IRMI）	状态水平（IRL）	质量指标（IRQ）	管理指标（IRS）
Cons	-2.962 (.721)	-1.718 (.875)	28.874 (.105)	-29.294 ** (.050)
ICI	.074 *** (.000)	.093 *** (.000)	.098 *** (.000)	.080 *** (.000)

续表

	总体水平（IRMI）	状态水平（IRL）	质量指标（IRQ）	管理指标（IRS）
HHI	-6.550 (.209)	7.924 (.265)	-10.894 (.237)	-22.615** (.016)
IBD	.046 (.598)	-.040 (.736)	.063 (.683)	.150 (.340)
LEV	-3.783 (.331)	-6.342 (.234)	-1.072 (.876)	-3.209 (.646)
GROW	-.012 (.647)	-.044 (.209)	.014 (.752)	-.012 (.789)
ROE	-2.942 (.653)	10.934 (.222)	-5.131 (.657)	-20.952 (.075)
SIZE	-.226 (.676)	-1.473** (.046)	.081 (.932)	.701 (.471)
IND	控制	控制	控制	控制
Obs	371	371	371	371
F 值	9.334***	8.227***	5.656***	4.144***
R^2	.336	.296	.234	.183
Adj-R^2	.300	.260	.193	.139

注：括号内标注的是显著性水平；*** 表示在 1% 水平下显著；** 表示在 5% 水平下显著；* 表示在 10% 水平下显著。

2. 分组检验

为检验在不同股权集中度的公司中，内部控制对投资者关系管理水平的作用强度是否存在显著差异，我们将全部样本按股权集中度由高到低均分为三组，分别对股权集中度最大组与最小组进行分组回归，我们对内部控制系数进行了邹式（Chow）检验以验证在股权集中度高和低的公司，内部控制对投资者关系管理水平的作用强度是否存在差异。检验结果见表 5，回归结果表明无论股权集中度高或低，内部控制对公司的投资者关系管理水平均具有显著的正向作用，且均在 1% 水平下显著，进一步支持了假设 1。高股权集中度公司样本组的内部控制回归系数均大于低股权集中度公司样本组，且 Chow 检验结果表明，内部控制对高 HHI 公司和低 HHI 公司的投资者关系管理总体水平、状态水平和管理指标的作用强度存在显著差异，但对质量指标的影响无显著差异，说明内部控制对高 HHI 公司的投资者关系管理的状态水平、管理指标和总体水平具有更强的正向作用，假设3基本得到支持。

表5 分组检验与结果

	总体水平（IRMI）		状态水平（IRL）		质量指标（IRQ）		管理指标（IRS）	
	高HHI样本组	低HHI样本组	高HHI样本组	低HHI样本组	高HHI样本组	低HHI样本组	高HHI样本组	低HHI样本组
Cons	-31.004* (.063)	10.123 (.504)	-23.202 (.316)	.874 (.967)	8.141 (.608)	28.916* (.064)	-83.563** (.010)	-1.836 (.942)
ICI	**.095*** (.000)**	**.052*** (.000)**	**.111*** (.000)**	**.069*** (.000)**	**.055*** (.000)**	**.038*** (.001)**	**.124*** (.000)**	**.051*** (.006)**
IBD	.001 (.993)	.268* (.097)	-.071 (.759)	.198 (.379)	-.065 (.682)	.313 (.059)	.152 (.638)	.287 (.280)
LEV	6.092 (.348)	-4.221 (.545)	9.982 (.270)	-20.167** (.041)	8.679 (.163)	4.721 (.509)	-.829 (.947)	1.881 (.870)
GROW	-.084* (.061)	.018 (.680)	-.153** (.015)	.004 (.952)	-.058 (.174)	.071 (.123)	-.044 (.610)	-.026 (.720)
ROE	15.517 (.208)	-7.639 (.457)	35.327** (.041)	.632 (.965)	5.733 (.626)	2.343 (.824)	6.426 (.786)	-27.456 (.108)
SIZE	-.679 (.344)	-.578 (.600)	-1.715* (.088)	-.371 (.810)	-.773 (.261)	-.713 (.528)	.485 (.726)	-.636 (.727)
IND	控制	控制	控制	控制	控制	控制	控制	控制
Obs	123	123	123	123	123	123	123	123
F值	6.497***	2.485***	4.922***	2.335***	3.369***	2.164***	3.048***	1.702*
R^2	.495	.287	.426	.274	.337	.259	.315	.216
Adj-R^2	.419	.171	.340	.157	.237	.140	.212	.089
Chow检验	F=7.3700*** (0.0066)		F=4.6014** (0.0319)		F=1.5443 (0.2140)		F=5.5864** (0.0181)	

注：括号内标注的是显著性水平；***表示在1%水平下显著；**表示在5%水平下显著；*表示在10%水平下显著。

（四）稳健性检验

本文进行以下稳健性检验：以第一大股东持股比例替代HHI作为股权集中度的衡量指标。检验结果与本文结论基本一致，说明本文结论具有较强的稳健性。

五、研究结论与启示

（一）研究结论

内部控制作为公司治理的制度基础，有助于提升公司投资者关系管理水平。但是，在股权集中度不同的公司，内部控制对投资者关系管理水平的促进作用是有差异的。本文选择2009年沪、深两市的部分上市公司作为调查样本，建立投资者关系管理指数用以衡量公司的投资者关系管理水平，并运用内部控制指数及公司财务数据，考察了内部控制对投资者关系管理水平的影响。

已有的实证研究表明公司治理环境和结构显著影响投资者关系管理水平，但是如果没有良好的内部控制将投资者关系管理纳入制度化和规范化的轨道，公司治理环境和结构就不可能对完善投资者关系管理起到促进作用。本文的研究发现，内部控制能够显著改善投资者关系管理的状态水平、质量指标、组织指标和总体水平；股权集中度除了对管理指标存在显著负向作用，对IRM其他指标的作用均不显著；相对于股权分散公司，股权集中度较高公司的内部控制对于提升投资者关系管理水平的作用更强，说明高股权集中度公司的投资者关系管理水平的提升更依赖内部控制的规范作用。本文的研究一方面从内部控制的角度为有效提升投资者关系管理提供了经验证据，丰富了投资者关系管理的相关文献；另一方面，本文的研究拓展了对内部控制功能和效应的认识，超越了COSO报告定义的内部控制在财务报告可靠性、经营合规合法性和经营效率、效果性方面的功能，证明了内部控制存在投资者保护方面的溢出效应。

（二）启示

1. 扩大内部控制建设范围，建立和完善投资者关系管理方面的内部控制规范

目前内部控制的完善和执行已经成为上市公司关注的焦点，但公司重点关注的是财务、生产和经营等内部流程环节的内部控制。本文的研究结论表明，内部控制的功能不仅局限于COSO报告，内部控制已经超越了“主内”的角色，在规范和促进与投资者沟通和权益保护方面也至关重要，这不仅应成为公司建立和完善内部控制的动力机制，而且也应该成为内部控制重点建设的内容之一。企业需要从投资者关系管理的机构设置、网站建设、回应投资者疑问、信息披露等方面建立和完善投资者关系管理的内部控制制度规范体系并严格执行，从而通过内部控制的规范作用促进投资者关系管理水平的提升。

2. 从建立健全公司内部控制规范入手提升投资者关系管理水平

投资者关系管理所产生的经济后果已经得到了理论界和实务界的认可，良好的投资者关系管理能够提升投资者满意度（李枫，2009）、降低融资成本和

代理成本（马连福等，2008；杨德明等，2006）、提升公司价值等（李心丹等，2007；张宏亮、崔学刚，2009），但关于如何提升投资者关系管理水平的研究不多，本文研究结论的启示在于，公司应该充分认识到内部控制规范功能对提升投资者关系管理水平的作用，上市公司应遵循财政部等五部委颁布的《内部控制基本规范》的基本框架，按照内部环境类指引、控制活动类指引、控制手段类指引的要求逐步建立和完善公司的内部控制体系，并强化执行，从而保证公司及时应对投资者的关切和疑问，提升投资者满意度，在资本市场营造良好的公司形象。

参考文献

[1]马连福,陈德球．投资者关系管理:一种新型的自主性治理机制[J]．董事会,2007(11):74-75.

[2]杨雄胜．内部控制范畴定义探索[J]．会计研究,2011(8):46-52.

[3]马连福,陈德球,胡艳．治理环境、股权结构与投资者关系管理[J]．当代经济科学,2008(3):101-109.

[4]张慧敏,陈德球.治理环境、董事会效率与投资者关系管理[J]．山西财经大学学报,2009(9):71-79.

[5] 林斌,辛清泉,杨德明,等.投资者关系管理及其影响因素分析——基于深圳上市公司的实证检验[J].会计研究,2005(9):32-39.

[6] 肖斌卿,李心丹,顾妍,等.中国上市公司投资者关系与公司治理——来自A股公司投资者关系调查的证据[J].南开管理评论,2007(9):51-60.

[7] 赵颖．股权结构与投资者关系管理——基于中国上市公司的实证研究[J]．山西财经大学学报,2011(8):92-100.

[8] 赵颖．我国上市公司投资者关系水平影响因素实证研究[J]．经济管理,2009(1):70-77.

[9] 张先治,张晓东．基于投资者需求的上市公司内部控制实证分析[J]．会计研究,2004(12):55-61.

[10] 杨德明,林斌,任英．内部控制、治理环境与投资者保护[J]．证券市场导报,2010(4):53-60.

[11] 杨有红,毛新述．内部控制、财务报告质量与投资者保护——来自沪市上市公司的经验证据[J]．财贸经济,2011(8):44-50.

[12] 杜海霞．内部控制的投资者保护路径研究[J]．北京工商大学学报:社会科学版,2012(1): 70-76.

[13]西蒙斯．控制[M]．北京:机械工业出版社,2004.

[14]安烨,钟廷勇.股权集中度、股权制衡与公司绩效关联性研究——基于中国制造业上市公司的实证分析[J]．东北师大学报:哲学社会科学版,2011(6):46-52.

[15]杨汉明.股权集中度、现金股利与企业价值的实证分析[J].财贸经济,2008(8):67-72.

[16]冯丽丽,林芳,许家林.产权性质、股权集中度与企业社会责任履行[J].山西财经大学学报,2011(9):100-107.

[17]吴淑琨.股权结构与公司绩效的U型关系研究——1997—2000年上市公司的实证研究[J].中国工业经济,2002(1):80-87.

[18] PORT A L,RAFAEL,SHLEIFER,et al.. Investor Protection and Corporate Governance [J]. Journal of Financial Economics, 2000(58):3-27.

[19]许年行,吴世农.我国中小投资者法律保护影响股权集中度的变化吗?[J].经济学,2006(4):893-922.

[20]于建霞.股权集中度、治理环境与公司治理模式的依赖[J].改革,2007(6):102-107.

[21]李心丹,刘玉灿,肖斌卿.中国上市公司投资者关系管理运作机制研究[J].中国管理科学,2005 (3):32-38.

[22]李心丹,肖斌卿,王树华,等.中国上市公司投资者关系管理评价指标体系及其应用研究[J].管理世界,2006 (9):117-128.

[23]BOTOSAN C A,Disclosure Level and the Cost of Equity Capital [J]. The Accounting Review, 1997(72):323-349.

[24]王宏,蒋占华,胡为民,等.中国上市公司内部控制指数研究[M].北京:人民出版社,2011:172-232.

[25]李枫.投资者类别对投资者关系管理与投资满意关系研究[J].财经问题研究,2009(11):75-80.

[26]马连福,胡艳,高丽.投资者关系管理水平与权益资本成本——来自深交所A股上市公司的经验证据[J].经济与管理研究,2008(6):23-28.

[27]杨德明,王彦超,辛清泉.投资者关系管理、公司治理与企业业绩[J].南开管理评论,2007(3):43-50.

[28]张宏亮,崔学刚.投资者关系、公司价值与投资者保护——基于金牌董秘评比结果的实证研究[J].财贸研究,2009(4):138-144.

Internal Control, Ownership Concentration and Investor Relations Management in China—Evidence from the Investor Relations Survey of a Listed Company

Abstract Investor relations management (IRM) is the corporate self-determination governance mechanism. The internal control (IC), as the institution basis of corporate governance will inevitably influence IRM. This paper firstly analysis the relation between the IC and IRM in theories, and then do the empirical test. The empirical research result indicates that the internal control is significantly and positively related to IRM levels; Ownership concentration has the significant and negative effect on IRS, but has no significant effect on the other elements of IRM.

The IC has stronger effect on the IRL, IRS, and IRMI to the corporate with low degree ownership concentration than to that with the high degree ownership concentration, but no significant differences on IRQ.

Key Words Internal Control Investor Relations Management Ownership Concentration Chow Test

上市公司财务柔性对非效率投资影响的实证研究

王满　姜慧琳

（东北财经大学会计学院/中国内部控制研究中心　大连　116025）

摘　要　本文选取2007—2011年我国沪深两市A股上市公司作为样本，运用理查德森的非效率投资度量模型，实证检验了我国上市公司财务柔性对非效率投资的影响。研究表明财务柔性对企业非效率投资的影响具有两面性：第一，财务柔性与投资不足显著负相关，表明上市公司储备财务柔性可以缓解融资约束，减少投资不足；与国有企业相比，财务柔性对非国有企业投资不足的负向影响程度更大。第二，财务柔性与投资过度显著正相关，表明财务柔性加剧委托代理问题，恶化投资过度行为；与非国有企业相比，财务柔性对国有企业投资过度的正向影响程度更大。

关键词　财务柔性　投资不足　投资过度　融资约束　委托代理

一、引言

由于我国资本市场尚不完善，上市公司既可能面临融资约束导致投资不足，也可能遭遇由委托代理问题引起的投资过度，这种非效率性投资将会导致企业资源配置的效率降低，阻碍企业的持续健康发展。目前，国内学者大都基于股权融资偏好探讨上市公司的非效率投资问题，而甚少就企业财务柔性视角研究投资效率。虽然国外已有少部分文献涉及这一领域，但不适用于我国资本市场环境和特殊的上市公司制度背景。本文通过实证研究探寻财务柔性对非效率投资的影响机制，以期为我国上市公司非效率投资的治理问题以及财务柔性经济后果研究提供借鉴和启示。

二、文献综述

（一）财务柔性内涵

美国财会准则委员会（1984）从现金持有政策的角度将财务柔性定义为企业采取有效行动改变现金流的数量和时间以对非预期需求和机会作出反应的

能力。Volderba（1998）认为财务柔性不仅具有强调企业对现金流量调控能力的预防属性，还包括应对不确定环境带来机遇的利用属性。随后，黄世忠（2008）、葛家澍（2008）指出财务柔性是一种超额现金的概念，可增强企业适应性。Graham 和 Harvey（2001）、Gamba 和 Triantis（2007）、Marchica 和 Mura（2010）等从财务杠杆政策角度，认为公司通过保持较低财务杠杆储备财务柔性，能够降低未来融资成本，把握投资机会。

近年来，出现将两种政策结合定义财务柔性的趋势。DeAngelo 和 DeAngelo（2007）认为基于柔性角度的最优政策应该是低杠杆加中度的现金持有量与高股利支付相结合。Gamba 和 Triantis（2008）认为财务柔性应该是综合考虑企业本身资本结构、流动性和对外投资战略决策的结果。Bates、Kahle 和 Stulz（2008）认为超额持有现金与低债务水平相关，应同时使用以预防企业陷入财务困境。Byoun（2008）发现发展中的小企业更倾向于寻求财务柔性，通常是通过低杠杆和高现金持有量来实现。Ozgur Arslan、Chrisostomos Florackis 和 Aydin Ozkan（2010）指出保守财务政策占主导地位，其次是持有大量现金。马春爱（2009）、宁宇和刘飞飞（2011）、刘得格和罗知地（2012）等也认同基于高现金持有和低财务杠杆的财务柔性有利于企业应对多变环境，提高投资能力。基于以往学者的研究，本文将财务柔性定义为持有超额现金流量和保留剩余举债能力，以使企业更好把握未来的有利投资机会，提高投资效率，这是企业低成本重构筹资的手段以及应对不确定环境的能力。

（二）财务柔性影响非效率投资

Graham 和 Harvey（2001）、Brounen 等（2004）及 Denis（2012）针对欧美企业问卷调研得结果表明财务柔性已成为影响财务决策的重要因素，尤其对公司投资决策有显著影响（Marchica 等，2010；顾乃康，2011）。高财务柔性企业可以直接调用现金储备和剩余举债能力为投资活动提供所需资金，财务柔性越高，公司追逐投资机会的能力越强（Bulan 等，2008；Marchica，2010；顾乃康等，2011；宁宇，2011；刘得格、罗知地，2012），从而减少投资不足，增加企业价值。Myers（1984）认为，保留借款能力的公司可以在保守财务政策之后几年轻松获得外部资金，进而逐渐扩大投资规模。Froot、Scharfstein 和 Stein（1993）认为保持财务柔性是为了避免投资不足导致的成本。Trigeorgis（1993）将财务柔性视做一种期权，有助于企业抓住更多投资机会并减弱各种不利于企业发展的影响因素。Daniel 等（2007）研究表明一旦财务柔性缺乏，公司首先削减投资，其次才是削减股利。Denis 等（2011）也证实公司保持财务柔性有助于缓解投资不足。Ozgur Arslan、Chrisostomos Florackis 和 Aydin Ozkan（2012）的实证研究表明高财务柔性公司在金融危机时期更可能获得投资机会，更少依赖内部资金，绩效更优异。Abe de Jong、Marno Verbeek 和 Patrick Verwijmeren（2012）的实证检验表明企业保留举债能力有助于未来非效率投资的减少，认为企业为未来可能的融资约束保留举债能力，财务柔性储备有助于企业应对经济周期影响及竞争环境的变化，对未来投资具有显著积极作用。

国外文献普遍认为财务柔性的存在减少企业投资不足，然而投资不足仅作为非效率投资的表现之一，较少研究将财务柔性、投资不足与投资过度纳入到同一分析框架中。马春爱（2011）运用描述性统计阐述了财务柔性与非效率投资的关系，但缺少实证检验。金余泉（2012）虽然运用实证检验的方法探讨财务柔性对企业非效率投资的影响，但研究还不够深入，存在理论解释不够具体细致、数据时间跨度较小且仅限于制造业上市公司、对财务柔性度量方法有待商榷等不足。本文将在理论分析的基础上实证检验财务柔性对企业非效率投资的影响情况，以期对此研究领域有所拓展。

三、理论分析与研究假设

（一）财务柔性、融资约束与投资不足

在完美市场中，无论企业所需资金来源于内部资金还是外部融资，只要投资项目净现值为正即可进行投资，有效的资本市场总能保证企业筹集足够资金，即企业的投资决策不存在融资约束，只与投资需求有关。然而现实并非如此，资本市场客观存在着信贷配给①不足问题，信息不对称的存在使得外部融资成本高于内部资本成本，由于无法获得充足资金，企业可能放弃净现值为正的投资项目，导致投资不足，即融资约束和信息不对称是造成企业非效率投资行为的重要影响因素。

财务柔性的存在使企业能够利用较低的交易成本来重构筹资，企业财务柔性越大，意味着企业可使用的内部资金和剩余举债能力越多。一方面企业超额现金流量可以满足优质项目的资金需求，另一方面剩余举债能力的增加，避免了由于负债比例过高使潜在债权人认为自己处于不利地位、将面临无法收回资金的高风险而导致外部融资困难从而丧失绝佳投资机会的情况。此外，当企业面临较低财务杠杆时，股东获得偿还债务后的剩余收益越多，股东更有动机进行投资。超额现金持有和剩余举债能力双管齐下，可以缓解由于资金短缺而不能及时把握投资机会的投资不足。

大量学者也对内外部资本市场间的关系进行研究，根据两者相互替代理论，对于保持高水平现金流量的企业来说，外部融资需求有所降低，这与融

① 现代最早研究信贷配给的是Roosa，1951年《资金可获性学说》表明货币政策可通过信贷渠道影响实际投资支出进而影响经济。宏观上信贷配给指在确定利率条件下，信贷市场上的贷款需求大于供给；微观上指贷款申请被部分接受或贷款申请额度只能部分被满足。

资优序理论观点一致，企业偏好内部融资。但 Heitor Almeida 和 Murillo Canpello（2007）实证检验发现内外部资本市场间的反向关系存在于面临低资金成本的企业，对于融资约束相对严重的企业，内外部资本市场呈现出互补的关系，即在使用内部资金保持现有资金需求或应对未来潜在投资机会的同时，也会进行外部融资加以补充，以避免资金短缺带来的投资不足，财务柔性正是这种思想的体现。财务柔性的存在使得企业保持较为充足的资金，缓解融资约束，减少投资不足现象的产生。基于以上分析，本文提出假设1：

H1：在其他条件一定的情况下，财务柔性与企业投资不足呈显著的负相关关系。

此外，国有企业在债务融资方面面临着“软约束”，并且国有企业对于留存收益有更灵活的运用方式，更容易利用内部融资。由于政府对国有上市公司的支持，其较少因融资约束而导致投资不足。相对而言，非国有企业融资渠道有限，银行对其贷款条件也相对苛刻，更容易因为信息不对称而导致融资成本相对较高。非国有企业由融资约束导致的投资不足问题显著（闫华红，许倩，2012）。因此，相对于国有企业，非国有企业的财务柔性越大，其对投资不足的缓解作用可能更加明显。基于以上分析，本文提出假设2：

H2：在其他条件一定的情况下，与国有企业相比，财务柔性对非国有企业投资不足的负向影响程度更大。

（二）财务柔性、委托代理与投资过度

财务柔性越大，企业可使用的超额现金流量和剩余举债能力越多，越可能加重股东与经营者、股东与债权人之间的代理问题，造成企业投资过度。

Jensen 和 Meckling（1976）的自由现金流理论指出企业拥有闲置资金时，经营者会倾向于将多余现金用于能够扩大企业规模的投资项目，而不是用于支付股利或偿还债务。Baumol（1959）、Marris（1964）、Willamson（1964）、Stulz（1990）及 Conyon 和 Murphy（2000）等观点类似，认为企业自由现金流充裕时，经理人可能不会考虑股东和债权人的利益，为了扩大企业规模，掌握更多资源、获得在职消费与个人名誉等私人利益，有动机投资于净现值为负的项目，造成明显的投资过度。Shin 和 Kim（2002）、Dittmar 和 Smith（2007）发现拥有大量现金的企业比拥有少量现金的企业容易作出非效率投资决策。Dechow、Richardson 和 Sloan（2005）证明了自由现金流下过度投资行为能导致企业业绩下降。可见，自由现金流量越大，越可能由于加剧代理问题引起企业投资过度行为。

Jensen（1986）指出债务在约束自由现金流滥用中起到一定作用。随后，Stulz（1990），Harris 和 Raviv（1990）、Hart 和 Moore（1995）及 Zwiebel

(1996) 将经营者帝国建造偏好的思想纳入模型中，并假定这种私有收益和企业的投资成正比。保持一定负债对于抑制股东与经营者的代理问题有一定作用，负债的存在使经营者面临未来还本付息、支出现金流量的压力，减少可供经营者支配的现金；负债也使经营者面临更多的监控和破产风险，一旦企业不能按期偿还债务，公司的控制权将归债权人所有，经营者将丧失从企业取得的各种收益。此外，债务融资数量的增加对于经营者的持股比例有放大的作用，其剩余索取权的比例将提高，这种激励作用使经营者减少偷懒、从事在职消费以及过度投资的可能性。可见，从不同角度来看，负债对企业过度投资有一定治理作用。

财务柔性越大，可获资金能力越强，一方面越可能加重经理人与股东间的代理问题造成过度投资；另一方面，股东为了自身利益最大化，冒险投资于高风险高收益的项目，这种项目一旦成功，股东可获得巨大利润，即使失败，也是由债权人承担到期不被偿付的风险，财务柔性越大，股东可借债务越多，冒险投资动机越大，加重了股东与债权人间的代理问题，更加恶化过度投资行为。同时，负债水平越小，其治理机制越不明显，越可能导致较为严重的过度投资行为。基于以上分析，本文提出假设3：

H3：在其他条件一定的情况下，财务柔性与企业投资过度呈显著的正相关关系。

此外，我国国有企业控股股东通常一股独大，控股股东与小股东之间代理问题严重，且国有企业控股股东具有对投资决策的控制权及对企业经营者的任免权，对经营者缺少激励机制，易造成过度的多元化投资以及一些短视性投资。不仅如此，国有企业在产权上表现为弱势控制，容易产生“内部人控制”现象，而在政治上却是强势控制，为了管理者的自身利益以及政治目的更容易产生过度投资现象。再者，国有控股的上市公司虽然历经多年改革与发展，但在公司治理机制方面往往并不健全，董事会难以发挥对管理层的监督与控制，国有企业比非国有企业存在更多过度投资行为。综上，相对于非国有企业，国有企业的财务柔性水平更大，越可能导致更大程度的过度投资。基于以上分析，本文提出假设4：

H4：在其他条件一定的情况下，与非国有企业相比，财务柔性对国有企业投资过度的正向影响程度更大。

四、研究设计

（一）样本选取与数据来源

本文以2007—2011年间我国沪深两市A股上市公司为样本，以企业非效率投资为研究对象。为了避免其他因素对研究的影响，针对样本进行以下筛选：①为排除财务数据特殊性，剔除金融保险类行业上市公司；②为排除财务异常，剔除当年被实施ST处理的上市公司；③为保证相同融资环境，剔除同时发行B股和H股的上市公司；④由于股权融资导致企业过度投资（潘敏，金岩，2003）不是本文研究重点，剔除当年IPO或当年实施过增发或配股记录的上市公司，这也保证财务柔性测度的相对准确性；⑤剔除财务会计数据或指标缺失的上市公司；⑥为控制极端值对回归结果的影响，本文对回归模型所有变量进行1%和99%分位数的Winsorize缩尾处理。本文所选样本数据来源于Wind资讯及国泰君安数据库，通过如上步骤进行手工整理得到2007—2011年间的5 106个样本，其中投资不足企业3 167个，包括国有企业1 794个和非国有企业1 373个；投资过度公司1 939个，包括国有企业1 124个，非国有企业815个。

（二）变量定义与模型构建

1. 被解释变量——非效率投资

本文赞同Richardson（2006）观点，认为新增投资支出是预期投资支出与非预期投资支出之和，可先计算公司预期投资支出，再将其与企业的实际支出作比较，差额部分即是企业的非预期支出，表现为回归模型的残差，残差大于零表示投资过度，残差小于零表示投资不足。经典模型中V/P_{t-1}的计算需要对贴现率和超额盈余的持续性参数进行估计，可能影响模型本身的准确性。多数研究采用托宾Q替代模型中的成长机会，例如杨华军（2008）研究自由现金流的过度投资时，也采用托宾Q这一替代变量。所以本文采用模型1度量非效率投资：

$$I_{New_t} = \alpha + \alpha_1(Tobin'Q_{t-1}) + \alpha_2 Lev_{t-1} + \alpha_3 Cash_{t-1} + \alpha_4 Age_{t-1} + \alpha_5 Size_{t-1} + \alpha_6 SR_{t-1} + \alpha_7 I_{New_{t-1}} + \sum Year + \sum Industry + \varepsilon \quad (1)$$

具体变量见表1。

2. 解释变量——财务柔性

本文认为，Marchica和Mura（2010）、Abe de Jong等从现金持有量或举债能力单一角度考察企业财务柔性，不能全面反映财务柔性实际情况；马春爱（2011）等采用构建财务柔性综合指数的方法虽然能够检验不同类型财务柔性企业之间融资能力的差异，但却难以对其具体融资方式作出合理预期与判断，且其度量方法涉及专家打分确定不同指标的权重，带有一定主观性（曾爱民等，2011）。因此，本文借鉴曾爱民（2011）的做法，将财务柔性量化为超额现金持有量与剩余举债能力之和，即现金柔性与负债融资柔性之和，其中，现金柔性=公司自身现金比率-行业现金比率均值，现金比率=（货币资金+交易性金融资产）/总资产；负债融资柔性=Max（0，行业负债比率均值-公司自身负债比率）。

表1 **非效率投资变量定义表**

变量类型	变量	变量计算方法
被解释变量	I_{New_t}	（t 年购建固定资产、无形资产和其他长期资产支付的现金-t 年处置固定资产、无形资产和其他长期资产收回的现金净额）/ t-1 期末总资产
解释变量	$Tobin'Q_{t-1}$	（流通股股数×流通股价格+非流通股股数×每股净资产+负责账面价值）/ t-1 期末总资产
	Lev_{t-1}	t-1 期末总负债账面价值/t-1 期末总资产
	$Cash_{t-1}$	t-1 期货币资金/t-1 期末总资产
	Age_{t-1}	LN（t-1 期末公司上市年限）
	$Size_{t-1}$	LN（t-1 期末总资产）
	SR_{t-1}	（t-1 年收盘价- t-1 年开盘价）/ t-1 年开盘价
	$I_{New_{t-1}}$	计算方法同 I_{New_t}
	Year	为控制年度的固定影响，设置 4 个年度虚拟变量
	Industry	为控制行业的固定影响，按照证监会《上市公司行业分类指引》规定，分为 12 类（剔除金融保险类），设置 11 个行业虚拟变量

3. 模型设计

本文在借鉴徐晓东、张天西（2009），马春爱（2011），金余泉（2012），吕峻（2012）等对于非效率投资研究的基础上，针对上文提出的四个假设，并考虑公司治理及财务信息对非效率投资的影响，设计以下两个模型，分别检验财务柔性对投资不足的影响及财务柔性对投资过度的影响。再将投资不足和投资过度的样本按照产权性质不同，分为国有上市公司样本及非国有上市公司样本，以此检验产权性质不同，财务柔性对非效率投资的影响程度。具体变量见表4。

模型2（针对 H1 和 H2）：

$$UI_t = \mu_0 + \mu_1 FF_{t-1} + \mu_2 ACR_t + \mu_3 OR_t + \mu_4 EC_t + \mu_5 Ind_t + \mu_6 TOP10_t + \mu_7 Tobin'Q_t + \mu_8 Size_t + \mu_9 Age_t + \mu_{10} \sum Year_t + \mu_{11} \sum Industry_t + \eta \quad (2)$$

模型3（针对 H3 和 H4）：

$$OI_t = \beta_0 + \beta_1 FF_{t-1} + \beta_2 ACR_t + \beta_3 OR_t + \beta_4 EC_t + \beta_5 Ind_t + \beta_6 TOP10_t + \beta_7 Tobin'Q_t + \beta_8 Size_t + \beta_9 Age_t + \beta_{10} \sum Year_t + \beta_{11} \sum Industry_t + \delta \quad (3)$$

表2 变量定义表

变量类型	变量	变量定义	计算方法
被解释变量	UI_t	投资不足	模型1残差小于零部分
	OI_t	过度投资	模型1残差大于零部分
解释变量	FF_{t-1}	财务柔性	t-1期超额现金持有量与剩余举债能力之和
控制变量	ACR_t	管理费用率	t期管理费用/t期末总资产
	OR_t	大股东占款比例	(t期其他应收款-其他应付款)/t期末总资产
	EC_t	高管薪酬	t期前三名高管薪酬之和取自然对数
	Ind_t	独立董事比例	t期独立董事人数/董事会成员人数
	$TOP10_t$	大股东持股比例	t期前十大股东持股比例
	$Tobin'Q_t$	成长机会	(流通股股数×流通股价格+非流通股股数×每股净资产+负责账面价值)/t期末总资产
	$Size_t$	公司规模	LN(t期末总资产)
	Age_t	上市年限	LN(t期末公司上市年限)
	Year	年度虚拟变量	同表1
	Industry	行业虚拟变量	同表1

五、实证结果与分析

(一)非效率投资回归结果

本文利用理查德森(2006)经典模型,利用2007—2011年间5 106个样本求出我国上市公司效率投资预期值,并与实际值比较求得残差作为非效率投资水平。模型具体回归结果见表3。

由表3可知,企业本期新增投资额与上一期托宾Q、资产负债率、货币资金、上市年限、公司规模、股票收益率以及上一期新增投资额等主要变量显著相关。具体结果为:

$$I_{New_t} = -0.127 + 0.016(Tobin'Q_{t-1}) - 0.027Lev_{t-1} - 0.022Cash_{t-1} - 0.017Age_{t-1} + 0.008Size_{t-1} + 0.010SR_{t-1} + 0.307I_{New_{t-1}} \quad (4)$$

(二)描述性统计

2007—2011年度企业非效率投资与财务柔性整体趋势如表4所示。在全样本下,我国非效率投资水平均值为0.005,结合样本投资不足企业3 167个、投资过度企业1 939个,表明我国上市公司投资不足情况比较普遍,但投资过

表 3　**非效率投资度量模型回归结果表**

	系数	标准差	T	P 值
（常量）	−0.127 ***	0.039	−3.253	0.001
$Tobin'Q_{t-1}$	0.016 ***	0.001	13.052	0.000
Lev_{t-1}	−0.027 ***	0.003	−8.938	0.000
$Cash_{t-1}$	−0.022	0.013	−1.604	0.109
Age_{t-1}	−0.017 ***	0.003	−6.624	0.000
$Size_{t-1}$	0.008 ***	0.002	4.781	0.000
SR_{t-1}	0.010 ***	0.002	4.236	0.000
$I_{New_{t-1}}$	0.307 ***	0.016	19.124	0.000
Year	控制			
Industry	控制			
样本量	5 106			
Adj-R^2	0.144			
F Value	43.912 ***			

注：*** 在 1% 水平（双侧）上显著；** 在 5% 水平（双侧）上显著；* 在 10% 水平（双侧）上显著。

度的程度（即残差绝对值）较大，而财务柔性平均指标为 0.164，表明经历亚洲金融危机以及次贷危机等非预期经济冲击后，我国上市公司大体上已经拥有了储备财务柔性的观念，并在具体的财务决策中采用了财务柔性战略。

将样本整体分为投资不足和投资过度两个组进行比较可得，投资不足企业的财务柔性平均值为 0.079，而投资过度企业的财务柔性平均值为 0.086，这表明投资不足的企业财务柔性相对较低，投资过度的企业财务柔性相对较高。

在投资不足企业中再分为国有企业和非国有企业两组。如表 4，投资不足中的国有企业财务柔性均值为 0.064，而投资不足的非国有企业财务柔性为 0.110，表明相比于国有企业，非国有企业由于面临着更大的融资约束，本身更注重储备财务柔性；非国有企业的投资不足水平（−0.250）低于国有企业的投资不足水平（−0.262）。这初步表明相比于国有企业，非国有企业的财务柔性对其投资不足的缓解作用可能更大。在投资过度的企业中，非国有企业储备的财务柔性水平（0.138）仍然高于国有企业的财务柔性水平（0.054）。但是国有企业的过度投资水平（0.300）高于非国有企业的过度投资水平（0.283），这同样可也初步说明，相比于非国有企业，财务柔性可能会导致国有企业更大程度的过度投资。

表4 企业非效率投资与财务柔性描述性统计表

样本类型		变量	极小值	极大值	均值	中位数	标准差
全样本		I	-1.357	3.900	0.005	-0.109	0.615
		FF	-0.198	1.204	0.164	0.081	0.273
投资不足	总体	I	-1.357	-0.007	-0.256	-0.314	0.256
		FF	-0.197	1.070	0.079	0.160	0.267
	国有企业	I	-1.357	-0.007	-0.262	-0.313	0.252
		FF	-0.195	0.994	0.064	0.131	0.235
	非国有企业	I	-1.346	-0.010	-0.250	-0.315	0.262
		FF	-0.197	1.070	0.110	0.198	0.299
投资过度	总体	I	0.005	3.900	0.291	0.527	0.670
		FF	-0.198	1.204	0.086	0.170	0.282
	国有企业	I	0.005	3.900	0.300	0.541	0.691
		FF	-0.198	1.204	0.054	0.131	0.253
	非国有企业	I	0.005	3.900	0.283	0.507	0.640
		FF	-0.198	1.204	0.138	0.225	0.310

（三）变量相关性检验

上市公司投资不足水平与各主要变量之间的相关性水平见表5。

表5 投资不足模型中变量的 Pearson 相关分析

	UI_t	FF_{t-1}	ACR_t	OR_t	EC_t	Ind_t	$TOP10_t$	Tobin'Q	$Size_t$	Age_t
UI_t	1.000									
FF_{t-1}	-0.116***	1.000								
ACR_t	-0.054***	0.032*	1.000							
OR_t	0.007	0.143***	-0.111***	1.000						
EC_t	0.003	0.035*	0.045**	0.046***	1.000					
Ind_t	-0.027	0.007	0.001	-0.031*	0.031*	1.000				
$TOP10_t$	-0.053***	0.181***	-0.032*	-0.014	0.151***	-0.014	1.000			
$Tobin'Q_t$	-0.273***	0.119***	0.355***	-0.068***	-0.007	0.045**	-0.114***	1.000		
$Size_t$	0.104***	-0.216***	-0.333***	0.041**	0.373***	0.027	0.220***	-0.396***	1.000	
Age_t	0.085***	-0.415***	0.012	-0.125***	-0.022	-0.004	-0.435***	0.093***	0.148***	1.000

注：*** 在1%水平（双侧）上显著；** 在5%水平（双侧）上显著；* 在10%水平（双侧）上显著。

由表5可知，投资不足水平与企业财务柔性水平、管理费用率、前十大股东持股比率、企业托宾Q、公司规模以及公司上市年限等解释与控制变量高度相关。其中投资不足水平与财务柔性呈显著的负相关关系，说明财务柔性水平确实可以抑制企业的投资不足情况。

上市公司投资过度水平与各主要变量之间的相关性水平见表6。

表6　**投资过度模型中变量的 Pearson 相关分析**

	UI_t	FF_{t-1}	ACR_t	OR_t	EC_t	Ind_t	$TOP10_t$	Tobin'Q	$Size_t$	Age_t
UI_t	1.000									
FF_{t-1}	0.073***	1.000								
ACR_t	-0.088***	0.073***	1.000							
OR_t	-0.029	0.111***	-0.121***	1.000						
EC_t	-0.034	-0.037	0.058***	0.018	1.000					
Ind_t	-0.010	0.005	-0.035	-0.053***	0.021	1.000				
$TOP10_t$	0.091***	0.160***	-0.004	-0.036	0.079***	0.023	1.000			
$Tobin'Q_t$	-0.019	0.133***	0.325***	-0.060***	0.022	0.021	-0.045**	1.000		
$Size_t$	0.058**	-0.307***	-0.343***	0.000	0.348***	0.029	0.079***	-0.399***	1.000	
Age_t	-0.019	-0.413***	-0.034	-0.182***	0.053**	-0.017	-0.435***	-0.051**	0.316***	1.000

注：*** 在1%水平（双侧）上显著；** 在5%水平（双侧）上显著；* 在10%水平（双侧）上显著。

由表6可知，投资过度水平与企业财务柔性水平、管理费用率、前十大股东持股比率以及公司规模有显著的相关关系。其中投资过度水平与企业的财务柔性水平呈显著的正相关关系，说明财务柔性可能导致更严重的投资过度水平。

（四）多元回归分析

由模型二、模型三进行多元回归得出结果见表7。

从表7的第二列FF系数为-0.045且在5%的水平下显著可知，在投资不足的企业中，财务柔性越大，企业投资不足越能得到一定程度缓解，即财务柔性与企业投资不足呈显著的负相关关系，因此可以证明假设H1的成立。从第二列我们还发现，企业上市年限系数为0.033且在1%水平下显著，表明企业上市时间越长，可能由于企业已经过了成长期，处于一种成熟状态，投资选择

表7 **模型二及模型三回归分析结果表**

	投资不足			投资过度		
	全样本	国有企业	非国有企业	全样本	国有企业	非国有企业
截距	-0.120	-0.125	-0.150	-0.578	-0.441	-1.061
	(-1.026)	(-0.823)	(-0.728)	(-1.381)	(-0.779)	(-1.506)
FF_{t-1}	-0.045**	-0.050*	-0.051*	0.239***	0.312***	0.158*
	(-2.423)	(-1.912)	(-1.883)	(3.911)	(3.519)	(1.839)
ACR_t	0.417**	0.477**	0.406	-1.872***	-1.576*	-1.944**
	(2.412)	(1.998)	(1.584)	(-3.082)	(-1.919)	(-2.024)
OR_t	0.036	0.145	-0.188	-.0518*	-0.681*	-0.324
	(0.391)	(1.252)	(-1.263)	(-1.697)	(-1.692)	(-0.665)
EC_t	0.005	0.017*	-0.008	-0.058**	-0.052	-0.068**
	(0.805)	(1.804)	(-0.844)	(-2.486)	(-1.597)	(-1.982)
Ind_t	-0.070**	-0.094**	-0.057	0.378***	0.091	0.761***
	(-2.097)	(-2.144)	(-1.089)	(3.294)	(0.562)	(4.606)
$TOP10_t$	-0.004	-0.010	0.005	0.052***	0.060**	0.057*
	(-0.798)	(-1.444)	(0.494)	(2.594)	(2.307)	(1.686)
$Tobin'Q_t$	-0.068***	-0.060***	-0.073***	0.023	-0.013	0.045*
	(-15.268)	(-9.559)	(-11.46)	(1.165)	(-0.42)	(1.667)
$Size_t$	-0.070	-0.028	-0.108	-0.246	-0.470	0.008
	(-0.796)	(-0.238)	(-0.813)	(-0.841)	(-1.197)	(0.018)
Age_t	0.033***	0.050***	0.012	0.030	-0.017	0.087*
	(3.648)	(3.837)	(0.855)	(0.97)	(-0.341)	(1.943)
Year	控制	控制	控制	控制	控制	控制
Industry	控制	控制	控制	控制	控制	控制
样本量	3 167	1 794	1 373	1 939	1 124	815
$Adj\text{-}R^2$	0.139	0.132	0.161	0.063	0.063	0.071
F Value	22.224***	12.375***	11.996***	6.436***	4.160***	3.585***

注：***在1%水平（双侧）上显著；**在5%水平（双侧）上显著；*在10%水平（双侧）上显著。

有限，因此存在更大程度的投资不足。另外，Tobin'Q的系数为-0.068且在1%水平下显著，由于Tobin'Q代表着公司的成长机会，所以当成长机会越大时，企业有充分的投资机会进行投资，其投资不足现象就越不明显。在其余变量中，管理费用率（ACR）与投资不足在5%水平下显著正相关；公司独立董事（Ind）与投资不足也在5%水平下显著负相关。

在投资不足的条件下，比较国有企业与非国有企业可知，第三列国有企业的FF系数为-0.050且在10%水平下显著，而第四列中非国有企业的FF系数为-0.051且在10%水平下显著，因此，非国有企业的财务柔性对投资不足的作用比国有企业的作用更大，即与国有企业相比，财务柔性对非国有企业投资不足的负向作用更为明显，从而证明假设H2成立。

由表7中第五列FF系数为0.239且在1%水平下显著可知，财务柔性与投资过度呈显著正向关系，即财务柔性会导致企业更严重的过度投资，从而证明假设H3成立。在其余变量中，管理费用率与过度投资在1%水平下显著负相关，说明管理费用越大，企业过度投资水平越低；公司独立董事与过度投资水平在1%水平下显著正相关，可能由于我国公司治理水平较低，独立董事只是形式上的存在，所以越高的独立董事比例，反而过度投资越严重；前十大股东持股比例也与过度投资在1%水平下显著正相关，说明由于我国股权分散度不够，前十大股东往往拥有公司的绝对决策权，所以其持股比例越大，越容易导致公司过度投资。其余变量中大股东占款比例（OR）与过度投资在10%水平下显著负相关，高管薪酬（EC）与过度投资在5%的水平下显著负相关。

在投资过度的企业中，比较第六、七列的FF系数可得，过度投资的国有企业FF系数为0.312且在1%水平下显著，而非国有企业FF系数仅为0.158且仅在10%水平下显著，这充分说明，与非国有企业相比，财务柔性对国有企业过度投资的正向影响更为显著，从而验证了假设H4的成立。

（五）稳健性检验

本文借鉴Denis（2011）去除随机误差的方法，将t年企业实际新增投资与通过模型（1）得出的t年新增投资拟合值上下浮动10%进行比较，即投资不足=t年企业实际新增投资-0.9新增投资拟合值，投资过度=t年企业实际新增投资-1.1新增投资拟合值，得出非效率投资数据并进行稳健性检验，回归结果见表8。

从表8可以看出，第二列FF系数为-0.042且在10%水平下显著，财务柔性与企业投资不足呈显著负相关关系，第五列FF系数为0.255且在10%水平下显著，财务柔性与企业投资过度呈显著正相关关系，即假设1和假设3再次被证实。但是根据产权性质分为国有企业和非国有企业时，虽然FF系数与预期相同，但非国有企业财务柔性对非效率投资影响并不显著，这可能是由于上下浮动10%的方法虽能从一定程度去除不利影响但可能带有一定主观性所致。

表8 **稳健性检验回归分析结果表**

	投资不足			投资过度		
	全样本	国有企业	非国有企业	全样本	国有企业	非国有企业
截距	-0.240	-0.198	-0.245	-1.815*	-0.877	-4.159*
	(-1.556)	(-1.049)	(-0.856)	(-1.933)	(-1.02)	(-1.893)
FF_{t-1}	-0.042*	-0.054*	-0.051	0.255*	0.458***	0.097
	(-1.733)	(-1.671)	(-1.369)	(1.864)	(3.365)	(0.375)
ACR_t	0.420*	0.585**	0.359	-2.32**	-1.45	-1.76
	(1.854)	(1.979)	(1.006)	(-1.804)	(-1.253)	(-0.624)
OR_t	0.190	0.428***	-0.216	0.297	-0.636	1.621
	(1.595)	(2.989)	(-1.04)	(0.435)	(-1.029)	(1.12)
EC_t	0.010	0.02*	0	-0.139***	-0.141***	-0.161
	(1.153)	(1.711)	(0.004)	(-2.671)	(-2.839)	(-1.531)
Ind_t	-0.142	-0.11	-0.14	-0.904	-0.936	-0.726
	(-1.238)	(-0.751)	(-0.759)	(-1.347)	(-1.514)	(-0.519)
$TOP10_t$	-0.132***	-0.138**	-0.159**	1.197***	0.354	2.252***
	(-3.014)	(-2.526)	(-2.189)	(4.596)	(1.416)	(4.435)
$Tobin'Q_t$	-0.063***	-0.056***	-0.066***	0.07	0.024	0.114
	(-10.815)	(-7.129)	(-7.454)	(1.617)	(0.516)	(1.47)
$Size_t$	0.006	-0.002	0.015	0.103**	0.095**	0.183*
	(0.781)	(-0.281)	(1.099)	(2.359)	(2.463)	(1.763)
Age_t	0.009	0.033**	-0.028	0.165**	-0.037	0.358***
	(0.774)	(2.004)	(-1.456)	(2.432)	(-0.497)	(2.777)
Year	控制	控制	控制	控制	控制	控制
Industry	控制	控制	控制	控制	控制	控制
样本量	3 167	1 794	1 373	1 939	1 124	815
$Adj\text{-}R^2$	0.139	0.132	0.161	0.063	0.063	0.071
F Value	22.224***	12.375***	11.996***	6.436***	4.160***	3.585***

注：*** 在1%水平（双侧）上显著；** 在5%水平（双侧）上显著；* 在10%水平（双侧）上显著。

六、研究结论

企业能否有效运用财务柔性策略，理性分析并作出合理的投资决策，保证投资效率对于企业目标的实现尤为重要。研究表明财务柔性对企业非效率投资的影响具有两面性：第一，财务柔性与投资不足显著负相关，即上市公司储备财务柔性可以缓解融资约束，减少投资不足；与国有企业相比，财务柔性对非国有企业投资不足的负向影响程度更大。第二，财务柔性与投资过度显著正相关，即财务柔性加剧委托代理问题，恶化投资过度行为；与非国有企业相比，财务柔性对国有企业投资过度的正向影响程度更大。

针对上述财务柔性对企业非效率投资影响的分析以及不同产权性质企业之间投资行为的不同，提出以下政策建议。第一，公司应该注重财务柔性思想，通过超额现金持有、保持低财务杠杆等多种方式综合储备适度的财务柔性，这不仅有利于应对非预期经济波动，更可以把握未来投资机会，提高企业投资效率。第二，努力打通我国债券市场融资渠道，尤其对于面临更强融资约束而导致投资不足的非国有上市公司，商业银行应合理分配贷款资源，为有发展潜力且财务状况优异的企业提供资金支持。第三，提高上市公司尤其是国有上市公司治理水平，建立良好激励机制以减弱股东与经营者代理问题，提高信息透明度以减弱“一股独大”和“内部人控制”现象，同时政府应减少行政干预，建立监管机制以完善对国有上市公司投资的市场监督。

参考文献

[1]白朝丽,杨邦文．OPM 战略下的财务弹性分析——基于鄂武商、武汉中商、武汉中百的案例[J]．财会通讯,2012(3):117-118.

[2]程新生,谭有超,刘建梅．非财务信息、外部融资与投资效率——基于外部制度约束的研究[J]．管理世界,2012(7):137-150.

[3]顾乃康,万小勇,陈辉．财务弹性与企业投资的关系研究[J]．管理评论,2011(6):115-121.

[4]吕峻．政府干预和治理结构对公司过度投资的影响[J]．财经问题研究．2012(1):31-37.

[5]刘得格,罗知地．财务弹性和投融资行为以及企业价值的关系研究[J]．经济研究导刊,2012(1):61-63.

[6]刘红霞,索玲玲．会计稳健性、投资效率与企业价值[J]．财务与会计研究,2011(5):53-63.

[7]金余泉．财务弹性影响企业非效率投资的实证研究[M]．合肥:安徽大学,2012.

[8]马春爱．中国上市公司的非效率投资研究:一个财务弹性的视角[J]．财贸研究,2011(2):144-148.

[9]宁宇,刘飞飞. 财务弹性视角下的企业价值与投资能力研究[J]. 企业纵横,2011(5):59-60.

[10]谢军,李千子. 公司治理结构能缓解非效率投资吗?——来自上市公司的证据[J]. 兰州商学院学报,2012(2):69-75.

[11]姜付秀,伊志宏,苏飞,等. 管理者背景特征与企业过度投资行为[J]. 管理世界,2009:(1):130-139.

[12]徐晓东,张天西. 公司治理、自由现金流与非效率投资[J]. 财经研究,2009(10):47-58.

[13]闫华红,许晴. 国有与非国有上市公司非效率投资比较的实证研究[J]. 公司治理,2012(7):96-99.

[14]俞红海,徐龙炳,陈百助. 终极控股股东控制权与自由现金流过度投资[J]. 经济研究,2010(8):103-114.

[15]赵华,张鼎祖. 企业财务柔性的本原属性研究[J]. 会计研究,2010(6):62-69.

[16]朱磊,潘爱玲. 负债对企业非效率投资行为影响的实证研究——来自中国制造业上市公司的面板数据[J]. 经济与管理研究,2009(2):52-59.

[17]张功富. 财务杠杆、投资行为与企业竞争优势——来自中国上市公司的经验证据[J]. 经济与管理研究,2009(2):44-51.

[18]曾爱民,傅元略,魏志华. 金融危机冲击、财务柔性和企业融资行为——来自中国上市公司的经验证据[J]. 金融研究,2011(10):155-169.

[19]周雪峰,兰艳泽. 债务融资对非效率投资行为的影响作用——基于中国民营上市公司的实证研究[J]. 暨南学报,2011(3):23-30.

[20] JONG A, VERBEEK M, VERWIJMEREN P. Does Financial Flexibility Reduce Investment Distortions? [J]. The Journal of Financial Research, 2012, 35(2):243-259.

[21] ARSLAN, OZGUR, LORACKIS C, OZKAN A. How and Why Do Firms Establish Financial Flexibility? [R]. Working Paper, ssrn. com, 2009.

[22] BULAN, LAARNI, SUBRAMANIAN N. A Closer Look at Dividend Omissions: Payout Policy, Investment and Financial Flexibility [R]. Brandeis University Working Paper, 2008.

[23] BYOUN, SOKU. Financial Flexibility and Capital Structure Decision [R]. Baylor University Working Paper, 2008.

[24] DENIS, MCKEON. Debt Financing and Financial Flexibility: Evidence from Pro-Active Leverage Increases [J]. Review of Financial Studies, 2012, 26(6): 1897-1929.

[25] DAVID J. Financial Flexibility and Corporate Liquidity [J]. Journal of Corporate Finance, 2011(17): 667-674.

[26] GAMBA, TRIANTIS. The Value of Financial Flexibility [J]. Journal of Finance, 2008, 63(5).

[27] DEANGELO H, DEANGELO L. Capital Structure, Payout Policy, and Financial Flexibility[R]. University of Southern California, Working Paper, 2007.

[28] GRAHAM, HARVEY. The Theory and Practice of Corporate Finance: Evidence from the Field [J]. Journal of Financial Economics, 2001(2-3):187-243.

[29] MARCHICA, MURA. Financial Flexibility, Investment Ability, and Firm Value: Evidence from Firms with Spare Debt Capacity [J]. Financial Management, 2010, 39(4):1339

-1365.

[30] MARCHICA, TERESA M, MURA R. Financial Flexibility and Investment Decision: Evidence from Low-Leverage Firms [R]. Manchester Business School Working Paper, 2007.

[31] STEWART M, MAJLUF N. Corporate Financing and Investment Decisions When Firms Have Information that Investors Don't Have [J]. Journal of Financial Economics, 1984, 13 (2): 187-221.

[32] RICHARDSON. Over-investment of Free Cash Flow [J]. Review of Accounting Studies, 2006(11):159-189.

An Empirical Research on the Effect of Listed Companies' Financial Flexibility on Inefficient Investment

Abstract This paper took the sample of A-share listed companies in Shanghai and Shenzhen stock exchanges from 2007 to 2011 and applied Richardson inefficient investment measurement model, empirically, to test how the financial flexibility influences the inefficiency of investment of the listed companies in China. Our study has showed that effects of financial flexibility on the inefficiency investment of the enterprises has two sides, one is that financial flexibility and under-investment has significant negative correlation, in another word, reserves of financial flexibility of listed company can alleviate the financing constraints, reducing under-investment and the negative correlation is more obvious of non-state owned enterprises than that of state owned enterprises. The other one is financial flexibility has significant positive effect on over-investment, which means financial flexibility worsen the agency problem and deteriorated the over-investment ; compared with non-state owned enterprises, financial flexibility has more significant positive influence on the over-investment of state owned enterprises.

Key Words Inancial Flexibility Under-investment Over-investment Financial Constraints Principal-agent Theory

特许权价值、公司治理和银行稳健性
——来自中国上市银行的经验证据

曲洪建[1]　张相贤[2]　王宇明[1,3,4]

（1. 上海工程技术大学　上海　201620；2. 威海商业银行　威海　264200；3. 东华大学　上海　200051；4．光大银行黑龙江分行　哈尔滨　250014）

摘　要　本文以2000—2012年16家上市银行为样本，实证分析了特许权价值、公司治理及其交互作用对银行稳健性的影响。研究结果表明：特许权价值存在自律效应；第一大股东性质和持股比例对银行稳健性没有显著影响，前十大股东的持股比例对银行稳健性有显著影响；董事会的监督管理能提高银行稳健性，而独立董事并没有起到应有的监督管理作用；高管持股能够增强银行稳健性，而高管薪酬却没有激励作用；银行规模和稳健性之间存在正相关关系，这也支持了“大而不倒”的观点；上市银行的杠杆效应没有充分发挥作用；特许权价值与前十大股东的持股比例、高管持股对于银行稳健性的影响起到相互替代作用。

关键词　特许权价值　公司治理　交互作用　银行稳健性

一、引言

2007年美国爆发了震惊世界的次贷危机，此次危机造成了多家知名投行破产，自2008年年初以来，美国已经有共计445家银行破产倒闭，上千家银行进入“问题银行名单”。为了应对全球金融危机的影响，各国采用非常规政策刺激经济，金融危机得到一定程度的缓解，但是金融市场的脆弱性尤其是商业银行稳健性引起了各国的重视。为了提高银行体系的稳健性，巴塞尔银行监管委员会召开会议，批准了加强《银行资本和流动性监管的政策建议（征求意见稿）》，各国也纷纷推出了各种措施提高银行体系稳健性。随着后危机时代的到来和巴塞尔协议Ⅲ的逐步实施，学者们越来越关注银行稳健性问题。

政府赋予商业银行特许经营的权力，它们基于自身经营优势和外在市场优势，具有获取超额收益的能力，这种牌照价值学术界称其为“特许权价值”。许多国家的实践都表明，特许权价值和银行稳健性密切相关，银行特许权价值降低，超额收益下降，银行经营者就会有冒险经营的冲动，银行稳健性就会降低。

公司治理风险是商业银行最大的风险之一，2008年金融危机以来倒闭的445家美国商业银行中，很大一部分倒闭的原因是公司治理风险。商业银行不完善的公司治理结构和内部控制会引发银行风险，降低银行稳健性。从国内银行的发展情况看，我国商业银行公司治理改革较晚，公司治理问题较多，对银行体系的稳健性产生许多负面影响。近几年来包括四大国有银行在内的商业银行纷纷上市，探索银行公司治理改革的思路，取得了一定进展。但与现代商业银行相比，我国商业银行的公司治理结构主要存在以下问题：银行产权主体不够明确；董事会、监事会、独立董事、经理层职责及任务、权力划分尚不清晰；对企业管理的有效监督机制尚未确立；缺乏清晰、市场化的激励约束机制等等。为此，2006 年银监会颁布《国有商业银行公司治理及相关监管指引》，提出了公司治理改革的主要目标：以改革管理体制、完善治理结构、转换经营机制、提高经营绩效为中心，将国有商业银行逐步建设成为资本充足、内控严密、运营安全、服务和效益良好、具有国际竞争力的现代化股份制商业银行。而完善公司治理是商业银行股份制改革的核心和关键，它直接影响到银行稳健性。

在这种情况下，有必要通过特许权价值的改变和公司治理机制的完善，提高商业银行的核心竞争力，促进商业银行稳健经营，维护整个金融系统的安全。因此本文基于上市银行的经验数据，研究特许权价值、公司治理及其交互作用对银行稳健性的影响。研究结果显示，特许权价值、前十大股东持股比例、董事会规模、高管持股能够提高银行稳健性；第一大股东性质和持股比例、独立董事比例、高管薪酬对银行稳健性没有显著性影响；银行规模和稳健性之间存在正相关关系，这也支持了“大而不倒”的观点；上市银行的杠杆效应没有充分发挥作用；特许权价值与前十大股东的持股比例、高管持股对于银行稳健性的影响起到相互替代作用。

本文的研究在以下两个方面有所拓展：（1）在银行风险研究的基础上，拓展到银行稳健性的研究，既考虑了银行稳定性（风险），又考虑了银行健康性（盈利性），对银行状态分析更加全面；（2）把特许权价值和公司治理机制纳入同一个模型，研究二者的交互作用对银行稳健性的影响，从一个新的视角研究银行稳健性问题，从而丰富了这一研究领域的文献。

二、理论分析与研究假设

国内外文献大多是特许权价值、公司治理对银行风险影响的研究，很少有对银行稳健性影响的研究，银行稳健性和银行风险之间还是存在一定差异的，稳健性包含两个方面的含义：稳定和健康，稳定主要是指银行风险小，而健康则说明银行要保持良好的盈利性。因此银行风险研究主要关注稳定因素，没有考虑银行的健康因素（即盈利性）。而从持续经营的角度看，单纯考虑风险，只能确保银行不倒闭，而不能保证银行的可持续发展。在影响银行风险承担的各种因素中，受学者关注较多的是特许权价值和公司治理，已有研究主要是从以下几个方面展开的：

（一）特许权价值和银行风险的研究

Diamond（1966）和 Rajan（1968）最早提出了银行特许权价值的概念，随后 Edward I. Aliman（1968），Caprio 和 Summers（1993）以及 Murdock 和 Stilglitz（1994）等研究了特许权价值对银行的重要影响。随着研究的深入，人们开始关注特许权价值和银行风险之间的关系，主要有两种不同观点：Marcus（1984）、Keeley（1990）、Rafael Repullo.（2002）、Frederick T. Furlong 和 Simon H. Kwan（2006）、Olivier De Jonghe，Rudi Vander Vennet（2008）等认为特许权价值会降低银行风险；而 Park（1997）、Saunders 和 Berry Wilson（1994）、Fisher 和 Gueyie（2001）等则认为特许权价值会增加银行风险。第二种观点也不是完全否定第一种观点，他们大都指出特许权价值降低银行风险必须符合一定的条件，如果不符合这些条件，特许权价值会增加银行风险。

国内研究比国外晚了许多，陆前进（2002）在国内最早提出了用资产负债法计算银行特许权价值。苑素静（2005）采用陆前进的公式计算了我国银行业特选权价值以及美国银行业的特许权价值，并对二者进行了比较，还通过对韩国商业银行的特许权价值的计算，得出了金融自由化降低了银行特许权价值的结论。李艳（2006）则提出了税前利润法计算特许权价值的公式，并选取1999—2003年的14家银行作为样本进行实证分析，发现中国商业银行特许权价值不高，因此特许权价值自律效应不足。韩立岩等（2006）、马晓军等（2007）、李燕平等（2008）用托宾Q值的计算方法计算特许权价值，并实证检验了上市银行的特许权价值和银行风险之间的负相关关系，得出了特许权价值存在自律效应的结论。而后孙犇等（2010）、彭寿康等（2011）、位华等（2011）、尚文程等（2012）也选取不同的样本进行实证分析，得出了相同的结论。曲洪建（2010，2011，2012）的研究发现，隐性保险制度削弱了特许权价值对银行稳健性的影响，而“隐性保险”对我国在所有商业银行进行了保护，与其所有制形式并无直接关联；并在文章最后提出了引入显性保险制度和加强监管等提高银行特许权价值措施，以增强银行稳健性。

从上述的文献研究可以看出，大部分的学者认为：特许权价值能够降低银行风险。基于以上分析，我们提出本文的第一个假设：

假设1：特许权价值越大，银行稳健性越好。

（二）公司治理和银行风险的研究

1. 股权结构对银行风险的影响

从股权结构的角度讨论商业银行风险承担的观点可以划分为两种：“道德风险论”和“公司控制论”。Amihud 等（1981）在 Merton（1977）等研究基础上，首次从“道德风险”的视角分析公司治理机制对银行风险承担的影响。他们通过研究认为，如果存在存款保险制度，银行股东作为贷款业务的主要决策者，往往通过追求更高风险来谋求自身利益最大化，由此引发银行股东决策的“道德风险”。随后 Saunders 等（1990）、Brewer 等（1996）都在这一思路指引下，进一步研究了道德风险对银行风险承担的影响。随着研究的进一步深入，反对的观点也逐渐出现。在随后几年的研究里，“公司控制论”逐渐被学者所接受。“公司控制论”认为：所有者-管理者之间的“委托代理失灵”问题，才是银行经营风险增加的最主要原因，股东不是银行贷款的决策者，高管才是银行贷款业务的真正决策者，他们直接控制银行风险（Gorton and Rosen，1995）。尽管银行股东可以在银行出现风险时，监督或者解聘高管，但是这种行为一般是在银行出现风险以后才进行的，因此滞后性强，为之付出的成本也比较昂贵。

Walter Dolde 和 John D. Knopf（2006）通过实证分析了公司治理机制和风险承担之间的关系，研究结果显示：内部人持股比例与风险承担之间不是简单的线性相关关系，而是呈 U 型关系，即二者之间先正相关，到达一定程度以后呈负相关关系；机构持股比例与风险承担之间呈负相关关系。股东性质和银行风险承担的研究也有很多，Fries 等（2005）通过研究认为，银行主体的所有权性质对风险承担有重要影响，在转型国家中，银行国有股比例越高，银行经营风险越大；金鑫等（2005）通过实证研究发现，合理的股权结构能够使上市商业银行的各个利益相关者的利益趋于一致，这样不仅能提高银行的经营业绩，还能够有效地降低银行风险。陈彩（2011）运用我国 2006—2009 年 34 家商业银行的 127 个面板数据进行实证分析，发现银行的第一大股东持股比例与银行的风险负相关。然而孔德兰等（2008）通过收集 2000—2007 年 5 家上市商业银行的大量数据，利用非平衡面板模型进行分析，发现大股东控制权力与银行风险承担呈显著正相关关系。曹艳华等（2009）首先构建一个多元回归模型，然后利用中国 14 家上市商业银行 2000—2007 年的数据进行实证分析，发现第一大股东的持股比例与银行风险承担之间存在正相关关系，而前五大股东的持股比例与银行风险承担之间存在负相关关系。张学陶等（2009）采用面板数据模型研究 14 家上市商业银行 2000—2008 年的数据，发现国有股比例和信用风险正相关，国有股比例和银行整体风险正相关；股权集中度和信用风险正相关，股权集中度和银行整体风险也是正相关。

然而反对的观点同样存在，Kenneth R. Spong 和 Richard J. Sullivan（2007）通过研究发现：股权集中度和银行风险负相关，即股权集中度越低，银行风险越大。曹廷求等（2006）对河南、山东 29 家中小商业银行的调查数据进行分析发现，银行第一大股东的性质和银行风险之间没有显著的相关关系。

从上述的文献研究可以看出，大部分的学者认为：第一大股东的持股比例越高（股权集中度越高），银行的风险越大；国家持股比例越高，银行风险越大。基于以上分析，我们提出本文的第二个假设：

假设 2a：第一大股东持股比例越低，国家持股比例越低，银行稳健性越好；

假设2b：前十大股东比例越大，银行稳健性越好。

2. 董事会对银行风险的影响

商业银行的董事会由股东大会选举产生，它要对所有股东的利益负责，负责经理层的雇佣和解聘，对公司增加或减少注册资本、分立、合并、终止和清算等重大事项提出方案。银行董事会如果相对独立，且具有监督权力，可以有效防止大股东和高管侵占公司利益，降低银行风险，有利于优化商业银行的公司治理结构。董事会人数较少时，监督权力就会受到一定的限制，银行的风险就会增加；可是当董事会人数较多时，董事会成员之间沟通协调就会变得困难，其监督能力就会下降，高管就会去追逐个人利益，从而增加银行风险。

巴曙松（2000）认为董事会和银行信用风险关系密切，因此保持董事会的独立性可以有效降低银行信用风险。陈晓蓉（2003）采用面板门槛模型，通过分析中国台湾1996—2001上市商业银行的数据，发现董事会规模和银行风险承担之间是负相关关系。王倩等（2007）的实证研究也表明董事会人数越多，风险越小。Kenneth R. Spong and Richard J. Sullivan（2007）也得出相同的结论。孔德兰等（2008）利用非平衡面板模型，收集2000—2007年5家上市商业银行的数据进行实证分析，研究发现独立董事的比例和银行风险承担之间是正相关关系，董事会的规模和银行风险承担是负相关关系。曹艳华等（2009）首先构建一个多元回归模型，然后利用中国14家上市商业银行2000—2007年的数据进行实证分析，也认为独立董事比例和董事会规模与银行风险承担之间存在负相关关系。张学陶等（2009）采用面板模型研究14家上市商业银行2000—2008年的数据，也发现独立董事比例和董事会规模与银行信用风险负相关的观点。高国华、潘英丽（2011）发现资本监管的边际风险约束力度随着公司治理结构中董事会规模、第一大股东持股比例和政府持股比例的增加而递减，对于银行风险行为的外部监管约束与内部治理机制之间存在一定的相互替代关系。陈彩（2011）运用我国2006—2009年34家商业银行的127个面板数据进行实证分析，发现董事会的规模与银行风险承担负相关。

虽然董事会规模大可以博采众长，Jenson（1993）指出：如果董事会规模过大，银行的信息传递过程就会出现失误，无法上传下达，决策的速度和准确性都会受到限制，董事会的监督功能就会削弱。Eisenberg等（1998）也发现芬兰中小型企业的董事会规模大小与公司业绩之间存在显著的负相关关系，董事会人数过多反而会影响董事会的监督约束能力，使得“委托代理失灵”问题更加严重、非常容易产生“搭便车现象”，从而降低公司经营绩效、增加经营风险。

从上述文献研究可以看出，大多数的学者认为：董事会的规模越大，银行的风险越小；独立董事规模越大，银行的风险越小。基于以上分析，我们提出本文的第三个假设：

假设3a：董事会规模越大，银行稳健性越好；

假设3b：独立董事比例越大，银行稳健性越好。

3. 经理层对银行风险的影响

经理层是负责公司日常经营的机构，直接决定了银行的风险承担行为。银行股东与经理层的效用函数不一样，经理层在商业银行的日常经营时，会出于自己利益的考虑，增加银行的经营风险。因此建立有效的经理层约束激励机制，使经理层的目标与上市商业银行目标趋于一致，解决“委托代理失灵”问题，能够有效控制商业银行经营风险。

Schreiber（1996）构建了一个期权定价模型来分析固定报酬制度和奖金报酬制度对高管风险行为的不同影响，他的研究发现管理层在固定报酬制度下，高管会限制甚至减少银行资产的经营风险；可是在奖金制度下，他们的利益与股东利益将趋于一致，因此他们会增加银行资产的经营风险。John（2000）认为合理的银行高管薪酬制度可以降低银行经营风险。

夏光等（2007）以上海证券交易所的上市公司为样本，运用相关性分析和多元回归分析，发现尽管高管持股比例与公司业绩正相关，但其结果并不显著；高管薪酬与公司经营业绩正相关，但这种正相关关系并不强，年薪制并未对高管起到其应有的激励作用。曹艳华等（2009）首先构建一个多元回归模型，然后利用中国14家上市商业银行2000—2007年的数据进行实证分析，发现高管薪酬与银行风险承担存在显著负相关关系。

而巩震等（2008）认为高管持股比例与公司经营绩效呈3次函数的关系：当高管持股比例在22.19%～54.83%之间时，高管持股比例与经营绩效正相关；在22.19%～54.83%之外时，高管持股比例与经营绩效存在负相关关系。张学陶等（2009）采用面板模型研究14家上市商业银行2000—2008年的数据，发现前3名高管薪酬数量与银行整体风险存在正相关关系，高管持股与银行信用风险存在负相关关系。陈彩等（2011）运用我国2006—2009年34家商业银行的127个面板数据进行实证分析，发现高管的薪酬与银行风险正相关。

从上述的文献研究可以看出，大部分学者认为：高管的薪酬越高，银行风险越小；高管的持股比例越高，银行风险越小。基于以上分析，我们提出本文的第四个假设：

假设4a：高管薪酬越多，银行稳健性越好；

假设4b：高管持股会提高银行稳健性。

（三）特许权价值和公司治理机制对银行风险的影响

曹廷求等（2010）开创性地将特许权价值和公司治理机制纳入同一个模型，研究二者对银行风险的影响，他们通过实证分析了特许权价值和公司治理机制（第一大股东持股比例、前十大股东持股比例、董事会规模、高管持股、独立董事比例等）对银行风险承担的影响。特许权价值能够降低银行风险，不同的银行由于其公司治理机制的不同，即使有相同的特许权价值，其风险承担行为也会有所不同，因此特许权价值和公司治理机制可能具有相互替代的作用。基于以上分析，我们提出本文的第五个假设：

假设5：特许权价值和公司治理对银行稳健性的影响有相替效应。

三、研究设计

（一）样本选择及数据来源

本文选择16家上市商业银行[①]2000—2012年间的数据作为样本，进行非平衡面板数据分析；其中股票价格来自于国泰君安数据库，其他数据根据上海证券交易所和深圳证券交易所网站公布的上市商业银行半年报和年报整理得到。

（二）变量选取

1. 被解释变量

芬兰银行和挪威银行除了考虑单体银行的稳健性指标，还把许多的宏观经济变量纳入分析的范围；美联储根据CAMEL评级系统，结合单体银行的情况，给出了银行整体稳健性的和单体银行稳健性的度量指标；《投资者报》数据研究部选取银行的资本充足率、不良贷款控制水平、拨备覆盖率水平以及流动性等四类指标衡量银行稳健性；曲洪建等（2010，2011，2012）认为银行的“稳健性”除了“稳定”的含义以外，还包含“健康”的含义，应该从这两个角度选取指标。根据曲洪建等（2010，2011，2012）的观点，参考《投资者报》的选取方式，本文选取贷款损失准备金比率、资本充足率、净资产收益率度量银行稳健性。

2. 解释变量

陆前进（2002）采用资产负债法计算特许权价值，李艳（2006）则采用税前利润法计算特许权价值，而这两种方法都无法计算特许权价值的预期收益，无法准确度量银行特许权价值。国外比较成熟的研究一般采用托宾Q值来计算特许权价值，目前两种计算方法比较流行：（1）使用银行资产的市场价值和重置价值之比来计算，托宾Q值=银行市场价值/重置价值=（股票价格×股票数量+负债账面价值）/银行总资产账面价值；（2）用股东权益或资产净值的市场价值和账面价值来计算。参考曲洪建等（2010，2011，2012）的观点，我们采用银行资产的市场价值和重置价值之比来计算特许权价值。

王光伟（2010）以第一大股东持股比例、前5大股东持股比例之和、公

---

① 北京银行、工商银行、光大银行、华夏银行、建设银行、交通银行、民生银行、南京银行、宁波银行、农业银行、浦发银行、平安银行、兴业银行、招商银行、中国银行、中信银行。

司前5位大股东持股比例的平方和H5（Herfindahl5指数）、管理者年薪、管理者持股、董事会规模、独立董事比例、监事会规模等度量银行公司治理机制；曹廷求等（2010）以第一大股东持股比例、第一大股东性质、前十大股东持股比例、高管持股、高管薪酬、董事会规模、独立董事比例等指标度量银行公司治理机制。本文采用曹廷求等（2010）的方法度量银行公司治理机制。

银行规模越大，其规模经济和范围经济的作用越明显，银行可能越稳健；而另外一个方面，银行规模越大，由于受到国家的隐性保护，可能表现出“太大而不能倒闭”的特征。资本杠杆是银行资本运营的一个手段，他们利用资本杠杆效应，以较少的公司股权资本支配尽量多的长期资本，这样一方面可以带来银行收益的增加，另一方面也加大了银行的风险。银行经营杠杆效应是指随着业务量的扩大，由于银行经营成本中固定成本比重降低，可以带来更多经营利润，增加银行稳健性。因此以银行规模、资本杠杆、经营杠杆作为其他解释变量。变量的具体定义见表1。

表1　**变量定义**

变量类型	变量名称	变量代码	变量定义
被解释变量	贷款损失准备金比率	LRR	贷款损失准备金/贷款总额
	净资产收益率	ROE	税后利润/净资产
	资本充足率	CAR	资产/风险
解释变量	特许权价值	FV	托宾Q值
	第一大股东性质	XZ	虚拟变量，第一大股东为国有时为1，否则为0
	第一大股东的持股比例	S1	第一大股东所持股份占全部股份的比例
	前十大股东的持股比例	S10	前十大股东所持股份占全部股份的比例
	董事会规模	BO	董事会中董事的人数
	独立董事比例	ID	董事会中独立董事所占的比重
	高管持股	MOS	虚拟变量，高管持股时取值为1，否则为0
	高管薪酬	SA	薪酬最高的前三名高管的平均薪酬
	银行规模	SIZE	Ln资产规模
	资本杠杆	CLV	所有者权益/总资产
	经营杠杆	OPLV	固定资产/总资产

（三）基本模型的设定

1. 稳健性公因子的提取

首先对稳健性的三个指标的样本数据进行因子分析，运用 SPSS17.0 软件进行 KMO 和 Bartlett 球形检验，检验结果见表2。

表2 KMO 和 Bartlett 的检验

取样足够度的 Kaiser-Meyer-Olkin 度量		.821
Bartlett 的球形度检验	近似卡方	1.935
	df	3
	Sig.	.003

一般认为，KMO 在0.9以上，非常适合因子分析；0.8–0.9，很适合因子分析；0.7–0.8 适合因子分析；0.6–0.7 不太适合因子分析；0.5–0.6，勉强因子分析；0.5 以下，不适合因子分析。Bartlett 球形检验的统计值显著性概率小于等于显著性水平时，可以做因子分析。从检验结果可以看出，该样本数据很适合进行因子分析，因此对样本数据进行因子分析，提取一个稳健性公因子，并将其保存为变量（BS）。

2. 基本模型的设定

在因子分析的基础上，以稳健性公因子（BS）作为被解释变量；以特许权价值（FV）、第一大股东性质（XZ）、第一大股东持股比例（S1）、前十大股东持股比例（S10）、董事会规模（BO）、独立董事比例（ID）、高管持股（MOS）、高管薪酬（SA）为解释变量；以银行规模（SIZE）、资本杠杆（CLV）、经营杠杆（OPLV）为控制变量，构建多元回归模型如下：

$$BS_{i,t}=\beta_{0i,t}+\beta_1 FV_{i,t}+\beta_2 SIZE_{i,t}+\beta_3 CLV_{i,t}+\beta_4 OPLV_{i,t}+\beta_5 XZ_{i,t}+\beta_6 S1_{i,t}+\beta_7 S10_{i,t}+\beta_8 BO_{i,t}+\beta_9 ID_{i,t}+\beta_{10} MOS_{i,t}+\beta_{11} SA_{i,t}+\eta_{i,t} \quad (1)$$

其中，$\beta_{0i,t}$是截距项，β_1、β_2、β_3、β_4、β_5、β_6、β_7、β_8、β_9、β_{10}、β_{11}分别代表特许权价值、银行规模、资本杠杆、经营杠杆、第一大股东性质、第一大股东持股比例、前十大股东持股比例、董事会规模、独立董事比例、高管持股、高管薪酬对于银行稳健性的回归系数，$\eta_{i,t}$是误差项。

四、实证结果与分析

（一）描述性统计（见表3）

表3列出了相关变量的描述性统计特征。其中，第一大股东持股比例、前十大股东持股比例、高管薪酬、资本杠杆的最小值和最大值相差甚远。例如高管薪酬最低15万元，最高约808万元，这说明不同银行的薪酬水平差距很大；

表 3　**变量描述性统计**

变量名	最小值	最大值	均值	标准差	中位数
LRR	.0056	.0474	.0235	.0077	.0231
ROE	.0432	.3671	.1585	.0639	.1549
CAR	.0230	.3067	.1126	.0348	.1105
FV	1.0010	1.6275	1.0966	.0959	1.0646
XZ	.0000	1.0000	.8593	.3486	1.0000
S1	.0590	.6796	.2412	.1840	.1783
S10	.2599	.9778	.5951	.2199	.5188
BO	13.0000	20.0000	16.3769	1.7476	17.0000
ID	.0000	.4444	.3201	.0711	.3333
MOS	.0000	1.0000	.3618	.4817	.0000
SA	15.0000	808.2133	233.9686	159.5159	200.0000
SIZE	10.8256	13.1897	11.9782	.5929	11.9305
CLV	.0201	.5391	.0530	.0396	.0522
OPLV	.0001	.0203	.0074	.0035	.0067

数据来源：根据上海证券交易所和深圳证券交易所网站公布的上市商业银行半年报和年报整理得到。

第一大股东和前十大股东比例差距较大，说明不同银行的股权状况存在很大差异。其他变量差异不是很大，这里不再冗述。

（二）相关性分析（见表 4）

表 4　**变量相关性表**

	BS	FV	XZ	S1	S10	BO	SA	ID	MOS	SIZE	CLV	OPLV
BS	1											
FV	.230**	1										
XZ	.097	.110	1									
S1	.288**	-.055	.174*	1								
S10	.413**	.043	.337**	.837**	1							
BO	.112	.058	.124	-.156*	-.015	1						
SA	.225**	-.100	-.229**	.249**	.118	-.006	1					
ID	.151*	-.259**	.094	-.020	.099	.299**	.224**	1				
MOS	-.041	.138	-.394**	-.377**	-.349**	-.342**	-.113	-.196**	1			
SIZE	.299**	-.271**	.202**	.707**	.724**	.073	.268**	.153*	-.526**	1		
CLV	.361**	.134	.032	.214**	.315**	-.106	.064	-.012	-.003	.189*	1	
OPLV	-.237**	.229**	.248**	.146*	.083	-.029	-.592**	-.321**	-.110	-.103	-.054	1

注：***、**、* 分别表示 1%、5%、10% 的显著性水平。

从表 4 的相关性分析的结果可以看出：银行稳健性指标 BS 跟其他变量的相关性较大，说明模型符合回归分析的要求；特许权价值和公司治理部分指标之间存在相关性较大的情况，说明解释变量之间存在多重共线性，如果直接单进行回归分析，可能会出现参数估计量不准确，变量显著性检验失去意义的问题。因此需要找出引起多重共线性的解释变量，将它剔除出去，以逐步回归法进行分析。

（三）多元回归结果分析

影响稳健性的因素很多，除了特许权价值和公司治理以外，还可能存在遗漏变量，如政府监管、外部宏观环境等，如果利用横截面数据或者时间序列方法估计，可能会出现异方差和序列相关性，导致回归结果不准确，因此采用面板回归分析方法。剔除相关变量（SA、ID、XZ、S1）以后，为了研究特许权价值与前十大股东持股比例、董事会规模、高管持股之间的交互影响关系，增加特许权价值和剩余变量（S10、BO、MOS）的交叉项，重新进行回归分析。模型的意义是，由于特许权价值对银行稳健性的影响系数为正，则若交叉项系数也为正，则特许权价值对银行稳健性的影响随着另一变量的增加而增加，两者存在一种互补关系；反之，若交叉项系数为负，则特许权价值对银行稳健性的影响随着另一变量的增加而减少，两者之间存在相互替代关系。具体的回归分析结果见表5。

表5 无交互作用的回归结果

	所有解释变量 回归（1）	剔除SA和ID后 回归（2）	剔除XZ和S1后 回归（3）	交互作用 回归（4）
FV	1.925** (.749)	1.950*** (.726)	1.915*** (.723)	15.693** (7.468)
XZ	.152 (.211)	.140 (.209)		
S1	.794 (.736)	.692 (.705)		
S10	.829 (.623)	.856 (.607)	1.317* (.420)	10.939*** (3.786)
BO	.098* (.041)	.107** (.039)	.094** (.037)	.765* (.473)
SA	-6.883E-5 (.000)			
ID	.406 (1.189)			
MOS	.385* (.176)	.356** (.172)	.294** (.158)	-1.406 (1.505)
SIZE	.215 (.185)	.201 (.182)	.227* (.176)	
CLV	5.886*** (1.631)	5.987*** (1.616)	5.827*** (1.605)	
OPLV	-84.509*** (23.017)	-76.683*** (19.077)	-70.540*** (18.094)	
S10*FV				-8.097** (3.436)
BO*FV				-.613 (.431)
MOS*FV				1.614 (1.355)
R^2	0.643	0.632	0.611	0.672
F	8.615	10.619	13.556	13.587

注：本表没有报告常数项的回归系数，***、**、*分别表示1%、5%、10%的显著性水平，括号中为标准误差（se）。

从表5的回归结果可以看出：

（1）特许权价值对银行稳健性的影响通过了显著性检验，且系数为正，即特许权价值和银行稳健性之间存在着正相关关系。实证结果支持假设1。这说明特许权价值存在自律效应，银行特许权价值越大，银行陷于财务危机以后破产成本越大，银行经营者越有动力去监督银行经营，规避银行风险，这非常有利于银行稳健经营。

（2）从股权结构的回归结果看：第一大股东性质对银行稳健性的影响没有通过显著性检验，这与曹廷求（2006，2010）的结论一致；第一大股东持股比例对银行稳健性的影响没有通过显著性检验；前十大股东的持股比例和银行稳健性正相关关系在回归结果（3）得到了支持。实证结果拒绝假设2a，部分支持假设2b，说明第一大股东性质和持股比例没有对银行稳健性产生显著影响，即不管哪种性质的股东，即使他们拥有了银行的控制权，也不会采取措施降低银行风险，提高银行的稳健性；除了第一大股东以外其他股东的股份比例越大，说明股权结构越集中，前几位股东控制权越集中，他们可以通过对第一大股东经营的干预，降低银行风险，增强银行稳健性。

（3）从董事会的回归结果看：董事会规模对银行稳健性的影响通过了显著性检验；独立董事比例对银行稳健性的影响没有通过显著性检验。实证结果支持假设3a，拒绝假设3b。这表明上市商业银行董事会充分发挥了监督管理职能，董事会能够提供多角度的决策咨询，帮助银行获得必要的资源，而且成员之间的监督与制衡，有利于吸收不同的意见，也有利于规避商业银行经营风险，实现稳健经营。独立董事监督管理职能没有得到体现，上市银行的独立董事大都受聘于银行，他们从银行获取报酬，经济上不独立，因此受到控股股东和公司管理层的限制，无法客观地监督约束银行经营，对银行稳健性影响不大。

（4）从薪酬激励的回归结果看：高管持股通过了显著性检验，且回归系数为正；高管薪酬没有通过显著性检验。实证结果拒绝假设4a，支持假设4b。这说明高管持股以后，其个人利益与银行利益趋于一致，部分解决了“委托代理失灵问题”，他们为了获得股权收益，必须加强银行管理，提高银行的稳健性；我国银行高管的薪酬激励没有通过检验，说明薪酬并不是银行稳健性的主要影响因素，这与我国商业银行高管的薪酬结构中股权、期权、股票期权支付比例较低，与银行稳健性的关联度较弱有关。其次，我国上市商业银行高管聘任不是完全的市场化，行政色彩比较浓，其薪酬高低与级别密切相关，且级别的高低往往与灰色收入成正比。

（5）银行规模对银行稳健性的影响在回归方程（3）中通过了显著性检验，即银行规模和稳健性之间存在正相关关系。这也支持了 Frederick T. Furlong（2006）“大而不倒”的观点。“大而不倒”的原因可能有以下四个：第一，由于规模经济和范围经济优势的存在，大银行垄断了大量的资源，与其他小银行竞争时优势明显，品牌效应显著；第二，银行规模大，对于宏观经济至关重要，不能倒闭；第三，我国政府变相帮助国有大银行，成立资产管理公司（长城、信达、华融、东方）冲销不良资产，上市的时候财政注资给予帮助；第四，政府对银行的救助，会使银行形成救助的预期，最后演变成“软预算约束”问题。

（6）从经济杠杆的回归结果看：资本杠杆对银行稳健性的影响通过了显著性检验，系数为正；经营杠杆对银行稳健性的影响也通过了显著性检验，系数为负。国外的研究结果表明，资本杠杆与银行稳健性是负相关关系，经营杠杆与银行稳健性是正相关关系。通过研究结果的比较可以看出，尽管资本杠杆和经营杠杆都通过了显著性检验，但是其结论却恰好相反。造成这一结果的原因可能是我国是转轨经济模式，商业银行还没有完全市场化运营，公司治理机制没有完善，杠杆效应无法充分发挥作用。

（7）从交叉项的回归结果看：①前十大股东的持股比例和特许权价值的交叉项通过显著性检验，回归系数为负；说明二者的相替效应通过了显著性检验，实证结果部分支持了假设5。这表明特许权价值对银行稳健性提高作用随前十大股东的持股比例的增加而减弱，即特许权价值与前十大股东的持股比例对银行稳健性影响相互替代。②高管持股和特许权价值的交叉项没有通过显著性检验，回归系数为正，说明二者的互补作用没有通过显著性检验，实证结果部分支持了假设5。这表明特许权价值对银行稳健性的提高作用随着高管持股的实施而减弱，即特许权价值与高管持股对银行稳健性影响相互替代。因此在提高银行稳健性的政策选择方面，特许权价值与前十大股东持股比例、高管持股之间是相互替代的关系，单独实行一个的效果更好，鱼和熊掌不可兼得。③董事会规模和特许权价值的交叉项没有通过显著性检验，回归系数为负，说明二者的相替作用没有通过显著性检验，实证结果拒绝了假设5。这表明特许权价值对银行稳健性的提高作用随董事会规模的增加而减弱，即特许权价值与董事会规模对银行稳健性影响相互补充。因此在提高银行稳健性的政策选择方面，特许权价值和董事会规模之间是互补关系，两者同时实行，效果更好。

五、稳健性检验

由于样本区间为2000—2012年，而2006年银监会颁布《国有商业银行公司治理及相关监管指引》，2006年4月开始实施，新旧制度的不同会使数据的可比性受到影响。为了检验上述研究结果的稳健性，本部分改用2007—2012年间的数据，对各部分分别作了回归分析。新的回归结果见表6，可以看出，除了董事会规模的显著性水平有一定差异以外，变量的系数大小、符号以及显著性水平没太大变化。这些稳健性检验的结果，说明本文的实证检验结果和结论都具有较高的稳定性和可靠性。

表 6　**有交互作用的回归结果**

	所有解释变量 回归（1）	剔除 SA 和 ID 后 回归（2）	剔除 XZ 和 S1 后 回归（3）	交互作用 回归（4）
FV	.092**（.865）	.125***（.851）	.143***（.840）	.198**（9.669）
XZ	.197（.261）	.163（.244）		
S1	.310（.846）	.198（.814）		
S10	.701（.793）	.786（.769）	.845*（.548）	5.446*（4.835）
BO	.019（.053）	.015（.049）	.018（.046）	.115（.614）
SA	8.393E-5（.000）			
ID	.752（2.144）			
MOS	.380*（.219）	.391**（.215）	.432***（.191）	-.018（1.804）
SIZE	.753***（.222）	.749***（.215）	.722***（.212）	
CLV	4.397***（1.747）	4.350***（1.730）	4.312***（1.699）	
OPLV	-86.026***（42.486）	-83.120***（39.301）	-77.250***（37.369）	
S10*FV				-5.531*（4.425）
BO*FV				.159（.564）
MOS*FV				.719（1.636）
R^2	0.621	0.619	0.616	0.511
F	5.544	6.831	8.784	5.082

注：本表没有报告常数项的回归系数，***、**、* 分别表示 1%、5%、10% 的显著性水平，括号中为标准误差（se）。

六、研究结论及政策建议

本文以 2000—2012 年 16 家上市银行为样本，实证分析了特许权价值、公司治理及其交互作用对银行稳健性的影响，通过研究得出以下结论：（1）特许权价值存在自律效应；（2）第一大股东性质和持股比例对银行稳健性没有显著影响，前十大股东的持股比例对银行稳健性有显著影响；（3）董事会的监督管理能提高银行稳健性，而独立董事并没有起到应有的监督作用；（4）高管持股能够增强银行的稳健性，而高管薪酬却没有激励作用；（5）银行规模和稳健性之间存在正相关关系，这也支持了“大而不倒”的观点；（6）上市商业银行的资本杠杆和经营杠杆效应没有充分发挥作用；（7）特许权价值与前十大股东的持股比例、高管持股对于银行稳健性的影响起到相互替代作用。根据上述研究结论，我们认为，可通过以下途径，提高银行特权价值，改变公司治理机制，增加银行稳健性的对策：（1）通过转变银行经营模式，拓展中间业务范围，开展业务创新增加银行特许权价值；（2）建立多元化的股权结构，引进战略投资者，改变银行以往的一股独大的局面，提升银行自身公司治理及经营管理水平，增加银行稳健性；（3）建立董事、监事尽责履职制度。董事应以个人身份承担相应的法律责任，忠实履行受托人职责和看管职责；监事应严格履行监督职责，对银行运营情况以及董事、高级管理人员和其他工作人员的尽职行为进行监督，避免其监督行为受到股东的干扰；（4）进一步完善高级管理人员持股制度，增加高管的薪酬结构中股权、期权、股票期权支付比例，最大限度地解决"委托代理失灵"问题；（5）减少政府对大银行的支持力度，重点扶持中小银行的发展，进一步完善破产清算制度，减少大银行对"隐性保险"制度的预期，走出"大而不倒"的恶性循环；（6）充分利用高负债经营的特点，使投资收益大于负债成本，利用资本杠杆效应，增加银行利润；此外，银行还可以提高固定资产的利用率，利用经营杠杆效应，提高银行经营业绩；（7）监管部门高度重视银行掩盖不良贷款的问题，加强对不良贷款审计检查力度，一旦发现问题，严格惩处相关责任人；（8）在制定相关政策时还需要注意各种政策之间的相互协调问题，如果政策之间有冲突，需要根据银行的具体情况进行取舍。

参考文献

[1] 巴曙松. 中国债券市场的发展及对利率政策、银行风险管理的影响 [J]. 金融研究，2000 (2)：67-72.

[2] 曹廷求，王营. 特许权价值、公司治理机制和商业银行风险承担 [J]. 金融论坛，2010 (10)：12-18.

[3] 曹廷求，郑录军，于建霞. 政府股东、银行治理与中小商业银行风险控制：以山东、河南两省为例的实证分析 [J]. 金融研究，2006 (6)：99-108.

[4] 曹艳华，牛筱颖. 上市银行治理机制对风险承担的影响 (2000—2007) [J]. 金融论坛，2009 (1)：43-48.

[5] 陈彩，朱博文. 资本约束、治理机制和银行风险承担 [J]. 金融发展研究，2011 (11)：60-65.

[6] 陈晓蓉. 中国台湾银行业公司治理机制与风险承担行为之关系 [J]. 风险管理学报，2003 (3)：363-391.

[7] 高国华，潘英丽. 资本监管、公司治理结构与银行风险行为 [J]. 软科学，2011 (8)：49-53.

[8] 巩震，金永生，王俊梓. 中国上市公司管理层持股与公司绩效实证分析 [J]. 北京邮电大学学报，2008 (6)：44-48.

[9] 韩立岩，李伟. 外资银行进入与中国商业银行特许权价值 [J]. 世界经济，2008

(10)：22-32.

［10］韩立岩，李燕平．中国上市银行特许权价值与风险行为［J］．金融研究，2006 (12)：82-91.

［11］金鑫．上市公司股权结构与公司治理［M］．北京：中国金融出版社，2005.

［12］孔德兰，董金．公司治理机制对商业银行风险承担影响的实证分析［J］．中央财经大学学报，2008 (11)：38-42.

［13］李文惠．公司治理的角度看银行风险承担问题之研究［DB］．台北：中山大学博士论文，2002.

［14］李艳，张涤新．中国商业银行特许权价值：基于面板数据的实证研究［J］．当代财经，2006 (3)：40-45.

［15］李艳．中国商业银行特许权价值：1994—2003［J］．上海金融，2006 (2)：26-30.

［16］李燕平，韩立岩．特许权价值、隐性保险与风险承担：中国银行业的经验分析［J］．金融研究，2008 (1)：76-87.

［17］陆前进．银行的特许权价值分析及政策含义［J］．立信会计高等专科学校学报，2002 (3)：16-33.

［18］马晓军，欧阳姝．中美两国商业银行特许权价值及影响因素的比较研究［J］．金融研究，2007 (4)：53-71.

［19］彭寿康，戴亭园．银行特许权价值的内生风险约束效应：基于中国上市银行的实证研究［J］．金融理论与实践，2011 (1)：3-8.

［20］曲洪建，孙明贵．特许权价值和单体银行稳健性的关系研究［J］．财经研究，2010 (12)：62-71.

［21］曲洪建，王建亭，周方召．中国上市银行特许权价值和银行稳健性关系的实证研究［J］．统计与信息论坛，2011 (4)：72-77.

［22］曲洪建，张相贤．特许权价值和银行稳健性的关系研究：基于中美上市银行的实证检验［J］．经济与管理评论，2012 (4)：29-98.

［23］尚文程，刘勇，张蓓．银行特许权价值、风险和竞争：来自于中国上市银行的证据［J］．财经问题研究，2012 (1)：38-44.

［24］孙犇，黄河．中国上市银行特许权价值的自律效应［J］．金融论坛，2010 (1)：5-9.

［25］王光伟．公司治理对我国商业银行风险承担行为影响的实证研究［DB］．苏州大学硕士论文，2010.

［26］王倩，黄艳艳，曹廷求．治理机制、政府监管与商业银行风险承担：基于山东省的实证分析［J］．山东社会科学，2007 (10)：96-101.

［27］位华，韩璐．隐性保险下的特许权价值自律效应［J］．山东社会科学，2011 (6)：57-60.

［28］夏光，宋莹．基于全球视角的人力资源理论与实践问题研究［G］．国际人力资源开发研究会第六届亚洲年会论文集，2007.

［29］苑素静．韩国金融危机中银行特许权价值降低的实证分析［J］．现代财经，2005 (12)：33-37.

［30］苑素静．中美银行特许权价值比较［J］．农村金融研究，2005 (5)：28-30.

［31］张学陶，李豪杰．我国上市银行公司治理对风险承担的影响研究［J］．求索，

审计师声誉的概念界定与因素量表开发①

王帆

（浙江工商大学财务与会计学院　杭州　310018）

摘　要　为了探索审计师声誉测量因素以指导我国事务所建设品牌，对审计师声誉概念进行界定，并在此基础上采用深入访谈、专家头脑风暴等定性研究方法与量表项目分析、探索性因素分析等定量研究方法进行量表开发，最终发现审计师声誉因素包括8方面16维度：综合业绩因素的维度是员工和成长及预期；产品和服务因素的维度是审计质量；社会责任因素的维度是对社会公众的责任；战略和领导力因素的维度是战略和领导力；环境状况因素的维度是沟通环境、法制环境和国际环境；诚信因素的维度是诚信状况；内部治理因素的维度是股东（合伙人）、决策与监督和质量控制；职业道德因素的维度是自我评价、密切关系和外在压力。

关键词　审计师声誉　概念界定　测量因素　量表开发

一、问题的提出

近年来，审计师声誉引起了我国审计实务界的高度重视，2007年的“做大做强”战略为我国事务所建立品牌声誉提供了潜在可能，2011年9月中注协发布的“十二五规划”更是明确指出我国事务所应“大力创建自主知名品牌”（王帆、张龙平，2012）。在2013年1月的中注协事务所品牌建设工作组第一次会议中，陈毓圭秘书长提出“做好品牌问题的研究与学习，应包括研究品牌的内涵、载体、要素等内容”，体现了研究审计师声誉概念与因素对事务所品牌建设的重要性。

然而，理论界并未有审计师声誉的权威定义，也无全面反映审计师声誉建设的因素。只在一些实证研究中发现，受到监管方惩罚的审计师将会遭受声誉破坏，从而引起经济损失（Firth，1990；Rollins and Bremser，1997；方军雄，2010）；事务所行业专门化既能影响审计质量和资本市场会计信息质量（陈丽红和张龙平，2010），也能提高审计师声誉（GAO，2003；Lee等，2004；Francis等，2005；Hertz，2006）；在法律不起主要作用的环境中，审计质量能

①　教育部人文社科青年基金资助项目（13YJC790139）；杭州市哲学社科规划课题（D13GL14）。

够决定审计师声誉（Skinner and Srinivasan，2010）；媒体和诉讼也同样影响审计师声誉（Peursem and Hauriasi，1999；McCracken，2003）。显然，这些因素只是建设审计师声誉要素的较少部分，一些诸如事务所内部治理、社会责任及战略与领导力等对声誉具有重大影响的因素并未被学者们研究。并且这些研究并未明确指明“审计师声誉”的真正含义，在不同研究中“审计师”一词的指代不同，多数研究认为该词应指事务所声誉（Weber et al.，2008；Nelson et al.，2008；Gao，2010），仅个别实验研究中涉及审计人员声誉（Rick Antle，1982；Mayhew，2001），从而误导事务所建立品牌声誉。因此，本文拟先对审计师声誉概念进行界定，随后在此基础上展开因素量表开发，以期拓展审计师声誉理论并为今后的实证研究提供测量工具，从而进一步推动事务所品牌建设。

二、概念界定与量表模型

（一）概念界定

声誉的概念在不同的场合有不同的表述方式，如商誉、名誉、品牌等。其中在管理学领域与声誉涵义最接近的是“品牌”，但品牌与声誉并不完全相同。声誉通常被看做是对驱动品牌权益贡献的“有差别回应”资产之一，并且品牌的范畴比声誉要窄，它支持并与一个单一的利益相关者群体（即顾客）发生互动，而声誉是与多样的利益相关者之间的互动（Aaker，1996）。但品牌建设与声誉形成密不可分，声誉是建立品牌的必要条件，而品牌是声誉的外在表现，因此与审计师创建品牌有关的研究必然会溯源到声誉形成的问题上来。

根据国际审计准则，审计师的概念有广义和狭义之分。狭义的审计师指审计师个人，广义的审计师既包括审计师个人又包括事务所①，而从学者们的研究来看与声誉有关的审计师主要指广义概念，即审计师声誉是社会公众及利益相关者对事务所与审计师个人保护投资者利益和维护职业道德规范活动的整体认知与评价。首先，审计师声誉是一种认知和评价，属于主观范畴，作出这种认知和评价的主体是社会公众和利益相关者（即客户、股东、债权人等）；其次，认知和评价的客体是事务所与审计师个人履行投资者利益保护和维护道德规范的活动。因此，在因素问卷量表开发中既要考虑审计师声誉评价主体的感受，也要从事务所与审计人员两方面出发设计问题。

---

① IAASB，Handbook of International Quality Control，Auditing Review，Other Assurance，and Related Services Pronouncements. 2012 Edition Volume I. “‘Auditor is used to refer to the person or persons conducting the audit，usually the engagement partner or other members of the engagement team，or，as applicable，the firm.”

、重文献、法规

…年会计师事务所综合评价前百家信息》，详情参见 http：//
… ax/201208/t20120828_ 35165. htm。

与相关网站以构建审计师声誉因素的维度及构面，具体见表1①。

表1 审计师声誉因素维度与构面表

因素	维度	构面	主要支持文献
综合业绩	市场	收入、客户	《会计师事务所综合评价前百家信息》（2002—2012）
	员工	人员素质、员工管理	《会计师事务所内部治理指南》（2008）
	成长及预期	分所发展、分所管理、证券审计资格	《会计师事务所分所管理暂行办法》（2010）
产品和服务	审计质量	专业胜任能力、独立性	Watts and Zimmerman（1981）；《中国注册会计师执业准则》（2010）；《中国注册会计师胜任能力指南》（2007）；《中国注册会计师职业道德守则》（2009）
	非审计服务	对独立性的影响、拓展非审计业务	《萨班斯—奥克斯利法案》（2002）；AICPA（1993，1999）；SCSAS（1997）
	专长及创新	行业专长、业务创新	Lee et al.（2004）；Francis et al.，（2005）；Hertz et al.，（2006）
社会责任	对社会公众的责任	承担社会义务、参加公益活动	普华永道、安永中国、毕马威中国、德勤中国官方网站均有对事务所承担社会责任的说明
	对行业的责任	维护行业声誉、支持行业建设	Doogar（2006）；Autore et al.（2009）；Huang and Li（2009）
战略和领导力	战略	职业规划、事务所发展战略	《特殊普通合伙会计师事务所协议范本》（2011）
	领导力	合伙人领导能力、事务所团队建设	
环境状况	文化环境	价值观文化、体制文化	周年洋等（2003）；常勋（2007）
	沟通环境	客户沟通、同业沟通、监管机构沟通、员工沟通	《中国注册会计师执业准则》（2010）；GAO（2007）
	法制环境	法律健全程度、法律执行程度	《中华人民共和国注册会计师法》（1993）
	国际环境	国际执业资格与能力、与境外事务所联盟	内地大型会计师事务所获准从事H股企业审计（中华人民共和国财政部网站，2010年12月）

① 由于篇幅所限，本文未对维度和构面进行详细说明。

续表

因素	维度	构面	主要支持文献
诚信	监督机制	受监管机构处罚惩戒、媒体曝光违规率	《违反注册会计师法处罚暂行办法》(2008)；Chaney and Philipich (2002)；Krishnamurthy et al. (2006)；方军雄等(2006)；朱红军(2008)
	追究机制	承担民事、刑事与行政责任	李明辉（2006）；吴溪(2008)
	诚信文化	执业中诚实守信、诚信文化建设	葛家澍（2003）
内部治理	股东（合伙人）	权利与义务、加入与退出机制、出资与股权转让制度	《会计师事务所内部治理指南》(2008)；《公司法》(2005)；《会计师事务所职业风险基金管理办法》(2006)；《财政部关于推动大中型会计师事务所采用特殊普通合伙组织形式暂行规定》(2010)
	决策与监督	拥有股东会（合伙人会议)、董事会（合伙人管理委员会)、监事会及事务所组织形式	
	质量控制	业务风险、收费标准、项目质量复核、报告签发制度	
职业道德	自身利益	自身利益	《中国注册会计师职业道德守则》(2009)
	自我评价	自我评价	
	过度推介	过度推介	
	密切关系	密切关系	
	外在压力	外在压力	

三、量表的开发

（一）初始题项与分析流程

1. 初始题项的产生

此次测量项目主要根据因素构面，采用开放式问卷、文献借鉴与深度访谈

到了0.000，说明问卷具有一定的校标关联效度。

（三）综合业绩量表开发

综合业绩共涉及市场、员工、成长及预期3个维度的14个题项（见表2）。我们按照分析流程对这些题项进行了分析，结果发现只需保留员工和成长及预期2个维度6道题就可解释该量表。具体步骤如下：①项目分析。从表3分析可见，A3、A4、A8和A11题的未达标准指标数分别为5、6、5和4，均超过了3个，因此删除这4题，保留10题。②探索性因素分析。把保留下来的题目纳入探索性因素分析，研究共进行5次因子旋转，在每次因子旋转前KMO检验值分别为0.614、0.643、0.676、0.717、0.693，Bartlett的P值均为0.000，在1%的水平上显著①（见表4），表明适合进行因子旋转。5次因子旋转的最终结果见表5，研究发现市场并不是综合业绩的主要维度，与市场有关的题项A1、A2被删除。经由因素分析后②，留下的题项为：A5、A6及A7（与员工有关），A12、A13和A14（与成长及预期有关）。③信度检验。随后采用两种方式对留下的6题进行信度检验，一种是a系数，经过检验发现量表的Alpha达到0.688（见表6），说明综合业绩层面的总体可信度较高；另一种是题项内部一致性分析，这是一种逐题检验信度的方法。从表6的分析可见，除了A7外其他题的“题项删除的Cronbach's Alpha值”均小于量表的a系数0.688。但由于A7题项删除的a值为0.699，与量表a系数仅差0.011，且一个维度的题目数最少在3个以上（吴明隆，2010）。此外如果删除此维度，成长及预期的解释变异量仅为24.937%（如表5所示），小于50%，该因素不成立。因此，为了保留此因素，我们不删除题项A7。

综合上述分析，综合业绩层面共保留员工（A5、A6、A7）和成长及预期（A12、A13、A14）两个维度，且这两个维度能够解释综合业绩的58.122%（如表5所示），超过了50%，符合统计学规定，可以代表该因素。

（四）职业道德量表开发

《中国注册会计师职业道德守则》（2009）把职业道德分为自身利益、自我评价、过度推介、密切关系以及外在压力五种可能产生不利影响的因素。本文依照这些规定设计了5种维度的25题（见表7），并依据探索性分析流程对它们进行分析，结果发现只需保留自我评价、密切关系、外在压力3个维度的11道题就可解释该量表。

① 当巴特莱特球体检验的统计值显著性概率小于等于显著性水平时，可以做因子分析。
② 在第一次旋转成分矩阵时删除了题项A9，在第二次旋转成分矩阵时删除题项A10。

表 2　　综合业绩题项及内容表

维度	构面	审计人员	事务所
市场	收入	A1 审计人员工作报酬	A2 事务所年度总收入
	客户		A3 事务所上市公司客户数量
员工	人员素质	A4 审计人员文化程度	A5 事务所内拥有证券执业资格及领军人才人数
	员工管理		A6 事务所员工聘用管理（业绩评价、人才晋升、薪酬管理）和权益保障
			A7 事务所安排培训时间、方式、内容，及培训质量
成长及预期	分所发展	A8 审计人员在分所中的晋升空间	A9 分所覆盖范围（业务或地域）
	分所管理		A10 分所不服从总所的人事、财务、执业标准、员工培训等方面控制
			A11 总所限制分所承接风险过大的业务
	证券审计资格	A12 审计人员在具有证券资格的事务所里工作过	A13 事务所拥有证券审计资格
			A14 不具备与具备证券审计资格事务所合并

表 3　　综合业绩层面项目分析摘要表

题项	极端值比较	题项与总分相关		同质性检验			未达标准指标数	备注
	决断值	题项与总分相关	校正题项与总分相关	题项删除后的 a 值	共同性	因素负荷量		
A1	3.393*	.405**	#.267	.759	#.139	#.373	3	保留
A2	4.898**	.552**	.445	.742	.334	.578	0	保留
A3	#2.639n.s.	#.366**	#.279	.756	#.160	#.400	5	删除
A4	#1.124*	#.328*	#.201	#.764	#.065	#.255	6	删除
A5	3.988**	.575**	.482	.739	.370	.608	0	保留
A6	4.235n.s.	.535**	.410	.744	.267	.516	0	保留
A7	3.187n.s.	.460**	#.328	.753	#.158	#.398	3	保留
A8	#1.961n.s.	#.392**	#.274	.757	#.121	.#348	5	删除
A9	5.498n.s.	.588**	.470	.738	.369	.608	0	保留
A10	3.044n.s.	.455**	#.321	.754	.201	#.448	2	保留
A11	#2.507n.s.	.438**	#.298	.756	#.186	#.431	4	删除
A12	5.292n.s.	.494**	#.369	.749	.280	.529	1	保留
A13	6.475n.s.	.673**	.569	.727	.495	.703	0	保留
A14	6.155**	.629**	.523	.732	.421	.649	0	保留
判标准则	≥3.000	≥.400	≥.400	≤.762	≥.200	≥.450		

注：0.762 为综合业绩层面的内部一致性 a（Cronbach's Alpha）系数，#未达指标值；** 为在 0.01 水平（双侧）上显著相关；* 为在 0.05 水平（双侧）上显著相关；n.s. 不显著。

表8 **职业道德层面项目分析摘要表**

题项	极端值比较	题项与总分相关		同质性检验			未达标准指标数	备注
	决断值	题项与总分相关	校正题项与总分相关	题项删除后的a值	共同性	因素负荷量		
H1	#2.338*	.405**	#.363	.854	.207	.455	2	保留
H2	4.748*	.547**	.499	.850	.344	.587	0	保留
H3	3.698n.s.	#.378**	#.332	.854	#.140	#.374	4	删除
H4	#1.749n.s.	#.350**	#.286	.855	#.122	#.349	5	删除
H5	3.502n.s.	#.307*	#.222	#.858	#.080	#.283	5	删除
H6	4.328*	.556**	.491	.849	.308	.555	0	保留
H7	4.189n.s.	.482**	.408	.852	.208	.456	0	保留
H8	4.134**	.550**	.482	.849	.306	.554	0	保留
H9	3.203n.s.	.460**	.403	.852	.215	.463	0	保留
H10	5.283**	.536**	.462	.850	.260	.510	0	保留
H11	3.070n.s.	.410**	#.333	.854	#.138	#.371	3	保留
H12	4.701*	.587**	.531	.848	.348	.590	0	保留
H13	3.142**	#.395**	#.318	.855	#.141	#.376	4	删除
H14	3.286**	#.312*	#.223	#.858	#.080	#.283	5	删除
H15	4.617**	.604**	.551	.848	.402	.634	0	保留
H16	4.229*	.550**	.493	.849	.314	.560	0	保留
H17	#2.191n.s.	.423**	#.346	.854	#.198	#.445	4	删除
H18	3.512*	.462**	#.398	.852	.226	.476	1	保留
H19	3.472**	.494**	.429	.851	.254	.504	0	保留
H20	#2.997**	.579**	.513	.848	.336	.580	1	保留
H21	3.309n.s.	.551**	.488	.849	.309	.556	0	保留
H22	3.889**	.648**	.590	.845	.440	.663	0	保留
H23	#1.837n.s.	#.318*	#.230	#.858	#.091	#.301	6	删除
H24	3.005n.s.	.467**	#.391	.852	#.199	#.446	3	保留
H25	4.671**	.588**	.507	.848	.340	.583	0	保留
判标准则	≥3.000	≥.400	≥.400	≤.857	≥.200	≥.450		

注：0.857为职业道德层面的内部一致性a（Cronbach's Alpha）系数，#未达指标值；**为在0.01水平（双侧）上显著相关；*为在0.05水平（双侧）上显著相关；n.s.不显著。

表9 **八次KMO和Bartlett的检验**

旋转次数		第一次	第二次	第三次	第四次	第五次	第六次	第七次	第八次
KMO样本测度		0.73	0.739	0.741	0.733	0.728	0.721	0.727	0.717
Bartlett的球形度检验	卡方	414.91	377.59	335.53	276.26	265.52	230.88	200.25	178.44
	Sig.	0.000	0.000	0.000	0.000	0.000	0.000	0.000	0.000

表 10 **职业道德层面探索性因素分析结果摘要表**

题项	自我评价	密切关系	外在压力	共同性
H10 自我评价	. 743	. 294	. 124	. 629
H11 自我评价	. 868	. 009	. 080	. 771
H12 自我评价	. 593	. 416	. 521	. 624
H15 密切关系	. 117	. 729	. 305	. 638
H16 密切关系	. 279	. 741	. 129	. 644
H18 密切关系	–. 182	. 738	. 141	. 597
H20 外在压力	. 177	. 069	. 636	. 441
H21 外在压力	. 073	. 190	. 676	. 499
H22 外在压力	. 238	. 092	. 758	. 639
H24 外在压力	. 134	. 176	. 525	. 325
H25 外在压力	–. 115	. 245	. 722	. 594
特征值	2. 656	1. 907	1. 838	
解释变异量（%）	24. 141	17. 335	16. 706	
累积解释变异量（%）	24. 141	41. 476	58. 182	

表 11 **职业道德层面信度分析表**

题项	题项已删除的刻度均值	题项已删除的刻度方差	校正的题项总计相关性	多相关性的平方	题项已删除的 Cronbach's Alpha 值
H10	19. 77	29. 911	0. 431	0. 336	0. 783
H11	19. 77	31. 877	0. 286	0. 454	0. 797
H12	19. 78	29. 8	0. 565	0. 53	0. 769
H15	19. 92	30. 518	0. 503	0. 44	0. 776
H16	19. 85	30. 943	0. 449	0. 351	0. 781
H18	19. 92	32. 518	0. 275	0. 303	0. 796
H20	19. 67	29. 718	0. 477	0. 341	0. 777
H21	20. 1	29. 922	0. 508	0. 341	0. 774
H22	20. 07	28. 538	0. 607	0. 474	0. 763
H24	19. 6	30. 108	0. 434	0. 309	0. 782
H25	19. 57	28. 148	0. 48	0. 485	0. 779
Cronbach's Alpha		基于标准化项的 Cronbach's Alpha			项数
0. 796		0. 798			11

四、结论与展望

本文参考了大量文献、相关机构网站与法规文件，采取深入访谈、关键事件法、专家头脑风暴法等定性研究方法，并通过量表项目分析、探索性因素分析、a信度检验与题项内部一致性分析等定量研究方法，最终确定了审计师声誉因素的正式研究量表。分析表明，该量表共保留8个因素的16个维度，共52题。其中，综合业绩因素的维度是员工和成长及预期；产品和服务因素的维度是审计质量；社会责任因素的维度是对社会公众的责任；战略和领导力因素的维度是战略和领导力；环境状况因素的维度是沟通环境、法制环境和国际环境；诚信因素的维度是诚信状况；内部治理因素的维度是股东（合伙人）、决策与监督和质量控制；职业道德因素的维度是自我评价、密切关系和外在压力。我们编制的审计师声誉因素量表实现了概念定义与实际测量的有效匹配，且信度与效度较好，是一个有效的测量工具。

此外，本文的研究成果对未来研究具有重大的启示意义：①未来可依照我们的思路继续进行审计师声誉因素的量表开发。本文的文献梳理可能遗漏了审计师声誉领域的一些重要文献和定义及测量工具，量表开发的测量项目有可能不全面，但却为今后的审计师声誉要素研究提供了思路。②为事务所品牌声誉建设研究提供依据。虽然我们的研究基于中国审计市场，但在一定程度上体现了评价主体对审计师声誉的整体认识，能够为监管机构或事务所研究如何建设品牌提供参考。③为审计师声誉的实证研究提供变量。本研究涉及审计师声誉8个因素的16个维度，今后可在实证研究中纳入这些维度，以验证其对审计师声誉的重要程度，从而进一步提出品牌建设应优先发展的因素。

参考文献

[1]陈丽红，张龙平．事务所行业专门化研究述评及展望[J]．会计研究，2010(11)：81-86.

[2]葛家澍．美国安然事件的经济背景分析(代序)，上市公司财务舞弊案例剖析丛书[M]．北京：中国财政经济出版社，2003.

[3]李明辉．试论注册会计师的刑事责任：兼谈我国相关法律的修订与完善[J]．审计研究，2006(6)：58-66.

[4]王帆，张龙平．审计师声誉研究：述评与展望[J]．会计研究，2012(11)：74-78.

[5]王广明，张奇峰．注册会计师"诚信"的经济学分析[J]．会计研究，2003(4)：41-48.

[6]王军．加快健全我国企业内控标准体系和会计师事务所内部治理机制[J]．会计研究，2006(9)：3-6.

[7]吴溪．监管处罚中的"重师轻所"及其后果：经验证据[J]．会计研究，2008(8)：23-31.

[8]朱红军,何贤杰,孙跃,等. 市场在关注审计师的职业声誉吗？基于“科龙电器事件”的经验与启示[J]. 审计研究,2008(4):44-52.

[9]BRIAN W,MAYHEW. Auditor Reputation Building [J]. Journal of Accounting Research, 2001,39(3): 599-617.

[10] DOUGLAS J, SKINNER, SRINIVASAN S. Audit Quality and Auditor Reputation: Evidence from Japan [R]. Chicago Booth School of Business Research Paper Series, Working Paper,2001.

[11]FOMBRUN C J,GARDBERG N A,SEVER J M. The Reputation Quotient Amulti-stakeholder Measure of Corporate Reputation [J]. Journal of Brand Management,2000,7(4): 241-255.

[12]GAO. Public Accounting Firms: Mandated Study on Consolidation and Competition [R]. Report to the Senate Committee on Banking, Housing, and Urban Affairs and the House Committee on Financial Service,2003.

[13]LEE H Y,MANDE V,ORTMAN R. The Effect of Audit Committee and Board of Director Independence on Auditor resignation [J]. A Journal of Practice Theory,2004,23(2):131-146.

[14]JERE R,FRANCIS,REICHELT K. The Pricing of National and City-Specific Reputations for Industry Expertise in the U. S. Audit Market [J]. The Accounting Review,2005, 80(1):113-136.

[15]GAO Y,JAMAL K,LIU QI LIANG,LUO LE. Does Reputation Discipline Big 4 Audit Firms? [R]. CAAA Annual Conference,2011.

[16]WEBER J,WILLEN M,ZHANG JIE YING. Does Auditor Reputation Matter? The Case of KPMG Germany and ComROAD AG [J]. Journal of Accounting Research,2008,46(4): 941-972.

[17] NELSON K, PRICE A, ROOFTREE B. The Market Reaction to Arthur Andersen's Shredding of Documents: Loss of Reputation or Confounding Effects? [J]. Journal of Accounting and Economics,2008,46(2): 279-293.

[18]KRISHNAMURTHY S, ZHOU JIAN, ZHOU NAN. Auditor Reputation, Auditor Independence, and the Stock Market Impact of Andersen's Indictment on its Client Firms [J]. Contemporary Accounting Research,2006,23(2):465-490.

[19]STEVEN F,CAHAN,EMANUEL D,SUN J. Are the Reputations of the Large Accounting Firms Really International? Evidence from the Andersen-Enron Affair [J]. Auditing: A Journal of Practice & Theory,2009, 28(2):199-226.

[20]SUSAN A,MCCRACKEN. Auditors' Strategies to Protect Their Litigation Reputation: A Research Note [J]. A journal of Practice & Theory,2003,22(1):165-179.

Definition and Factor Scale Development of Auditor Reputation

Abstract In order to explore the auditor reputation factors to guide our firm to build the brand, it's necessary to define the concept of auditor reputation and use the quantitative research methods, such as in-depth interviews, expert brainstorming qualitative research and scale project analysis, exploratory factor analysis, to make a scale development. And through this trying we found that the auditor reputation factors include eight aspects and 16 dimensions: the dimension of the consolidated results factor is the employees, growing and expectation; the dimension of the product and service factor is the quality of audits; the dimension of social responsibility factor is the responsibility to the public; the dimension of strategy and leadership factor is strategy and leadership; the dimension of the environment factor is communication environment, legal environment, and international environment; the dimension of the integrity factor is integrity situation; the dimension of the internal governance factor is the shareholder (partner), decision-making, supervision and quality control; the dimension of professional ethics factor is self-evaluation, close relations and external pressure.

Key Words Auditor Reputation Definition Measurement Factors Scale Development

全面风险管理、财务困境与企业业绩——基于中央上市企业的实证研究①

宋丽梦　孟泽锐

（中南财经政法大学　武汉　430074）

摘　要　本文使用中央上市企业2008年至2011年全面风险管理数据实证检验了企业实施全面风险管理对业绩的影响。研究发现，相比于未实施全面风险管理的企业，实施了全面风险管理的企业具有更好的财务业绩；企业实施全面风险管理的程度越高，企业财务业绩越好；全面风险管理的实施有利于降低企业高财务杠杆带来的财务困境风险。为避免内生性带来的结果偏差，本文利用联立方程组模型对全面风险管理、财务困境和企业业绩三者之间的关系进行研究，结果显示全面风险管理能通过降低企业财务困境风险进而提升企业业绩，而且还能通过其他途径提高企业价值。使用托宾Q值替代财务业绩情况下得出的结果与前面一致。研究结果为相关政策提供了经验证据，同时扩展了该领域现有的研究成果。

关键词　全面风险管理　COSO报告　财务困境　企业业绩　联立方程

20世纪八九十年代，英国巴林、日本三井住友及大和等知名银行相继倒闭；而后在21世纪初，美国安然事件、世通事件、施乐公司财务舞弊事件等极大地打击了证券市场倡导的诚信，损害了股权持有人的利益与信心，最重要的还是挫伤了各地经济发展的元气。这些事件使得资本市场监管者意识到来自企业董事和高层管理者的舞弊意图很难被经营管理层面的内部控制程序所阻止，企业急需一个能够填补公司层面风险管理空白的方案。

2004年COSO发布的《企业风险管理——整合框架》提出了全面风险管理概念并将其在企业管理和公司治理中的地位推向了顶峰。由于决策层、投资者和企业管理者相信全面风险管理能够更好地管理企业风险和创造企业价值，使得全面风险管理在企业管理实践中的运用成为一种世界性的趋势。近十年来越来越多的欧美企业建立风险管理部门甚至是设立风险管理委员会（Risk Management Committee）和聘用首席风险官（Chief Risk Officer）。同时，国际评级机构诸如穆迪指数、标准普尔指数将企业是否实施全面风险管理作为其评级考核内容之一（Ramirez 2008）。2006年中国国有资产管理委员会参照COSO

① 本文受中南财经政法大学研究生创新教育计划——“研究生参加学术会议”的资助；曾获中国会计学会财务成本分会2013学术年会优秀硕博论文奖。

报告（2004）制定了《中央企业全面风险管理指引》（以下简称《指引》），要求中央企业开展全面风险管理建设，在具备条件的情况下建立全面风险管理体系。

在全面风险管理这一研究领域，美国处于领先水平，但我国与美国有完全不同的价值体系和文化传统，如果盲目引进西方经验而不加以验证，可能得不偿失。更何况国外关于全面风险管理能否创造企业价值在学术和实务层面都尚未达成共识，因此，《指引》是否能满足国资委的初衷，即全面风险管理能否为企业创造价值值得深入研究。

一、文献回顾

（一）全面风险管理

全面风险管理又被称为企业风险管理（Enterprise Risk Management）、整合的风险管理（Integrated Risk Management）。目前广为认可的全面风险管理定义源于COSO报告（2004），其中定义：企业风险管理是一个由企业的董事会、管理当局和其他人员实施，应用于企业战略制定并贯穿于企业各种经营活动中，旨在识别潜在的影响企业价值的事件并使风险保持在偏好范围内的，为企业目标的完成提供合理保证的过程。该报告从内部控制出发将风险管理理念纳入到企业的各种活动中，结合企业战略目标，构建整合框架，将企业内部控制提升到一个新的高度。虽然也有学者对COSO整合框架的有效性提出质疑（Gordon et al. 2009），但COSO框架是目前较为完整、认可度较高的框架。而国资委发布的《指引》文件直接借鉴了COSO整合框架。

虽然实务界及学术界对全面风险管理的定义尚未统一，但都有共同的特征：首先，全面风险管理相对于传统内部控制更加强调风险观，其将内部控制从被动防止纯粹风险发展为主动利用风险，将战略目标纳入全面风险管理体系。其次，全面风险管理强调了风险管理的整合观。相比于传统的风险管理将每种风险作为个体进行单独管理，全面风险管理强调应该将所有的风险进行整合管理，其中每一种风险都是企业总风险组合里的一个部分。再者，全面风险管理贯穿于整个企业的所有部门及所有活动。最后，全面风险管理的基本目标是保护和增加股东财富。

（二）全面风险管理与企业财务困境

传统风险管理能为企业带来好处，全面风险管理在传统风险管理的基础上引入整合观，被认为不仅能够起到保护股东价值的功能而且是创造公司价值的手段（Lam，2004；Meulbroek，2002；Nocco和Stulz，2006）。只要在同一企业的名下，每一项商业活动都会影响整体风险，而这种影响并不是每个单项风险的简单累计；而有时若干风险对公司的总影响可能会小于单个风险对公司的影响（Kleffner et al.，2003）。通过将所有的风险整合，企业可以利用自然对冲来避免风险管理的重复性支出（Harrington et al.，2002）。实施全面风险管理的企业往往对这种作用有更深的理解，就能够更客观地配置资源，进而提高资本效率和收益。

财务困境成本被认为是财务困境发生的概率乘以发生时的损失。正确使用财务对冲可以降低企业陷入财务困境或者破产的概率，从而减少财务困境成本或企业破产成本（Smith 和 Stulz，1985）。相对于传统风险管理中单独的风险管理可以降低特殊风险（例如纯粹风险），整合的风险管理可以控制累加的整体风险（Liebenberg 和 Hoyt，2003），因此实施全面风险管理可以避免风险的过度累加而导致的财务困境。财务困境对企业的影响巨大，当企业遇到财务困境需要强制出售资产时往往会被低估本身的价值，即使是预期可能会出现的财务困境也会对企业产生重大影响（Meulbroek，2002），而全面风险管理观又从损失总量的角度重新认识了财务困境成本，避免片面地从财务等单个方面估计损失，进而避免错估风险导致的企业破产。

（三）全面风险管理与企业价值

根据现代投资组合理论（Markowitz，1952）和 MM 理论（Modigliani 和 Miller，1958），外部投资者可以通过调整自己的投资组合来调整其面临的风险，最终只需承担系统风险，不必承担公司的特有风险。因为投资者可以轻易地提高或者降低他们所要面临的风险，因此该理论的支持者认为企业风险管理已再无价值，只会带来资源的浪费（Meulbroek，2002）。

然而现代投资组合理论的建立基础是有效资本市场假设，即投资者有效运用这种手段的前提是：能够清楚地知道企业所面临的风险。然而由于信息不对称，这种完美市场假设在实际活动中并不成立。出于竞争考虑，企业不可能完全披露自己的战略计划或者投资动向，而这些活动本身就伴随着系统风险，因此外部投资者很难了解企业的具体风险。但是管理者可以根据这些外部投资者所不知道的信息来进行风险管理，并通过全面风险报告将企业整体风险信息予以披露（Liebenberg 和 Hoyt，2003，2011）。因此在某种程度上，企业实施及披露全面风险管理可以降低管理者与股东之间的信息不对称（Liebenberg 和 Hoyt，2003），即全面风险管理可以在不完美市场和有代理成本的条件下增加企业价值（Stulz，1996）。而且以有限的上市企业进行全面风险管理代替资本市场大量投资者搜集、分析信息并决定投资策略的工作，一般投资者可以享受规模效应带来好处（Meulbroek，2002）。Pagach 和 Warr（2011）使用 Cox 模型研究得出企业实施 ERM 是为了直接经济利益而不仅仅是迎合监管的需要。Hoyt 和 Liebenberg（2011）在研究中剔除政府管制及市场差异的影响，利用联立方程模型对美国保险业进行实证研究，结果显示全面风险管理的实施情况与企业价值成显著正相关。Baxter et al.（2012）通过使用全面风险管理质量（ERMQ）来衡量企业的全面风险管理实施情况，研究发现越复杂、资源约束越少、公司治理越好的企业的全面风险管理质量越高；在控制这些变量的情况下，实施全面风险管理能提高会计指标和企业价值。

也有一部分研究表明全面风险管理需要在特定条件下才能创造企业价值。Beasley，Pagach 和 Warr（2008）通过研究资本市场对企业任命 CRO 的反应发现：全面风险管理的成本和收益因企业性质不同而不同。对于非金融企业，报告期收益与企业的规模、前期盈余波动成正相关，与财务杠杆、负债现金流成负相关；但对于金融企业，报告期收益与企业特征并无太多关系，他们将此结论归因于诸如监管约束等因素强行推动了金融企业的全面风险管理。Gordon et al.（2009）认为全面风险管理是否创造价值取决于特定公司的全面风险管理实施程度与企业面临的环境是否匹配，当全面风险管理的实施程度与该公司的具体经济环境较为匹配时方能创造价值。Pagach 和 Warr（2010）在研究企业实施全面风险管理（以是否设立 CRO 为衡量标准）前后的变化时发现企业实施全面风险管理后确实降低了收入的波动性，但是总体上尚不能得到支持全面风险管理能够创造企业价值的证据。McShane et al.（2011）以风险管理程度与企业价值关系的角度对全面风险管理进行了研究，其利用标准普尔给出的风险管理程度评级指标将企业实施的风险管理水平分为5级，最高级别为设立完整的全面风险管理体系。结果显示在一定程度范围内的风险管理与企业价值成正相关，当超过特定范围后这种相关性并不显著。

在国内，全面风险管理研究以规范类和理论上的阐述居多，实证分析较少。唐国储和李选举（2003）等国内学者大多从全面风险管理体系构建以及在金融行业的具体实施方法角度研究全面风险管理。朱华建，张盛勇，高宏伟（2011）通过对2000年至2010年国内主要期刊主题的研究发现，内部控制研究中实证研究只占19.6%，其中经验研究只占10.2%，尚未有全面风险管理与企业价值的关系研究。刘红霞，刘晓川（2012）利用A股中央上市企业截面数据研究了权变因素、全面风险管理目标和企业绩效之间的关系，但其在研究全面风险管理目标设定时从各目标单一角度出发衡量全面风险管理目标设定，并没有把握全面风险管理四大目标整合一体化的内涵。

总体来说国内外对于全面风险管理的研究多集中于规范性研究，实证研究文献较少，且结果颇有争议。本文从国内新兴资本市场出发研究全面风险管理与企业业绩之间的关系，并从财务困境角度验证全面风险管理创造企业价值的途径，具有以下三方面创新：（1）从实证角度验证全面风险管理对企业业绩的影响，为相关的政策提供经验支持。（2）从财务困境这一角度探讨了全面风险管理创造价值的具体途径。（3）立足中国新兴资本市场，研究非金融企业全面风险管理实施情况，拓展了现有全面风险管理的研究领域。

二、研究设计

（一）研究假设

在信息不对称条件下，全面风险管理要求完善职能机构设置，将风险控制在董事会认可的范围内，使管理者个人风险偏好与企业风险偏好相对独立，因此能有效避免管理层一意孤行带来的损失，减少代理成本。同时全面风险管理使风险保持在偏好范围内，能将企业系统风险锁定在特定目标，外部投资者由此保证了自己所面临的系统风险的确定性继而愿意接受股权交易中稍高的溢价，从而带来企业再融资成本的降低（Meulbroek，2002）。此外，通过将所有的风险整合，企业可以利用自然对冲来避免风险管理的重复性支出（Harrington et al.，2002）。如果实施全面风险管理带来的好处能够弥补实施全面风险管理的成本，则全面风险管理能增加企业业绩，因此本文提出假设：

H1：实施全面风险管理的企业拥有更好的业绩。

H2：企业实施全面风险管理程度越高，企业业绩越好。

正确使用财务对冲可以降低企业陷入财务困境或者破产的概率，从而减少财务困境成本或企业破产成本（Smith 和 Stulz，1985），而全面风险管理在传统风险管理的基础上引入整合观，不仅能够起到保护股东价值的功能而且是创造公司价值的手段（Lam，2004；Meulbroek，2002；Nocco 和 Stulz，2006），因此全面风险管理能降低财务杠杆引起的财务风险，预防企业陷入财务困境。财务困境对企业的影响巨大，当企业遇到财务困境需要强制出售资产时往往会被低估本身的价值，从而影响企业的业绩，即使是预期可能会出现的财务困境也会对企业产生重大影响（Meulbroek 2002）。因此财务困境的降低能够提高企业业绩。由此本文提出假设：

H3：全面风险管理能降低企业陷入财务困境的可能性，由此能够提高企业业绩。

（二）样本选择

全面风险管理正式出现在国内资本市场源于国务院国有资产监督管理委员会 2006 年出台的《中央企业全面风险管理指引》（以下简称《指引》）。《指引》中提出中央企业可以根据自身实际情况贯彻执行该指引，但并未强制企业服从规范条例，而对于其他企业尚未提出任何关于全面风险管理的要求，因此《指引》的出台其实为国内全面风险管理的实施提供了一个试点。鉴于此，本文选择中央控制的上市企业作为样本，包括国资委、中央部委等作为实际控制人的企业，样本来源于 CSMAR 最终控制人数据库，时间跨度为 2008—2011 年，全面风险管理指标由手工收集，其他数据来自 CSMAR 数据库。数据处理过程中剔除了如下样本：（1）金融类企业样本，因为金融类公司财务特征与其他公司显著不同；（2）数据不完整的样本。最后得到887个样本。本文运用stata软件进行后续的数据处理及模型估计。

（三）模型构建

1. 全面风险管理的衡量指标

全面风险管理衡量指标的构建是本研究领域中的一个重要难题，在已有文献中主要有CRO指代法（Beasley et al.，2008；Pagach和Warr，2011）、评级法（Beasley et al.，2005；Paape和Speklé，2012）、指数拟合法（Gordon et al.，2009）、标准普尔ERMQ指数（McShane et al.，2011；Baxter et al.，2013）、问卷调查法（Kleffner et al.，2003）。本文综合客观性及可行性选择Hoyt和Liebenberg（2011）使用的方法，即字眼查找法，同时结合了内容分析法：收集中央上市企业2008年至2011年的年报、内部控制报告并搜索网络新闻，查找"全面风险管理"、"企业范围风险管理"、"风险管理委员会"、"首席风险管理官"、"风险管理部"等关键词，对查找结果按照本文给出的全面风险管理特征进行判断。首先参照Beasley et al.（2008）、Pagach和Warr（2011）的方法设立哑变量erm1，企业开始实施全面风险管理则取1；相反则取0。其次参照Beasley et al.（2005）、Paape和Speklé（2012）的方法构建程度变量erm2，从"没有报告任何全面风险管理"到"建立完整全面风险管理体系"将全面风险管理分为3个等级。

2. 企业业绩的衡量指标

在企业业绩评价的理论研究与实践应用中有两种常用评价指标：一个是会计指标，另一个是市场价值指标。这两种评价指标各有优劣。会计指标与企业经营结果直接相关，但有一定的滞后性，经营者从事经营的许多方面无法在当期会计指标中反映出来；市场价值指标能够反映市场对企业整体的评价，在这点上可以弥补会计指标的不足，但其受市场因素、宏观政策的影响较大，尤其在中国新兴资本市场上本指标含有大量的噪音，即准确性较低（陈共荣、刘应文2003）。在具体实务中，国家对国有企业的业绩考核以"实现利润"和"上缴利税"为主，因此以企业的会计指标作为业绩衡量指标研究中央企业实施全面风险管理对其业绩的影响是可行的。

3. 实施全面风险管理的企业业绩的模型设立

借鉴Baxter et al.（2012）的研究方法并结合本文研究需要构建全面风险管理与企业业绩之间的多元回归模型（1）、（2）：

$$roa=\alpha+\beta_1 erm1_{j,t}+\beta_2 lnasset_{j,t}+\beta_3 beta_{j,t}+\beta_4 lev_{j,t}+\beta_5 mb_{j,t}+\beta_6 Outdirector_{j,t}+\beta_7 holdratio_{j,t}+\beta_{8-11} year+\mu_{j,t} \quad (1)$$

$$roa=\alpha+\beta_1 erm2_{j,t}+\beta_2 lnasset_{j,t}+\beta_3 beta_{j,t}+\beta_4 lev_{j,t}+\beta_5 mb_{j,t}+\beta_6 Outdirector_{j,t}+\beta_7 holdratio_{j,t}+\beta_{8-11} year+\mu_{j,t} \quad (2)$$

其中被解释变量 roa 表示企业业绩。由于资产收益率能够反映企业经营收益能力，故本文用资产收益率 roa 来衡量企业业绩。解释变量 erm1、erm2 都表示全面风险管理的实施情况。此外，本文引入企业规模、财务杠杆、成长性、系统风险、独立董事规模、前三大股东持股比例、年份作为控制变量。各变量的具体定义见表 1。

4. 企业实施全面风险管理与财务困境模型设立

$$z=\alpha+\beta_1 erm1_{j,t}+\beta_2 lev_{j,t}+\beta_3 beta_{j,t}+\beta_4 lnasset_{j,t}+\beta_5 mb_{j,t}+\mu_{j,t} \quad (3)$$

$$z=\alpha+\beta_1 erm1_{j,t}\times lev_{j,t}+\beta_2 lev_{j,t}+\beta_3 beta_{j,t}+\beta_4 lnasset_{j,t}+\beta_5 mb_{j,t}+\mu_{j,t} \quad (4)$$

模型中被解释变量 z 表示企业的财务困境指标，其根据 Altman（1968）提出的 z 值模型（$z=0.012\times X_1+0.014\times X_2+0.033\times X_3+0.006\times X_4+0.999\times X_5$）计算得出。其中 X_1 为营运资金/资产总额；X_2 为留存收益/资产总额；X_3 为息税前利润/资产总额；X_4 为股东权益市场价值/负债总额；X_5 为主营业务收入/资产总额。z 值越小企业财务风险越大，发生财务困境的可能性越大。Lev 表示企业的财务杠杆。erm1×lev 为全面风险管理与财务杠杆的交乘项。模型（3）研究在控制企业财务杠杆、系统风险、规模、成长性对企业财务困境的影响下，全面风险管理对企业财务困境的影响程度；模型（4）研究在控制企业系统风险、规模、成长性对企业财务困境的影响下，全面风险管理对财务杠杆所引起的财务困境的影响。

相关变量定义见表 1。

表 1 **变量定义**

	变量	变量名称	变量描述
主要变量	全面风险管理	erm1	哑变量：企业开始实施全面风险管理则取 1；相反则取 0
		erm2	如果企业已构建完整的全面风险管理体系则取 3；如果尚未构建完整的全面风险管理体系，只设立风险管理委员会、首席风险管理官等则取 2；如果尚未着手全面风险管理则取 1
	财务困境	z	根据 Altman（1968）提出的 z 值模型计算
	企业业绩	roa	净利润与期末资产总额之比
控制变量	规模	lnasset	总资产取对数
	财务杠杆	lev	企业负债总额占总资产比重
	系统风险	beta	beta 系数
	独立董事规模	outdirector	外部董事人数占全部董事人数比例
	成长性	mb	（股权市场价值+负债账面价值）/总资产账面价值
	股权激励	holdratio	管理层持股比例
	年份哑变量	Year	2008 年至 2011 年设置 3 个哑变量

三、实证检验

（一）描述性统计

表2给出了2008年到2011年中央上市企业实施全面风险管理的比例。

表2 中央上市企业全面风险管理实施情况

年份	2008	2009	2010	2011
实施企业占比	3.32%	20.75%	36.51%	46.47%

从表2可以得知，在《指引》文件出台之前全面风险管理在央企中尚未普及，至2011年年底，已将近半数企业健全全面风险管理体系或正在建设当中，从中可以看到相关政策对公司治理的影响。从另一方面讲，企业或许只为相应号召，即为满足合规性要求而进行全面风险管理，如果全面风险管理未能满足其初衷（保护并增加企业价值），那么这种合规性行为势必会损害企业价值。

表3给出了所有研究变量4年数据的描述性统计结果。

表3 总样本描述性统计

变量	平均数	中位数	标准差	最大值	最小值
erm1	0.28	0	0.45	1	0
erm2	1.51	1	0.84	3	1
roa	0.03	0.03	0.06	0.21	-0.31
z	0.85	0.71	0.58	4.5	0.05
beta	0.99	1.03	0.19	1.49	-0.04
lev	0.54	0.56	0.21	1.29	0.04
lnrev	22.06	21.75	1.75	28.55	16.21
lnasset	22.52	22.16	1.69	28.28	19.56
outdirector	0.37	0.33	0.06	0.8	0.25
mb	1.77	1.39	1.18	11.18	0.62
holdratio	0	0	0.02	0.34	0

从表3可知，总体样本中有27%的样本已经或者正在建设全面风险管理体系。

表4给出了主要变量在分组统计中的结果及t检验结果。

表 4　　主要特征变量分组统计及 t 检验结果

	NonERM（N=674）		ERM（N=258）		差额及 t 检验	
变量	平均数	标准差	平均数	标准差	平均数	标准差
roa	0.0294	0.0024	0.0411	0.0032	−0.0117***	0.0045
z	0.8162	0.0225	0.9517	0.0359	−0.1355***	0.0426

注：***、**、* 分别代表在 1%、5% 和 10% 的显著性水平下显著。

由表 4 可知，实施了全面风险管理的企业其总资产收益率、z 值都比未实施全面风险管理的企业要大，差额在统计意义上显著。

表 5 给出了所有变量之间的相关系数。

表 5　　Spearman 秩相关系数与 Pearson 相关系数表

	roa	erm1	erm2	z	lnasset	beta	lev	mb	holdratio
roa		0.121***	0.121***	0.188***	0.073**	−0.067**	−0.399***	0.154***	0.083**
erm1	0.1668***		0.973***	0.105***	0.152***	−0.006	0.044	0.008	−0.061*
erm2	0.1682***	0.9926***		0.102***	0.167***	−0.033	0.063*	0.007	−0.059*
z	0.2575***	0.1281***	0.1302***		−0.095***	−0.016	−0.111***	0.159***	−0.003
lnasset	0.0729**	0.1480***	0.1542***	−0.1481***		−0.401***	0.374***	−0.447***	−0.041
beta	−0.0902**	0.0071	−0.0071	0.0438	−0.3324***		−0.139***	0.078**	0.023
lev	−0.3733***	0.0227	0.0306	−0.1306***	0.3931***	−0.1321***		−0.306***	−0.074**
mb	0.1777***	0.0708**	0.0678*	0.2047***	−0.5997***	0.2250***	−0.3461***		−0.017
holdratio	0.0764**	−0.006	0.0031	−0.0311	−0.0277	0.0027	0.0024	0.0279	

注：***、**、* 分别代表在 1%、5% 和 10% 的显著性水平下显著。

表 5 中左下角为 Spearman 秩相关系数，右上角为 Pearson 相关系数。从表 5 中可见，所有变量之间相关性基本在可接受范围之内，只有规模与成长性之间的相关性超过 0.5，在后面将对此计算 vif 值。两种相关系数计算方法得出的结果基本一致，只有 beta 与 erm1 的相关系数用两种方法计算出来的方向相反。由于一种方法采用数值计算，一种采用秩计算，因此在计算两者相关性时结果有所偏差。

（二）模型参数估计

1. 全面风险管理与当期企业业绩

为检验假设 1、2，证明实施全面风险管理对企业业绩的影响，本文先利用全部样本对模型（1）、（2）进行估计，异方差问题用 stata 中的 robust 命令解决，回归结果列示于表 6 中 A、B 两列。

表6 模型（1）和模型（2）的回归结果

	roa（全样本）		roa（制造业）	
	A	B	C	D
erm1	0.0152*** (3.64)		0.0146*** (2.98)	
erm2		0.00819*** (3.72)		0.00801*** (3.19)
lnasset	0.0107*** (7.65)	0.0107*** (7.62)	0.0122*** (5.53)	0.0121*** (5.49)
beta	−0.011 (−1.12)	−0.0101 (−1.03)	0.00246 (0.15)	0.0028 (0.18)
lev	−0.129*** (−14.12)	−0.129*** (−14.19)	−0.149*** (−7.89)	−0.149*** (−7.92)
mb	0.00674*** (3.54)	0.00668*** (3.51)	0.00337 (1.33)	0.00328 (1.3)
outdirector	−0.0727** (−2.50)	−0.0719** (−2.47)	−0.0914** (−2.33)	−0.0881** (−2.25)
holdratio	0.198*** (2.74)	0.197*** (2.73)	0.293*** (6.13)	0.292*** (6.07)
year	控制	控制	控制	控制
_cons	−0.118*** (−3.24)	−0.127*** (−3.49)	−0.152** (−2.66)	−0.159*** (−2.79)
N	887	887	584	584
F-stat	29.32***	29.4***	23.00***	20.94***
Adj R-squ	0.2422	0.2427	0.2541	0.2548
MeanVif	1.48	1.48	1.49	1.49

注：括号内为t统计量。***、**、*分别代表在1%、5%和10%的显著性水平下显著。

从表6可知，方程的F统计量都在1%的显著性水平上通过检验。方差扩大因子（Vif）的平均值都小于2，说明模型没有出现多重共线性问题。A、B两组回归结果基本一致，即在控制企业规模、企业系统风险、成长性下，财务杠杆越高，企业业绩越低，表明目前运用财务杠杆作用为企业带来的效益无法弥补其对企业带来的损失，例如还贷压力；管理者持股对企业业绩具有正影响，表明管理者持股能起到激励作用，促进企业业绩的提升，这与已有研究一致；独立董事规模对企业业绩影响为负，证明目前国内企业中独立董事的设置不仅没有起到预期的作用，反而增加了企业费用支出，降低了经营业绩；全面风险管理的两个指标与企业业绩都成正相关，说明实施全面风险管理的企业拥有更好的业绩，并且全面风险管理实施程度越高，企业业绩越好。具体的，从A估计式可知所有行业中实施全面风险管理对总资产回报率的平均贡献为1.52%，即实施全面风险管理的企业的总资本回报率比未实施的高0.0152。从B估计式可知全面风险管理实施程度每上一个台阶，总资产收益会提高0.819%。

本模型未控制行业变量对企业业绩的影响。由于样本总体局限于中央上市企业，若分行业则会导致样本量无法满足模型估计的要求。观察发现所有样本中制造业企业最多，故为使研究结果更具有可信性，本文将样本细致到制造业进行检验。结果如表6中C、D列所示。从表中可见，在调整样本规模后模型的估计结果与之前基本一致。从C估计式可知在制造业实施全面风险管理对总资产回报率的平均贡献为1.46%。从D估计式可知全面风险管理实施程度每上一个台阶，总资产收益会提高0.801%。

2. 全面风险管理与延期企业业绩

由建设全面风险管理体系设计到风险评估技术的提高、职能机构的设置、人员的培训、全面风险管理观文化的树立，因此实施全面风险管理本身带有巨大的投资性质。一般而言，业绩越好的企业越有能力实施全面风险管理，由此就带来了全面风险管理的实施与企业业绩的内生性。为解决此问题，本文拟从时间角度检验全面风险管理与企业业绩的关系，即研究全面风险管理的滞后项与企业业绩的关系。仍然利用模型（1）、（2），用全面风险管理滞后项回归后结果见表7。

表7　**全面风险管理对企业业绩的滞后效果**

	roa（全样本）				roa（制造业）			
	A	B	C	D	E	F	G	H
L. erm1	0.0151 *** (3.12)				0.0173 *** (2.64)			
L2. erm1		0.0111 * (1.77)				0.0199 ** (2.18)		
L. erm2			0.00792 *** (3.07)				0.00873 *** (2.58)	
L2. erm2				0.00646 * (1.94)				0.0086 * (1.95)
lnasset	0.0109 *** (7.18)	0.0128 *** (6.08)	0.0110 *** (7.18)	0.0127 *** (6.08)	0.0128 *** (5.25)	0.0126 *** (4.03)	0.0127 *** (5.24)	0.0126 *** (4.02)
beta	-0.0147 (-1.42)	0.0095 (0.66)	-0.0138 (-1.33)	0.00967 (0.68)	-0.01 (-0.68)	0.0059 (0.33)	-0.00937 (-0.64)	0.00619 (0.35)
lev	-0.122 *** (-12.53)	-0.131 *** (-7.49)	-0.123 *** (-12.58)	-0.131 *** (-7.51)	-0.155 *** (-7.55)	-0.161 *** (-6.94)	-0.155 *** (-7.57)	-0.161 *** (-6.91)
mb	0.00684 *** (3.65)	0.00660 ** (2.96)	0.00682 *** (3.64)	0.00656 *** (2.93)	0.00281 (1.07)	0.000586 (0.18)	0.00281 (1.07)	0.0006 (0.19)
outdirector	-0.0706 ** (-2.35)	-0.0761 * (-2.45)	-0.0697 ** (-2.32)	-0.0758 ** (-2.43)	-0.0957 ** (-2.35)	-0.0759 (-1.58)	-0.0927 ** (-2.27)	-0.0738 (-1.53)

续表

	roa（全样本）				roa（制造业）			
	A	B	C	D	E	F	G	H
holdratio	0.196 ** (2.21)	0.0559 (1.34)	0.195 ** (2.2)	0.0558 (1.34)	0.327 *** (8.89)	7.018 *** (4.73)	0.326 *** (8.79)	6.985 *** (4.71)
year	控制	控制	控制	控制	控制	控制	控制	控制
_cons	-0.121 *** (-2.92)	-0.182 *** (-3.29)	-0.136 *** (-3.34)	-0.188 *** (-3.40)	-0.143 * (-2.24)	-0.155 * (-1.90)	-0.153 ** (-2.38)	-0.164 ** (-2.00)
N	671	437	671	437	443	290	443	290
F-stat	26.91	23.53	26.87	23.61	21.88	21.04	21.78	20.79
Adj R-squ	0.2582	0.2582	0.2579	0.2932	0.2983	0.3568	0.2973	0.3539
MeanVif	1.36	1.36	1.37	1.33	1.39	1.42	1.39	1.42

注：括号内为t统计量。***、**、* 分别代表在1%、5%和10%的显著性水平下显著。

表7中L. erm1、L. erm2表示全面风险管理实施情况的滞后一期指标，其研究当期全面风险管理的实施对第二年企业业绩的影响。L2. erm1、L2. erm2表示全面风险管理实施哑变量的滞后二期指标，其研究全面风险管理的实施对第三年企业业绩的影响。从表7中可以看到企业实施全面风险能在未来一定期间提高企业业绩，滞后一期的影响最大，而且显著性水平最高，结果更稳健。而其他指标与企业业绩的关系与前面研究结果基本一致。

3. 全面风险管理与财务困境

为检验假设3，证明实施全面风险管理对财务困境的影响，本文先利用全部样本对模型（3）、（4）进行估计，异方差问题仍用stata中的robust命令解决，回归结果列示于表8。

表8 **模型（3）和模型（4）的回归结果**

	z	z
	A	B
erm1	0.139 *** (3.23)	
erm1×lev		0.289 *** (3.97)
lev	−0.220 ** (−2.19)	−0.292 *** (−2.87)
beta	−0.169 (−1.54)	−0.176 (−1.61)
lnasset	−0.018 (−1.23)	−0.0204 (−1.40)
mb	0.0548 *** (2.86)	0.0534 *** (2.79)
_cons	1.414 *** (3.57)	1.511 *** (3.81)
N	887	887
F-stat	7.94 ***	9.05 ***
Adj R-squ	0.0375	0.0432
MeanVif	1.29	1.31

注：括号内为t统计量。***、**、* 分别代表在1%、5%和10%的显著性水平下显著。

表8中A栏显示，在控制企业规模、系统风险这两个基本特征下，财务杠杆越大，z值越小，即企业陷入财务困境的可能性越大，这与已有研究相符；企业成长性越高，市场接受度越高，则陷入财务困境的可能性越小；实施全面风险管理能够提高z值，即降低企业陷入财务困境的可能性。B栏中所用模型解释了全面风险管理如何缓解财务杠杆对财务困境的影响。由B栏lev的系数可知当企业财务杠杆提高一个单位，对应的z值降低0.22个单位，即企业财务杠杆越高，其陷入财务困境的可能性越大；而全面风险管理与财务杠杆的交乘项erm1×lev系数为正，即在实施全面风险管理的情况下，财务杠杆对企业陷入财务困境可能性的影响比未实施全面风险管理的企业要低，仅为0.03。

4. 全面风险管理、财务困境与企业业绩

由前面可知，全面风险管理的实施有助于降低企业陷入财务困境的可能性，而这种财务困境成本的降低能为企业带来利益，进而提高企业业绩。同时，已有研究显示，资产透明度、企业复杂度、董事会独立性、企业系统风险及能源行业、交通运输业、医药制造业等特种行业都会影响企业实施全面风险管理（Meulbroek，2002；Kleffner et al.，2003；Beasley et al.，2005，2008；Liebenberg 和 Hoyt，2003，2011；Pagach 和 Warr，2010，2011）。故如果用单一方程研究全面风险管理与财务困境或者企业业绩的关系就有可能出现变量内生性问题，而内生性会导致模型的估计结果出现偏倚。为保证研究结果的可信性，本文借鉴Hoyt 和 Liebenberg（2011）、姜付秀（2009）中联立方程组模型并用三阶段最小二乘法来分析三者之间的关系。

$$
\begin{aligned}
erm1 &= \alpha+\beta_1 gassetratio_{j,t}+\beta_2 lnrev_{j,t}+\beta_3 outdirector_{j,t}+\beta_4 beta_{j,t}+\beta_5 energy_{j,t}+ \\
&\quad \beta_6 transport_{j,t}+\beta_7 medicine_{j,t}+\beta_{8-10} year+\mu_{j,t} \\
z &= \alpha+\beta_1 erm1_{j,t}\times lev_{j,t}+\beta_2 lev_{j,t}+\beta_3 beta_{j,t}+\beta_4 lnasset_{j,t}+\beta_5 mb_{j,t}+\beta_{6-8} year+\mu_{j,t} \\
roa &= \alpha+\beta_1 z_{j,t}+\beta_2 erm1_{j,t}+\beta_3 beta_{j,t}+\beta_4 lev_{j,t}+\beta_5 lnasset_{j,t}+\beta_6 outdirector_{j,t}+ \\
&\quad \beta_7 holdratio_{j,t}+\beta_8 mb_{j,t}+\beta_{9-11} year+\mu_{j,t}
\end{aligned}
\tag{5}
$$

模型（5）中，第一个方程为全面风险管理影响因素方程，被解释变量为企业是否实施全面风险管理，用哑变量erm1表示。解释变量中gassetratio为固定资产占总资产比重，描述企业资产的透明度；lnrev为企业收入的对数，描述企业的复杂程度；outdirector为独立董事人数占董事会人数之比，表示企业董事会的独立性；beta为企业系统风险；energy、transport和medicine为哑变量，表示该企业是否为能源业、交通业、医药制造业。此外还控制了年份变量。第二个方程为风险方程，被解释变量为企业财务困境风险，用z值表示。erm1×lev为全面风险管理与财务杠杆的交乘项。此外添加企业财务杠杆、系统风险、规模、成长性和年份作为控制变量。第三个方程为业绩方程。被解释变量为企业资产净利率，代表企业的业绩水平。解释变量为erm1和z值，添加财务杠杆、系统风险、规模、董事会独立性、股权激励、成长性和年份作为控制变量。holdratio 为管理层持股，代表企业股权激励水平。表9为联立方程模型用三阶段最小二乘法估计得出的结果。

表9　　全面风险管理、财务困境与企业业绩联立方程回归结果

erm 影响因素方程		财务困境风险方程		企业业绩方程	
	erm1		z		roa
gassetratio	−0.241*** (−3.36)	lev_ erm1	0.434*** (5.72)	z	0.0149*** (4.25)
lnrev	0.0421*** (4.52)	lev	−0.283*** (−2.78)	erm1	0.0190*** (4.26)
outdirector	0.394* (1.69)	beta	−0.173 (−1.58)	beta	−0.00996 (−1.00)
beta	0.195** (2.5)	lnasset	−0.0193 (−1.29)	lev	−0.125*** (−13.78)
energy	0.189*** (2.86)	mb	0.0670*** (3.21)	lnasset	0.0106*** (7.66)
transport	0.141** (2.51)	_cons	1.496*** (3.72)	holdratio	0.176** (2.17)
medicine	0.321*** (3.43)	year	控制	mb	0.0057*** (3.00)
_cons	−1.173*** (−4.89)			outdirector	−0.0791** (−2.74)
year	控制			_cons	−0.129*** (−3.53)
				year	控制
N	887	N	887	N	887
chi2	210.88***	chi2	67.10***	chi2	317.98***
R-squ	0.1842	R-squ	0.0489	R-squ	0.2601

注：括号内为t统计量。***、**、*分别代表在1%、5%和10%的显著性水平下显著。

从表9可见，全面风险管理影响因素的回归结果与已有研究完全一致。企业实施全面风险管理与企业财务困境风险的关系与前文回归结果基本一致，即实施全面风险管理能降低企业财务杠杆带来的负面效应。

在企业业绩模型中，企业财务困境风险越低（z值越大）则企业业绩越好。模型中erm1变量与企业业绩成显著正相关，由此可知除了能够降低财务

困境风险进而提高企业业绩，全面风险管理的实施还能从其他方面增加企业业绩。已有研究显示：全面风险管理对企业所有风险进行整合，避免重复性风险管理支出（Harrington et al.，2002）；平稳收入，能够降低债务成本（Liebenberg 和 Hoyt 2003，2011；Meulbroek，2002）；在一定程度上避免了信息不对称引起的代理成本（Liebenberg 和 Hoyt，2003；Meulbroek，2002；Ramirez，2008），从而影响了当期利润，使企业业绩得到了提升。因此本文研究结果与相关领域的理论研究结果一致。

在控制企业规模、企业系统风险的情况下，财务杠杆越高，企业业绩越低，表明目前运用财务杠杆作用为企业带来的效益无法弥补其给企业带来的损失，例如还贷压力；管理者持股对企业业绩具有正影响，表明管理者持股能够带来激励效应，促进企业业绩的提升；成长性好的企业能够拥有更高的业绩，这与已有研究一致；独立董事规模对企业业绩影响为负，证明目前国内企业中独立董事的设置不仅没有起到预期的作用，而且增加了企业费用支出，降低了经营业绩。

（三）稳健性检验

虽然之前提到，用会计指标 ROA 衡量企业业绩来研究全面风险管理对企业业绩的影响可行，但为提高结论的可靠性，本文利用市场价值指标 Tobin's Q 进行稳健性检验。同时考虑到企业业绩对财务困境风险的影响，修改模型（5），利用滞后一期企业业绩拟合财务困境风险方程，结果见表 10。

表 10　**全面风险管理、财务困境与企业业绩（Tobin's Q）联立方程回归结果**

erm1 影响因素方程		财务困境风险方程		企业业绩方程	
	erm1		z		tobin's q
gassetratio	-0.265*** (-2.92)	lev_erm1	0.487*** (6.16)	z	0.196** (2.52)
lnrev	0.0627*** (5.25)	lev	-0.225*** (-1.75)	erm1	0.201** (2.25)
outdirector	0.589** (-2.02)	beta	-0.310** (-2.51)	beta	-1.038*** (-4.78)
beta	0.273*** (2.80)	lnasset	-0.0654*** (-4.08)	lev	-1.145*** (-5.68)
energy	0.207** (2.44)	L. roa	1.369*** (3.21)	lnasset	-0.410*** (-14.42)
medicine	0.460*** (3.79)	_cons	2.632*** (6.44)	holdratio	-1.783 (-0.95)
transport	0.184** (2.53)	year	控制	outdirector	0.192 (0.3)
_cons	-1.477*** (-4.79)			_cons	12.59*** (17.23)
year	控制			year	控制
N	671	N	671	N	671
chi2	80.88***	chi2	66.70***	chi2	382.57***
R-squ	0.0911	R-squ	0.0539	R-squ	0.3497

注：括号内为 t 统计量。***、**、*分别代表在 1%、5% 和 10% 的显著性水平下显著。

从表10可知，回归结果与之前基本一致。但是由于市场业绩具有较大的噪音，以及全面风险管理无法完全为市场接受，因此在结果的显著性水平上有所不足。同时，关于董事会独立性以及股权激励对企业市场价值的影响也与之前结论有所不同。股权激励对企业业绩的影响方向由正变为负，可能是由于股权激励使得管理者只顾眼前财务业绩而忽略了企业长期价值。综合来看，本文的研究结果具有一定的稳健性。

四、结论

本文以2008年至2011年中央控制上市企业为研究样本，收集了全面风险管理实施情况指标，对企业全面风险管理、财务困境和企业业绩三者进行了实证检验，结果显示：相比于未实施全面风险管理的企业，实施了全面风险管理的企业具有更好的业绩；企业实施全面风险管理的程度越高，其获得的效益越好。具体的，全面风险管理的实施有助于企业降低财务困境风险，并且在其他方面也对企业业绩的提升有所帮助。本文从实证角度为《指引》提供了依据。对于中央企业，实施全面风险管理这种合规性行为不仅没有给自身带来成本的上升，反而增加了企业价值；对于非中央企业，实施全面风险管理能带来绩效提升，所以值得股东及管理层将其纳入企业管理体系。本文为后续全面风险管理研究提供了新的视角，但亦有不足：

首先，研究的样本局限于中央控制上市企业。虽说央企在全面风险管理的实施过程中起到了示范的作用，但是一般企业由于各自情况不同，在具体实施全面风险管理时要结合自身情况进行。

其次，控制变量的选择尚不全面，例如财务困境风险方程的拟合度小于0.1；控制变量的衡量不够全面，例如关于企业复杂性的衡量，这些都有待扩展。

最后，本文虽然试图从全面风险管理创造价值的途径研究其对企业业绩的影响，但也只限于财务困境风险控制这一角度。本文结果显示除了通过降低财务困境风险，全面风险管理尚有其他影响企业业绩的途径。因此本文有很大的后续研究空间。

参考文献

[1]陈共荣,刘应文. 企业业绩评价指标若干问题研究[R]. 转型经济下的会计与财务问题国际学术研讨会,2003.

[2]刘红霞,刘晓川. 权变因素、ERM目标与企业绩效研究[J]. 北京工商大学学报:社会科学版,2012,27(1):57-62.

[3]朱华建,张盛勇,高宏伟. 21世纪以来我国内部控制研究主题及述评[J]. 会计研究,

2011,(11):57-64,93.

[4] AABO T et al.. The Rise and Evolution of the Chief Risk Officer, Enterprise Risk Management at Hydro One [J]. Journal of Applied Corporate Finance,2005,17(3):62-75.

[5] EDWARD A. Financial Ratios, Discriminate Analysis and the Prediction of Corporate Bankruptcy [J]. Journal of Finance,1968(4):589-609.

[6] RYAN B et al.. Enterprise Risk Management Program Quality: Determinants, Value Relevance, and the Financial Crisis [J]. Contemporary Accounting Research,2013.

[7] MARK B et al.. Enterprise Risk Management: an Empirical Analysis of Factors Associated with the Extent of Implementation [J]. Journal of Accounting and Public Policy,2005, 24(6):521-531.

[8] MARK B et al.. The Information Conveyed in Hiring Announcements of Senior Executives Overseeing Enterprise-Wide Risk Management Processes [J]. Journal of Accounting, Auditing & Finance,2008,23(3):311-332.

[9] PERRIN S, TILLINGHAST. A Changing Risk Landscape a Study of Corporate ERM in the U. S. [R],2006.

[10] COLQUITT L, LEE et al.. Integrated Risk Management and the Role of the Risk Manager [J]. Risk Management & Insurance Review,1999,2(3):43-61.

[11] COSO. Enterprise Risk Management: Integrated Framework: Executive Summary,2004.

[12] CHRISTINE C, BEVERLY H. The Challenges of Risk Management in Diversified Financial Companies [J]. Economic Policy Review,2001,7(1):1-17.

[13] LAWRENCE G et al.. Enterprise Risk Management and Firm Performance: A Contingency Perspective [J]. Journal of Accounting and Public Policy,2009,28(4):301-327.

[14] HARRINGTON S et al.. Enterprise Risk Management: The Case of United Grain Growers [J]. Journal of Applied Corporate Finance,2002,14(4):71-81.

[15] HOYT R, LIEBENBERG A. The Value of Enterprise Risk Management [J]. Journal of Risk and Insurance,2011,78(4):795-822.

[16] HUSSIN M R et al.. Enterprise-Wide Risk Management as a Value Added Tool in Enhancing the Economic Value of Business Enterprises [J/OL]. http://www.ensany.ir/storage/Files/20101129 075128-p0586300010831-KHNGA.pdf,2012.

[17] LAM J. Enterprise Risk Management: From Incentives to Controls [R]. PRMIA Chicago Meeting,2004.

[18] KLEFFNER A et al.. The Effect of Corporate Governance On the Use of Enterprise Risk Management, Evidence From Canada [J]. Risk Management and Insurance Review,2012,6(1): 53-73.

[19] LAM J. Enterprise-Wide Risk Management and the Role of the Chief Risk Officer [J/OL]. http://www.jameslam.com/media/ERM_and_Role_of_CRO_ERisk_Mar_2000_A16.Pdf,2000.

[20] LIEBENBERG A, HOYT R. The Determinants of Enterprise Risk Management: Evidence From Appointment of Chief Risk Officers [J]. Risk Management and Insurance Review, 2003,6(1):37-52.

[21] MACKAY P, MOELLER S. The Value of Corporate Risk Management [J]. The Journal of

Finance,2007,62(3):1379-1419.

[22] MANAB N A et al.. Enterprise-Wide Risk Management Practices: Between Corporate Governance Compliance and Value Creation [J]. International Review of Business Research Papers, 2010,6(2):239-252.

[23] MCSHANE M K et al.. Does Enterprise Risk Management Increase Firm Value? [J]. Journal of Accounting, Auditing & Finance,2011,26(4):641-658.

[24] MEULBROEK L K. A Senior Manager's Guide to Integrated Risk Management [J]. Journal of Applied Corporate Finance,2002,14(4):56-70.

[25] MILLER K D. A Framework for Integrated Risk Management in International Business [J]. Journal of International Business Studies,1992,23(2):311-331.

[26] NOCCO B W, STULZ M. Enterprise Risk Management, Theory and Practice [J]. Journal of Applied Corporate Finance,2006,18(4):8-20.

[27] ÖNDER S, ERGIN H. Determiners of Enterprise Risk Management Applications in Turkey: An Empirical Study with Logistic Regression Model On the Companies Included in ISE (Istanbul Stock Exchange) [J]. Business and Economic Horizons,2012,7(1):19-26.

[28] OPLER T et al.. The Determinants and Implications of Corporate Cash Holdings [J]. Journal of Financial Economics,1999,52(1):3-46.

[29] PAAPE L, SPEKLÉ R. The Adoption and Design of Enterprise Risk Management Practices: An Empirical Study [J]. European Accounting Review,2012,21(3):1-32.

[30] PAGACH D, WARR R. The Characteristics of Firms that Hire Chief Risk Officers [J]. Journal of Risk and Insurance,2011,78(1):185-211.

[31] PAGACH D, WARR RICHARD. The Effects of Enterprise Risk Management on Firm Performance[R]. Working Paper,2010.

[32] QUON T K et al.. Enterprise Risk Management and Business Performance During the Financial and Economic Crises [J]. Problems and Perspectives in Management, 2012, 10(3): 95-103.

[33] RIZAL R, MOHD T. Review of the Literature on Enterprise Risk Management [J]. Business Management Dynamics,2011,1(5):8-16.

[34] SIMKINS B, RAMIREZ S. Enterprise-Wide Risk Management and Corporate Governance [J]. Loyola University Chicago Law Journal,2008,(39):571-594.

[35] SMITH C, STULZ R. The Determinants of Firms' Hedging Policies [J]. The Journal of Financial and Quantitative Analysis,1985,20(4):391.

[36] STULZ R. Optimal Hedging Policies [J]. The Journal of Financial and Quantitative Analysis,1984,19(2):127.

[37] STULZ R. Rethinking Risk Management [J]. Journal of Applied Corporate Finance, 1996,9(3):8-25.

[38] SUBHANI M, AMBER O. The Essence of Enterprise Risk Management in Today's Business Enterprises in Developed and Developing Nations [J]. European Journal of Social Sciences,2011,25(4):515-524.

[39] TUFANO P. Who Manages Risk? An Empirical Examination of Risk Management Practices in the Gold Mining Industry [J]. The Journal of Finance,1996,51(4):1097-1137.

Enterprise Risk Management, Financial Distress and Firm Performance— An Empirical Study Based on Public Enterprise Controlled by Central Government

Abstract By using data of central public enterprises from 2008 to 2011, an empirical study of the effect of enterprise risk management on firm performance was conducted, together with the further study about the mechanism of this effect. The study found that compared to those had no ERM, enterprises that had already taken part in ERM program would have a better firm performance. Enterprise risk management could reduce the financial distress probability by mitigating the negative effect brought by firms' high level of financial leverage, and by this way ERM could add firm value. Considering the probably endogenous problem, we used simultaneous equations model to test the relationship among enterprise risk management, financial distress and firm performance, and the result showed that ERM could not only promote firm performance by reducing financial distress probability, but also through other ways. The result was robust when ROA was replaced of Tobin's Q. This study would provide empirical evidence for relevant policy.

Key Words Enterprise Risk Management (ERM)　COSO Report　Financial Distress　Firm Performance

“BBB明智捐款联盟”的评价标准体系

樊子君　李灿　赵秋爽

（东北财经大学会计学院/中国内部控制研究中心　大连　116025）

摘　要　美国的慈善事业之所以成功，除了其拥有完善的法律法规体系外，独立于政府监督的第三方监督也起到了不可替代的作用。“BBB 明智捐款联盟”就是众多第三方监督机构之一。本文首先对“BBB 明智捐款联盟”进行了简要介绍，然后详细说明了联盟的慈善组织评价标准及应用指引，以及其评估报告的类型和内容，最后总结评价标准体系的特点，提出针对我国慈善评估机构建立与完善的启示。

关键词　BBB 明智捐款联盟　慈善组织评价标准　慈善组织评价应用指引

美国是慈善事业最为成功的国家之一，据美国 2010 年慈善捐赠年度报告，2010 年美国的慈善捐款总额达 2 908.9 亿美元（其中个人捐款达 2 117.7 亿美元，占捐款总量的 72.8%）①。美国的慈善事业之所以发达，不仅因为其创新的现代慈善理念、发达的慈善组织体系、良好的社会信任机制，以及完善的慈善立法和税收制度，还因为其有独立于政府监管的另一种监督形式——独立的慈善组织评估机构（以下简称“评估机构”），为美国慈善事业的良性发展起到了极大的促进和激励作用。

美国的评估机构大多由民间发起，按照运作模式主要分为三种类型：第一种采用大众点评的模式，如成立于 2007 年的“卓越的非营利组织（Great Nonprofits，GN）”；第二种采用认证的模式，如成立于 1992 年的“马里兰州非营利组织联合会（Maryland Association of Nonprofit Organizations）”；第三种采用对慈善组织进行评估或排名，但不提供资格认证的模式，如成立于 2001 年的“慈善导航（Charity Navigator）”。与第一种和第二种相比，第三种评估机构规模和影响力更大，评估人员多为相关领域的专家，评估的透明性、专业性、准确性也更强。

美国“BBB 明智捐款联盟”具有历史渊源长和评估经验丰富的特点，属于上述第三种类型。本文将对其基本情况、运行机制及评价标准进行详细介绍，以期对建立和发展我国第三方慈善评估机构提供借鉴。

---

① 2010 美国慈善捐赠报告，GivingUSA Report。

一、联盟概况

BBB 明智捐款联盟（以下简称"联盟"）是由美国国家慈善信息局①和更好事务局委员会（Council of Better Business Bureau，CBBB）② 下属机构公益咨询服务部（PAS）于2001年合并后成立的，隶属于更好事务局委员会，并纳入该委员会的合并财务报表。

联盟是一个非营利组织，其使命是通过评估面向全国筹款的慈善机构是否遵守20条严格的评价标准（Standards for Charity Accountability）③ 来帮助捐赠者做出决策，并促进慈善行业公信力的不断提高。如果某慈善机构满足联盟所有的20条评价标准，联盟会鼓励其购买使用"BBB 慈善认证标志"的权利，慈善组织（以下简称"组织"）可以把该标志放在它们的网站上、发送的邮件里以及报纸和杂志的广告中，以迅速有效地吸引更多潜在的捐赠者。

联盟有自己独立的董事会，日常工作人员主要有总裁（兼首席执行官）、首席运营官、编辑、分管发展和慈善评估的董事、报告分析员、行政协调员等，但其人事、媒体、会计、信息技术、法律和行政方面的工作由 CBBB 的职员承担。联盟的活动资金主要来源于个人、企业和基金会的捐赠。

二、慈善评价标准及应用指引

联盟的慈善组织评价标准（以下简称"评价标准"）包括治理与监督、绩效评估、财务及筹资和信息披露4个方面，共计20条。该20条标准是在其他国家的慈善组织信息局标准、BBB 基金会及其下属的捐赠服务机构标准的基础上，进行独立和有效的研究，同时利用网络与捐赠者充分讨论，以保证这些标准能够反映普通大众的意见，力求鼓励公平诚实的劝募，提倡慈善组织的道德诚信，并争取公众对慈善事业的支持。

联盟还制定了应用指引，用来帮助理解评价标准，每条评价标准的应用指引都包含两个方面：慈善机构需提交的基本资料以及标准的具体应用。

慈善组织评价标准的制定得到了小型和大型慈善组织代表、会计专业人士、公司中负责公益事务的管理人员、资助型基金会、制定规章的机构、研究机构和 BBB 系统等专业与技术上的支持。

---

① 美国国家慈善信息局，成立于1918年，是纽约州立非营利组织，与联盟有相同的使命。

② CBBB，成立于1912年，是更好事务局系统的全国性办事处。

③ Standards for Charity Accountability，直译为"慈善问责标准"。在当前语境下，我们将其译为"慈善组织评价标准"。

（一）治理与监督

1. 具体标准

对任何一家慈善组织来说，董事会都是最终的监督机构。本部分标准旨在确保志愿董事会①是活跃的、独立的和无内幕交易的。

标准1：设立对组织的运作及其成员进行充分监管的董事会。

充分的监管是指（但不限于）对CEO的业绩进行有计划的定期评估，以及对组织开支进行相应的监控。例如，董事会对组织的预算和筹资活动进行批准，出台利益冲突政策，建立保护组织财务安全的会计程序。

标准2：董事会的成员中至少有5位拥有投票权。

标准3：董事会会议每年至少召开3次且间隔相等，董事会的大多数成员应亲自到会。

标准4：董事会最多只能吸收一位直接领取报酬（如领薪雇员）或间接领取报酬（如领薪雇员的配偶或家人）的个人作为其投票成员，且该成员不能担任董事会主席或财务主管。

标准5：董事会成员或组织中的其他成员不得在关联交易中因任何关系或商业联系而与组织发生重大利益冲突。

在判断关联方交易是否会造成利益冲突以及这种冲突是否重大时，应当考虑的因素包括（但不限于）：组织是否建立了公平交易程序（arm's length procedure）；与组织可能的支出相对应的关联交易规模；利益主体是否参与了董事会对关联交易的投票；是否寻求了竞争性招标；关联交易是一次性的、重复性的还是连续发生的。

2. 应用指引

慈善组织应提交的资料包括：董事会投票委员花名册、董事会会议的日期和出席信息、国税局990表、财务报表、相关补充信息表格以及关联方交易信息表格。

与标准1相关的指引内容。联盟应要求慈善组织确认其董事会实施了下列每一项监督活动：（1）至少每两年对首席执行官的绩效进行一次正式评估；（2）有正式批准的预算；（3）确保与外部筹资机构之间的活动有书面文件；（4）有正式批准的调解利益冲突的政策并进行日常监督以确保其得到持续遵守；（5）委派一名拥有投票权的董事会成员（例如，财会委员会主席或者类似的职位）来监督组织的财务状况并向董事会报告；（6）确保没有人同时担任行政主席和财务主管的两项职位；（7）每年都要接收组织的下列资料：①国税局990表；②经审计的财务报表（如果没有进行审计，就提供组织未经审计的财务报表）；③审计师的管理建议书（如果已经发布）。如果前述的任

① 志愿董事会，即董事会是由志愿者成员组成的。

何一项活动没有得到实施，那么组织就不符合标准 1 的要求。

与标准 2 相关的指引内容。联盟对投票委员花名册进行检查，确定是否包含至少 5 名拥有投票权的董事，并对组织进行询问，对每一位无投票权的董事会成员进行确认。

与标准 3 相关的指引内容。询问组织关于其过去一年的董事会会议的日期和出席信息，确定是否满足以下要求：（1）董事会会议的频率——每年至少召开 3 次董事会会议（其中一次可以是电话会议）；（2）董事会会议的出席人数——大部分董事会成员（平均至少 50%）应该出席会议；（3）代替出席人数——在确定组织是否满足出席人数要求时，代替出席人员不计入到人数内。

与标准 4 相关的指引内容。联盟对国税局 990 表和财务报表等表格中有关报酬的信息进行分析，并根据以下定义和原则来确定组织是否满足本标准：（1）直接领取报酬的董事会投票成员是指从组织接受报酬（以现金和/或非现金形式）的成员（即受薪员工，受薪顾问等等）；（2）间接领取报酬的董事会投票成员是指上述直接领取报酬成员的直系亲属（如配偶、父母、兄弟姐妹以及子女）；（3）董事会投票人员接受酬金认为是直接领取报酬，仅报销发生的费用不认为是领取报酬；（4）董事会投票人员从其隶属公司领取工资，且该公司与组织在财务和管理上存在关联方关系，并按照公认会计准则需要编制合并报表，则认为投票人员直接领取报酬。

与标准 5 相关的指引内容。联盟对国税局 990 表和财务报表中有关关联方交易的相关信息进行分析，组织如果有下列一个或多个情形时将不满足这一标准：（1）组织与董事会成员或职员有大量交易且关联公司没有采取措施以确保公平交易；（2）如果交易的数额巨大或影响时间长，那么该项交易不可能是公允的；（3）关联交易在整个财务年度多次发生，虽然每一次交易数额比较小，但合计起来就构成重大关联方交易。

（二）绩效评价

1. 具体标准

一个组织应当定期评估其完成使命的有效性。本部分标准试图确保组织有一个明确而适当的评估程序，以评价项目是否成功，以及项目对组织实现其目标的影响，同时指出组织在实现其目标的过程中存在的不足。

标准 6：董事会应出台一项政策，要求组织至少每两年一次地对组织的业绩和效益进行评估，并制定为实现组织使命所需的改进措施。

标准 7：组织应向其董事会呈交一份书面报告，并报请董事会批准。报告内容包括上述绩效评估的结果和对未来行动的建议。

2. 应用指引

针对这部分标准，组织需要提交绩效评估政策的复印件，并在联盟调查表[①]中说明董事会是否收到书面绩效评估报告并对其进行批准。

与标准6相关的指引内容。联盟应证实组织正在实施绩效评估政策，且至少每两年进行一次评估。该政策应清楚表明，组织会对实现其使命和目标过程中所取得的成功和造成的影响进行正式评估。

与标准7相关的指引内容。联盟应确认绩效评估已经得到实施，但并不评价其质量和内容。因此，联盟不要求组织提供其评估报告副本。

（三）财务

1. 具体标准

这部分标准试图确保组织诚实谨慎地运用其资金，并与组织声明的筹资目的相一致。

标准8：组织用于慈善活动的支出不得低于总支出的65%。

公式为：$\frac{\text{总项目费用}}{\text{总费用}} \geqslant 65\%$

标准9：组织筹资所发生的费用不得超过捐赠收入总额的35%。

公式为：$\frac{\text{总筹资费用}}{\text{总收入}} \leqslant 35\%$

标准10：组织应避免积累可以用于开展当前项目活动的资金，为满足这一标准，组织的可使用净资产不应超过上一年的费用或本年度预算两者中较高者的3倍。（特别说明：慈善组织如果没有达到第8、9和/或10条标准的要求，可以提供证据说明其对资金的使用是合理的。如较高的筹资成本、新成立的组织的行政成本、捐赠人对资金使用的限制、特殊的遗赠，以及非组织所能控制的环境或政治事件，尽管它们并不符合在此陈述的财务评估标准，但也构成导致合理开支的因素）

标准11：及时提供根据公认会计准则编制的完整年度财务报告。

当组织的年度总收入超过＄500 000时，财务报表应当依照公认审计准则接受审计；对于年度总收入大于＄250 000少于等于＄500 000的组织，由注册会计师审核即可达标；对年度收入少于＄250 000的组织，内部编制的完整的财务报表即可达标。

标准12：财务报告应包括各种开支（如工资、差旅费、邮费等）的分类细目，并说明这些开支分配到项目、资金筹集和行政活动上的具体金额。

标准13：在财务报表中准确地报告组织的支出状况，包括对共同费用的分配。

标准14：及时提供经董事会批准的年度预算，陈述预期用于主要项目活动、筹资和行政管理的支出。

2. 应用指引

依据上述标准，组织应根据其收入规模提供经审计（或审核）的财务报

---

① 联盟调查表需由慈善组织填写完成，能提供联盟评估所需的大部分信息。

表、内部编制的财务报表或者国税局 990 表、预算表、计划表、本年度财务预算副本以及资金募集资料。

与标准 8 相关的指引内容。联盟按照下列方法计算组织的项目费用比率：(1) 如果组织有经审计或审核的财务报表，联盟用报告的所有项目的活动费用除以所有费用来确定项目费用比率。(2) 如果组织没有经审计或审核的财务报表，联盟就用国税局 990 表来计算这一比率，即用第 13 行（所有项目的服务费用）除以第 17 行（所有费用）确定项目费用比率。(3) 如果组织没有经审计或审核的财务报表或国税局 990 表，联盟就使用可获得的最近的未审计的财务报表计算项目费用比率，方法如 (1)。(4) 如果组织没有经审计或审核的财务报表或未经审计的财务报表，但完成了国税局 990-EZ 表，联盟就用这个表来计算该比率，即用第 32 行（所有项目的服务费用）除以第 17 行（所有费用）确定项目费用比率。(5) 如果组织没有满足 65% 的项目费用标准但认为有标准中特别说明的事项（如新成立组织的行政成本较高），应将这些事项告知联盟。

与标准 9 相关的指引内容。联盟按照下列方法计算组织的筹资费用比率：(1) 如果组织有经审计或审核的财务报表，联盟用报告的所有筹资费用除以所有捐赠收入来确定筹资费用比率。(2) 如果组织没有经审计或审核的财务报表，联盟就用国税局 990 表来计算该比率。首先将第 1 行（所有的捐赠）、第 3 行（会员费）和第 9 行（特殊筹款收入）相加得出总捐赠收入，然后用第 15 行（总筹资费用）除以总捐赠收入来确定筹资费用比率。(3) 如果组织没有经审计或审核的财务报表或国税局 990 表，联盟就使用最近可获得的未审计的财务报表计算筹资费用比率，方法如 (1)。(4) 如果没有经审计或审核的财务报表也没有未经审计的财务报表，组织即使完成了国税局 990-EZ 表也不能使用其计算该比率，因为 990-EZ 表不能确定总筹资费用。(5) 如果组织没有满足 35% 的项目筹资费用比率标准但认为有标准中特别说明的事项（如较高的筹资成本），应将这些事项告知联盟。

与标准 10 相关的指引内容。联盟按照下面的方法计算可使用净资产比率：(1) 第一步，使用经审计或审核的财务报表确定全部可使用净资产数量（通常，被审计的财务报表的净资产有三类：可使用的、暂时受限的、永久受限的）；第二步，用最近一期经审计的财务报表中显示的总费用或者当年的计划年度总费用两者中较高者作为计算比率时的总费用；第三步，用总的可使用净资产除以总费用，确定其比率是否小于等于 3。如果比例大于 3，联盟应该重新评估可使用的净资产，净资产中如果包含任何固定资产（如土地、建筑物、设备等），应该在剔除这些资产价值后重新计算该比率。(2) 如果组织无法提供经审计的财务报表，联盟使用国税局 990 表计算该比率，即用第 67 行（可使用净资产）除以第 17 行（总费用）计算该比率；如果组织无法提供国税局 990 表，联盟使用未审计的财务报表计算该比率，方法如 (1)；如果组织只能提供990-ZE表，由于该表没有对净资产进行分类（即分为可使用的净资产、暂时受限的净资产、永久受限的净资产），联盟无法计算该比率，则组织就不符合该标准的要求。（3）如果组织可使用净资产数量超过了该标准的要求，但组织认为自己不满足这一标准是由特殊情形所引起，应做出说明；如果不存在特殊情形，但联盟按照以下要求对信息进行了披露，则可视同组织满足该标准：①在直接邮件诉求中，应在邮件显著的位置用正式的语言清晰地陈述可使用净资产与总费用的关系，如：X组织大约有＄XXX，XXX，XXX的不受限制的慈善资金储备，或者净资产大约是最近一年费用＄XXX，XXX，XXX的X倍；②其他受时间或地点限制的诉求（如电话诉求、公益广告诉求）不要求组织披露上述信息。但如果潜在募捐者要求的话，组织应该寄送相关书面材料；③在组织网站上应该有专门区域按照在直接邮件诉求中的格式描述组织的可使用净资产。

与标准11相关的指引内容。联盟使用下列准则评估组织提交的财务报表：（1）如果组织的年度总收入超过＄500 000，其财务报表应得到外部审计师的审计，审计意见是“标准无保留”意见时表明其财务报表是按照公认会计准则编制的。（2）如果组织的年度总收入超过＄250 000但小于等于＄500 000，其财务报表应该得到外部审计师的审核，审核能提供一定程度的保证，但并不需按公认审计准则进行，审核的报表与审计的一样，也应包括财务状况表、日常活动表、现金流量表、附注等。（3）如果组织的年度总收入小于等于＄250 000，组织可以只提供内部编制的财务报表，但也应该包括财务状况表、支持声明、收入费用表、附注以及其他适用的表格。如果组织没有内部编制的财务报表，只提供了国税局990表或990-EZ表，也视同组织符合该标准。（4）如果组织的财务报表中包括了共同费用的分配，组织应根据公认会计准则，分别披露总费用和分配到项目服务、筹资以及行政费用中的数目。

与标准12相关的指引内容。联盟对该标准作了进一步的解释：（1）根据公认会计准则的要求，所有的健康和福利型慈善组织都应该制作一个按照功能对费用进行详细分类的表格。联盟则要求所有组织的财务报表中均包含这种表格。（2）这个表格展示详细的费用分类，它对每一个主要的项目服务、筹资和行政费用按照费用的性质进行罗列和汇总。表的纵栏是费用的性质（如工资、房屋租金、差旅费、津贴、电话费、邮费、办公费、印刷费等，最后是费用合计），表的横栏是项目服务名称、筹资费用、行政费用以及总费用。

与标准13相关的指引内容。联盟根据以下指导方针评估组织提供的财务信息：（1）如果组织的财务报表和/或国税局990表没有报告筹资费用或行政费用（比如财务报表或国税局990表中筹资项目或者是空白的或者是＄0），那么组织不满足该标准。（2）如果组织在其财务报表和/或国税局990表中以净捐赠的形式进行披露以至于不适当地减少了报告的筹资费用，那么组织不满足该标准。换句话说，组织所有的筹资费用都应该包含在财务报表和/或国税局990表的筹资费用项目中。(3) 在一些特殊的筹资活动中，捐赠者有时会因为他们的捐赠得到一些有价值的服务或礼物（如一顿饭或一张音乐会的门票)。许多组织报告的都是减除了这些费用后的筹资收入，国税局990表许可使用这种方法，这在美国会计准则也是允许的。但与该筹集活动相关的所有筹集费用，如邀请费、邮费、咨询费应该包括在财务报表和国税局990表的筹资费用目录中。

与标准14相关的指引内容。联盟以下面的准则评估组织提交的信息：(1) 预算必须清楚地说明组织本财务年度的预期总费用。(2) 如果组织的预算仅确定了组织按性质分类的费用（如工资、邮费、差旅费等）但不提供显示每一个主要项目服务（如项目A、项目B等)、筹资以及行政管理的总预期费用的费用明细，则不满足该标准。(3) 预算必须得到董事会的批准。

（四）筹资和信息披露

1. 具体准则

筹资诉求（fund raising appeal）常常是捐助者与组织直接联系的开端，并且可能是捐助者捐赠的唯一动力来源。这部分标准在于确保组织对公众所作的陈述是准确、完整和可信的。

标准15：用尽可能多的方式传播准确、可信、不误导他人的全部或部分的劝募书和相关信息资料。

标准16：拟定一份可以向所有人公开的年度报告，内容包括：

(1) 组织使命的陈述；

(2) 上一年度的项目服务成果的总结；

(3) 董事会成员和其他管理人员花名册；

(4) 财务信息，包括：①上一财务年度的总收入；②财务报告中说明的各类项目、筹资和行政管理的开支；③期末净资产。

标准17：所有通过组织网站进行网上募捐的活动，都应同时公布组织年度报告所涉及的所有信息、组织的通讯地址及其最新的国税局990表的电子访问路径。

标准18：通过以下做法关注捐助者的隐私。

(1) 每年至少一次为初次和多次捐赠者提供一种方式（例如，可在相关方格内打钩的表格，即Check-off Box)，使他们能告知组织是否希望自己的名字和地址在组织以外被共享。

(2) 在组织的所有网站上公示清楚、醒目和易于访问的隐私保护政策，告知访问者：①他们的哪些信息（如果有的话）正在被组织所收集，以及这些信息将被如何使用；②如何联系组织以检查被收集的个人信息，并要求更正；③访问者不希望在组织以外共享其个人信息时，如何通知组织；④组织采取了哪些安全措施来保护个人信息。

标准19：明确披露组织如何从产品或服务的销售（例如，与慈善事业相关的买卖交易）中获益。在筹资时，应当公开以下销售信息：

（1）组织所能获得的购买价格中的实际或预期比例（例如，每卖一件x公司的产品向a组织捐赠5美分）；

（2）商业活动持续的时间；

（3）任何一笔捐款的最高或最低保证金额（例如，最多可达200 000美元）。

标准20：联盟和更好事务局委员会提请组织关注其筹资活动、违反隐私保护政策的行为及其他问题所招致的投诉，组织对此应做出快速反应，并且采取行动。

2. 应用指引

针对该部分标准，联盟要求组织提供的资料有：劝募书和相关信息资料样本，包括直接邮件诉求、电话诉求、印刷广告（如报纸、杂志）、电视脚本和电台诉求、捐赠建议、网络诉求等，以及最近的年度报告、组织网址、与慈善营销相关的资料以及回复相关投诉信件的复印件。

与标准15相关的指引内容。联盟围绕以下关键点来评估组织提交的材料：（1）如果组织的捐赠诉求中表明捐赠物将在某个特定的时间（如发生灾难时）和/或将为特殊的目的（如帮助受灾人员）使用，组织应该能证实其确实遵循了这些承诺。（2）捐款诉求应该包括对所募集资金的特殊项目活动的描述，如果募捐书中对问题的描述缺乏组织对这些问题的解决方法，则组织不满足该标准。（3）联盟应该要求组织确认其诉求中所陈述信息的准确性，包括但不限于下列情形：①募捐书中用到的财务资料是否与组织财务报表中的数据一致；②过时的报道、照片和/或数据（即时间长于3年）能否代表目前的状况；③有关组织绩效的资料（例如，接受帮助的人数）是否准确。

与标准16相关的指引内容。联盟从以下几方面具体评估组织的年度报告：（1）报告应包括标准16中提到的从（1）到（4）的所有项目，缺少任何一项则表明联盟不满足该标准。（2）年度报告可以用除“年度报告”之外的标题，如“成绩报告”、“年度评估”、“进展报告”等，只要将标准中提到的所有信息包含在内，组织就符合标准。（3）组织可以只在网上披露年度报告，但如果有人要求寄送纸质报告，组织就必须满足其要求。

与标准17相关的指引内容。联盟围绕下列关键点评估组织的网站：（1）如果组织有相应的网站并利用网站进行了募捐，那么，网站应该提供满足标准16要求的年度报告信息，并给出组织的邮寄地址、最近的国税局990表的电子访问路径；如果组织没有利用网站进行募捐，这一要求不适用。（2）如果组织由于下列某一原因没有完成国税局990表，那么这部分标准不适用：①组织是新成立的，还没有填报过990表；②组织在过去3年平均年收入少于＄25 000，不用完成990表；③组织是教会、犹太教堂、清真寺或类似机构，不需要申请填写990表。

与标准18相关的指引内容。对标准中（1）部分，组织如果对外公布捐赠者的名字和地址，应至少每年一次提供一个书面申请样本，使捐赠者有机会告知组织是否希望他们的名字被公布；对标准中（2）部分，组织如果拥有网站，需要提供网址并指出有关隐私政策在网站的什么位置。联盟围绕以下关键点评估组织提供的信息：（1）书面申请书，①至少每年一次在给捐赠者的书面募捐书中包括捐赠者可以告知组织是否希望自己的名字在组织之外被共享的方式（如可以采用在相关表格中打钩的方式）；②如果捐赠者第一次向组织进行捐赠，且本年没有后续募捐，在对捐款者的地址和名字披露时应该包括对他们的慷慨捐赠的感谢；③如果组织没有对捐赠者信息进行披露，该标准不适用。（2）网站，①不论是否募集资金，组织都应通过在网站主页上设置的链接提供清晰、醒目、易于访问的隐私政策；②即使不通过网站进行慈善募捐，也可能为了其他目的要求访问者提供他们的名字、地址和其他个人信息，这种情况下也适用该标准；③标准中提到的隐私政策因素都应该包括在组织的隐私政策中，缺少任何一个都表明组织不符合该标准。

与标准19相关的指引内容。如果组织涉及慈善营销，要提供与这些营销相关的资料。组织应该按照下面的建议进行披露：（1）组织应该运用如下陈述方式进行披露，如X公司每销售一盒早餐，将捐赠5分钱给A组织；（2）披露数目应该以货币计量（如将有25美分捐赠给组织）或者以销售价格的比例计量（如销售价格的3%将捐赠给组织）；（3）在进行慈善营销时就应该向潜在的购买者披露组织受益的相关信息，披露方式可以是产品的广告中或者产品的包装和挂牌上；（4）如果组织仅在披露中陈述组织将从该营销中获得"收益"、"利润"、"净收益"或其他财务收益，则不符合该标准。

与标准20相关的指引内容。组织对相关投诉应提供回复信件的复印件。如果没有投诉，该标准不适用。联盟按照下列要求评估相关信件：（1）组织应该对所有的投诉进行回复，回复中应包括组织将采取什么行动来解决投诉中提出的问题；（2）投诉可能涉及的领域有：①组织没有按照捐赠者的要求使用捐赠者的捐款；②组织没有应捐赠者要求从其通讯录中移除捐赠者的地址或电话号码；③组织用激进的方式募集资金等。

三、出具评估报告

根据20条慈善评价标准及其应用指引对组织做出评估后，联盟将按照一定的格式对其出具评估报告。依据不同的结果，评估报告主要有三种类型：第一种是无法对组织是否符合标准做出评估结论的报告；第二种是组织不符合一条或多条标准的报告；第三种是组织符合所有标准的报告。每份报告主要包括组织的联系方式（包括地址、电话和网址）、"BBB明智捐款联盟"的评价、该组织实施的主要项目、治理层、筹资情况、税收地位以及财务状况7个部分。

第一种评估报告，是由于组织没有提供联盟要求的信息资料，联盟无法对其是否符合20条标准做出评估，但报告会在评价部分做出“尽管组织是否接受联盟的评估是自愿的，但联盟认为没有参加评估表明该组织可能缺乏透明性”的特别说明。第二种评估报告会在联盟评价部分详细地罗列该组织不满足哪些标准以及不满足的原因。第三种评估报告在联盟评价部分会说明该组织满足所有20条标准。

联盟的评估报告只对组织是否满足标准做出客观陈述，不对组织做出排名。捐赠者是否向该组织进行捐款，需要其自己做出判断。

四、结语

联盟的评估标准体系具有很多特点：（1）全面性，如在指引的多处指出“如果前述的任何一项活动没有得到实施，那么组织就不符合标准X的要求”；（2）重要性，紧紧围绕组织的治理与监督、财务活动、绩效评价、筹资和信息披露四个主要方面，突出重点；（3）细致性与清晰性，如“大部分董事会成员（平均至少50%）应该出席会议”、“代替出席人员不计入到人数内”、“间接领取报酬的董事会投票成员是指上述直接领取报酬成员的直系亲属（如配偶、父母、兄弟姐妹以及子女）”等；（4）可操作性，如“组织用于慈善活动的支出不得低于总支出的65%”、“如果组织没有经审计或审核的财务报表或国税局990表，联盟就使用可获得的最近的未审计的财务报表计算项目费用比率，方法如a”，考虑到了不同规模的组织和各种情况；（5）证据性，如要求组织提供的资料有各种相关资料及回复相关投诉信件的复印件；（6）严格性，如“缺少任何一个都表明组织不符合该标准”；（7）客观性，联盟只对组织做出客观陈述，不对组织排名，捐赠者需要自己做出判断。

2009年，Greg Chen对慈善组织是否遵守20条慈善评价标准与慈善组织接受捐款数额之间的关系进行的实证研究表明，在控制了一些重要因素后，遵守20条评价标准的慈善组织具有较高的捐赠收入水平。可见，评价标准体系准确反映了组织的内部管理和信息披露水平。近年来，我国慈善组织的透明度低、信息披露严重不足、违法背德行为屡屡发生、相关评估工作薄弱，导致公众慈善捐赠热情由热趋冷，慈善行业陷入困局。为此，我国应加快建立独立的慈善评估机构，构建科学合理的评价标准体系，制定可操作性强的评价指引，突出技术要领，明确分类界限，深入细致讲解，为公众提供客观公正的慈善机构评估信息，以便不断提升慈善事业的公信力，促进我国慈善事业健康持续地发展。

参考文献

[1]沈慎．美国慈善评估机构概述[J]．社会管理研究,2012(2):40-43.

[2]邹世允,吴宝宁．扩大我国慈善透明度研究[J]．财经问题研究,2012(2):15-20.

[3]饶锦兴．美国慈善事业发展印象[J]．社会管理研究,2011(1):25-28.

[4]BBB 明智捐款联盟网站．http://www.bbb.org/us/charity/.

[5]美国慈善捐款报告．http://www.givingusareports.org/.

[6] BRODY E. Sunshine and Shadows on Charity Governance: Public Disclosure as a Regulatory Tool [J]. Florida Tax Review, 2012, 12(4): 175-206.

[7] SZPER R. Playing to the Test: Organizational Responses to Third Party Ratings [J]. VOLUNTAS: International Journal of Voluntary and Nonprofit Organizations, 2012, 23(1).

[8] GARCIS M R, CAVANNA J M, GONZALEZ L. Assessing and Advancing Foundation Transparency: Corporate Foundations as a Case Study [J]. The Foundation Review, 2012, 4(3): 77-89.

[9] SAXTON G, GUO CHAO. Accountability Online: Understanding the Web-Based Accountability Practices of Nonprofit Organizations [J]. Nonprofit and Voluntary Sector Quarterly, 2011, 40(2): 270-295.

[10] JONES K. Nonprofit watchdogs: Do they serve the average donor [J]? Nonprofit Management and Leadership. 2011, 21(4): 381-397.

[11] REBECCA S, ASEEM P. Charity Watchdogs and the Limits of Information-Based Regulation. VOLUNTAS: International Journal of Voluntary and Nonprofit Organizations [J]. 2011 (22): 112-141.

[12] MCALLISTER B, CLAUSEN T, CLAIBORNE M. The Benefactor: Assessing the Financial Performance of Charitable Organizations [J]. The Accounting Educators' Journal, 2011 (11): 19-31.

[13] GORDON T, KHUMAWALA S, et al.. Five Dimensions of Effectiveness for Nonprofit Annual Reports [J]. Nonprofit Management and Leadership, 2010, 21(2): 209-228.

[14] CHEN G. Does Meeting Standards Affect Charitable Giving? —An Empirical Study of New York Metropolitan Area Charities [J]. Nonprofit Management & Leadership, 2009, 19(3): 349-365.

[15] BBB Wise Giving Alliance. Standards for Charity Accountability [S]. http://www.bbb.org/us/standards-for-charity-accountability/. 2003.

The Evaluation Standards System of BBB Wise Giving Alliance

Abstract America's perfect laws and regulations system greatly contributes to the success of its philanthropy; in addition, the third party supervision which is independent of the government also plays an irreplaceable role. BBB Wise Giving Alliance is one of the third party supervision mechanisms. This paper first briefly introduces the BBB Wise Giving Alliance, and then presents the Alliance's Charity evaluation standards and application guides in details. After that, the paper gives a sketch of the type and contents of the Alliance's assessment report. Finally, we summarize the features of the evaluation standards system and put forward some recommendations about establishing our own charity appraisal institution.

Key Words BBB Wise Giving Alliance Charity Evaluation Standards Charity Implementation Guides

引入内部控制的出版企业业绩评价体系研究
——基于出版传媒上市公司的实证检验①

耿云江　车晓丽

（东北财经大学会计学院/中国内部控制研究中心　大连　116025）

摘　要　随着2011年最后一批出版社转企改制名单的发布，我国出版体系中的出版社改制部分全部完成，出版企业日益成为自主经营、自负盈亏的现代市场经济主体，面临前所未有的机遇与挑战。在此种背景下，如何构建科学合理、适应出版企业特点的业绩评价体系，对刚刚完成改制的中国出版企业而言刻不容缓。本文在传统业绩评价体系的基础上，引入内部控制的相关指标，进而构建了过程与结果相结合、经济效益与社会效益兼顾的出版企业业绩评价体系，并以出版传媒等出版业上市公司为例，进行了实证检验。

关键词　业绩评价　内部控制　出版企业

进入21世纪以来，国家高度重视文化产业的发展，“文化产业”一词也在《中共中央关于制定国民经济和社会发展第十个五年计划的建议》中首次被提出，标志着文化产业已经成为中国经济和社会发展的重要组成部分。值得一提的是，在党的十八大报告中，明确指出了“文化产业成为国民经济支柱性产业被列入2020年全面建成小康社会的指标体系”。由此可见，文化产业正处于并持续处于重要的发展时期。与此同时，作为文化产业的组成部分，出版业的体制改革也在持续开展，尤其是随着2011年最后一批出版社转企改制名单的发布，我国出版体系中的出版社改制部分已全部完成。出版企业既具有一般企业属性，又具有意识形态特殊性，需要兼顾经济利益和社会利益，因此面临着更加激烈的竞争。如何抓住机遇，保持自身的健康有序发展，成为我国出版企业亟待解决的重要课题。而尽快完善业绩评价体系，构建更加合理、更能适应出版企业特点的业绩评价体系，对刚刚完成改制的出版企业来说刻不容缓。本文在传统业绩评价体系的基础上，引入内部控制的相关指标，进而构建了过程与结果相结合、经济效益与社会效益兼顾的出版企业业绩评价指标体系，并以出版传媒等出版业上市公司为例，进行了实证检验。

---

①　本文系国家社科基金青年项目（13CGL060）、辽宁省高校优秀人才支持计划（WJQ2011041）、辽宁省社科基金项目（L11DGL020）、东北财经大学会计学院青年学者培育项目“企业集团内部绩效评价模式的构建与实证研究”的阶段性成果。

一、引入内部控制构建出版企业业绩评价体系的原因分析

（一）内部控制评价融入业绩评价指标体系的现实必要性

COSO报告指出，内部控制本身不是目的，而是实现目标的手段。内部控制的目标在于帮助企业实现经营目标、完成使命和减少经营过程中的风险。由此可见，内部控制并不是独立于企业业绩之外，而是与企业经营管理与绩效密切相关，是企业实现经营目标的重要保证。内部控制是否有效，将直接影响企业绩效的高低。因此，企业业绩评价体系有必要在一定程度上反映内部控制的有效性，将内部控制评价融入业绩评价体系之中。这不仅有助于体现内部控制的有效性对企业业绩的影响，而且有助于更加全面、系统、持续地反映企业的真实绩效。

（二）内部控制评价融入业绩评价指标体系的理论可行性

内部控制理论的蓬勃发展，为其融入企业业绩评价体系提供了坚实的理论支持。

内部控制概念于20世纪40年代首次正式提出。此后，内部控制理论不断发展完善。1992年9月，COSO委员会发布了内部控制发展史上里程碑式的文件《内部控制——整体框架》（简称COSO报告），并于1994年进行了增补。2002年7月，《萨班斯-奥克斯利法案》正式生效，作为《萨班斯-奥克斯利法案》中最重要的404条款，要求上市公司必须在年报中提供内部控制报告和内部控制评价报告。2004年9月，COSO委员会正式发布了《企业风险管理——整合框架》（简称“ERM框架”）。ERM框架进一步补充和发展了COSO报告。

根据COSO报告，内部控制是一个过程，它受到董事会、管理人员和其他职员的影响，以期为实现经营的效果和效率、财务报告的可靠性及遵守相关的法律法规提供合理的保证。从内部控制的定义和COSO内部控制框架可以看出，内部控制是一个过程，而且是一个多方向交叉的反复的过程，是影响企业未来发展的过程因素。因此，如果将内部控制作为一个过程因素融入现有的业绩评价体系中，理论中先进业绩评价体系与我国现有的业绩评价体系之间的矛盾就可以得到解决，完善后的业绩评价体系更能够促进企业业绩的可持续发展。此外，内部控制的目标与保证企业的经营效果和效率密切相关，是企业经营管理过程中的一个机制，因此将内部控制融入到业绩评价体系中是合理可行的。

在我国，内部控制理论也正处于蓬勃发展中。2007年3月，企业内部控制标准委员会发布了《企业内部控制基本规范》，自2009年7月1日起首次在

上市公司中实施。随后，财政部发布了《企业内部控制应用指引》和《企业内部控制评价指引》。我国初步形成了完整的企业内部控制标准体系。

二、引入内部控制的出版企业业绩评价体系的构建

（一）构建思路

目前，很多研究认为业绩评价不再是单纯的事后管理活动，而是一个反馈和循环的过程，是为实现企业战略经营目标服务的，应把业绩评价纳入战略管理的全过程。其中，陈鹰、张蕊（2013）提到，Band（1990）认为业绩评价应该形成业绩评价的反馈及循环机制。Maskell（1992）建议，新的一流水平的业绩评价应该随着公司的需要和战略的调整而调整，业绩评价的目的是促进企业管理的改进，而不只是监测。还有学者直接指出，绩效评价本身也是一个过程，并被引申为以绩效评价为核心的绩效管理（梅艳晓，2009）。作为一种较为先进的业绩评价方法，平衡计分卡将企业创造价值的动因——顾客、内部业务流程、学习与成长纳入到企业业绩评价中，体现了业绩评价是过程的思想。可见，先进的业绩评价体系是一个完整过程，不仅应对事后的业绩结果做出价值判断，而且应将业绩评价纳入企业的战略管理中。目前，国内比较权威的业绩评价规范是2002年财政部等有关部门颁布的《企业效绩评价操作细则(修改)》，以及2006年国资委公布的《中央企业综合绩效评价管理暂行办法》。但这两大业绩评价体系均偏重财务指标，可能导致企业注重眼前利益而忽视长远利益，容易产生短期经营行为和利润操纵行为。同时，这两大体系也存在弱化财务指标的监控作用等不足（马英华，胡国强，2009），不能形成有效的反馈机制。

国内学者对于内部控制评价体系与业绩评价指标体系的融合也持不同的观点。梅艳晓（2009）认为内部控制在纳入绩效评价系统时宜采用过程因素纳入法，即以原来的业绩指标结果乘以控制有效系数。马丽英（2011）认为，一方面企业财务绩效评价已覆盖了企业内部控制定量评价，内部控制定量评价与企业绩效评价的融合是“天然”的；另一方面，可以用内部控制定性评价指标取代现有的绩效评价指标。周红燕（2011）研究了价值管理视角下企业业绩评价体系中内部控制指标的选择，并认为，此选择与其说是业绩评价体系与内部控制指标体系的融合，不如说只是内部控制指标的自我完善，应将内部控制指标作为企业业绩评价体系的一部分的核心理念。谭文浩、饶庆林(2010）认为企业必须建立起基于绩效评价机制的内部控制体系，并着重强化绩效的评价与考核。

我们同样认为，内部控制评价与绩效评价的融合是必要的、可行的。具体操作过程中，应将内部控制作为过程因素融入业绩评价体系。具体而言，首先

针对出版企业的特点，分别对其内部控制和以结果为导向的企业业绩进行评价，进而将内部控制评价结果转换为百分数，作为控制调整系数对以结果为导向的业绩评价结果进行修正，最终实现对出版企业业绩创造过程及结果的全面评价。

（二）内控评价指标的设计

内控调整系数的确定过程就是对内部控制进行评价的过程。同时，根据《企业内部控制评价指引》，内部控制评价是对企业内部控制有效性进行评价，形成评价结论，出具评价报告的过程。因此，内部控制评价是对内部控制有效性的评价，是对内部控制的再控制。

COSO内部控制框架、《企业内部控制基本规范》和《企业内部控制评价指引》均指出，建立与实施有效的内部控制应包括内控环境、风险评估、控制活动、信息与沟通和内部监督等5个要素。因此，本文首先从这5个要素出发，本着全面性、系统性、重要性、成本效益及适用性等原则，设计出反映出版企业特点的内部控制评价指标体系的5个准则层。在此基础上，依据层次分析法的基本思想，将5个基本要素层层分解成更细的维度和指标。比如，将内控环境要素分解为发展战略、企业文化、董事会与审计委员会、管理层、人力资源和社会责任等6个二级评价维度，然后在每个二级维度下设计多个评价指标。最终形成包括5大维度、60个指标的内部控制评价指标体系，见表1。

表1　　内部控制评价指标体系

评价维度		评价指标
内控环境	发展战略	1. 企业有明确的长远发展目标与战略规划
		2. 董事会下设战略委员会，或指定相关机构负责发展战略管理工作
		3. 制定并实施了战略管理制度
	企业文化	1. 建立和形成了具有自身特色的企业价值观
		2. 企业价值观与企业发展战略相一致
		3. 全体员工对企业价值观的认同感较高
	董事会与审计委员会	1. 董事会的独立性
		2. 董事会成员的专业胜任能力
		3. 董事会成员与各职能部门主管之间能有效沟通
		4. 审计委员会的独立性
	管理层	1. 管理层具有企业发展所需要的知识结构及素质
		2. 管理层的从业经验
		3. 制定了相关的规范、准则，约束和评价企业家行为

续表

<table>
<tr><th colspan="2">评价维度</th><th>评价指标</th></tr>
<tr><td rowspan="8">内控环境</td><td rowspan="4">人力资源</td><td>1. 有明确的人力资源发展目标以及年度人力资源需求计划</td></tr>
<tr><td>2. 能够通过恰当的渠道招聘员工</td></tr>
<tr><td>3. 各工作岗位人员职责权限、任职条件明确</td></tr>
<tr><td>4. 有长效的员工培训机制</td></tr>
<tr><td rowspan="4">社会责任</td><td>1. 建立了严格的安全生产管理体系与操作规范</td></tr>
<tr><td>2. 有规范的生产流程及产品质量控制和检验制度</td></tr>
<tr><td>3. 有环境保护与资源节约制度</td></tr>
<tr><td>4. 依法保护员工合法权益并积极促进就业</td></tr>
<tr><td rowspan="14">风险评估</td><td rowspan="3">目标设定</td><td>1. 目标设定主体素质高，程序合理</td></tr>
<tr><td>2. 风险评估的目标与企业战略目标协调一致</td></tr>
<tr><td>3. 目标合理且具有良好的预见性</td></tr>
<tr><td rowspan="4">目标保证</td><td>1. 风险评估的目标有具体的衡量标准</td></tr>
<tr><td>2. 公司全体成员认可该目标</td></tr>
<tr><td>3. 风险评估目标能够在实践中贯彻实施</td></tr>
<tr><td>4. 能够对企业风险评估目标的实施进行监督、检查及调整</td></tr>
<tr><td rowspan="3">风险识别</td><td>1. 相关人员善于识别和分析风险</td></tr>
<tr><td>2. 建立了适合企业特点的风险识别程序</td></tr>
<tr><td>3. 重要活动有较完善的风险预警机制</td></tr>
<tr><td rowspan="4">风险应对</td><td>1. 企业相关层级能够及时准确的判断风险的严重程度</td></tr>
<tr><td>2. 能辨别风险发生的可能性</td></tr>
<tr><td>3. 有明确的防范和降低风险的措施</td></tr>
<tr><td>4. 重要活动设定有应急预案</td></tr>
<tr><td rowspan="7">控制活动</td><td rowspan="3">活动控制</td><td>1. 各项活动有规范的内部控制制度</td></tr>
<tr><td>2. 具体事项有规范的操作程序</td></tr>
<tr><td>3. 控制制度和程序能有效执行</td></tr>
<tr><td rowspan="4">业绩控制</td><td>1. 相关领导重视企业业绩评价</td></tr>
<tr><td>2. 有切实可行的业绩评估体系</td></tr>
<tr><td>3. 针对具体事项有全面可量的业绩评价计量指标</td></tr>
<tr><td>4. 业绩评估体系能够有效激励和约束员工行为</td></tr>
</table>

续表

评价维度		评价指标
信息与沟通	信息	1. 建立完善的信息系统
		2. 设立专门的机构负责信息系统的建设、维护与管理工作
		3. 有完善的信息系统维护和安全维护措施
		4. 相关人员能准确辨识所获信息
		5. 企业内部信息的传递渠道畅通
	沟通	1. 各级人员清楚自己的工作职责
		2. 有开放的上下级沟通渠道
		3. 沟通出现偏差时，各级员工都能以大局为重
内部监督	监督主体	1. 设立专门的内部控制监管部门与人员
		2. 监督主体具备相应的能力
		3. 监督主客体间遵循回避原则
	监督组织	1. 内部审计直接受托于董事会，对经营管理层实施监督
		2. 监督组织内部有定期的讨论制度
		3. 对内部控制系统进行持续复核和管理
	监督活动	1. 企业有自我监督机制
		2. 各监督活动有一定的制度安排
		3. 企业重视监督活动的评价及结果
		4. 针对存在的内部控制缺陷，能够及时予以改正

（三）基于结果的出版企业业绩评价指标体系的构建

中国出版企业转企改制后，参与市场竞争，一大批市场主体如雨后春笋般涌现，形成了120家各类新闻出版企业集团，出版行业实力显著提高，企业之间的竞争力和机遇也随之增多。从结果来看，我们的图书、报纸、期刊、音像、印刷等主要产品都实现了空前的高增长，发展速度是惊人的。随着科技的发展，新媒体也得到了蓬勃发展，表现形式也日益丰富，例如互联网、网络电视、数字杂志、数字报纸等。新媒体的出现对传统媒体造成了极大的触动和冲击。中国出版企业在面临巨大机遇的同时，也面临着各方面的挑战。

《企业绩效评价操作细则》和《中央企业综合绩效评价管理暂行办法》是比较权威的业绩评价规范。但是，这些业绩评价指标体系并没有行业针对性，而且多为职能体系经营结果的财务指标，缺乏对企业长期发展能力的评价。这些缺陷的存在，使现有的业绩评价指标体系并不能全面持续有针对性地对出版企业做出合理的业绩评价。因此，针对出版企业的特点，因地制宜地设计一些体现行业特色的指标，符合当前阶段出版企业迫切需要健康有序发展的目标。

出版企业是文化产业的重要组成部分，与文化有着直接的联系。出版产业包括编辑出版、印刷和发行三大基础产业，将初始的知识进行创作、选择、编辑、印刷和发行流通，所生产出的出版物既有经济活动属性又有文化商品属性，因此，出版企业既有一般产业属性，也有意识形态特殊性。作为知识经济的基础产业，出版企业不仅是国民经济不可或缺的一部分，而且担负着传播文化思想的重大社会责任，体现在出版企业业绩评价体系的设计中就是要坚持经济效益和社会效益并重的原则，全面反映出版企业的经济效益和社会效益水平。

在《企业绩效评价操作细则》和《中央企业综合绩效评价管理暂行办法》的基础上，参考部分学者有关出版企业业绩评价指标体系的研究，本着数据可得性原则、客观性原则、适用性原则、财务指标与非财务指标相结合的原则以及经济效益和社会效益并重的原则，来设计出版企业的业绩评价指标体系。本文设计的业绩评价指标体系由经济效益指标和社会效益指标两大体系构成，缺一不可。出版企业业绩评价指标体系见表2。

表2　**出版企业业绩评价指标体系**

<table>
<tr><th colspan="2">评价维度</th><th>具体指标</th><th>指标的说明</th></tr>
<tr><td rowspan="19">经济效益指标体系</td><td rowspan="3">盈利能力</td><td>销售净利率</td><td>净利润/销售收入</td></tr>
<tr><td>总资产净利率</td><td>净利润/总资产</td></tr>
<tr><td>权益净利率</td><td>净利润/股东权益</td></tr>
<tr><td rowspan="4">营运能力</td><td>应收账款周转率</td><td>销售收入/应收账款</td></tr>
<tr><td>存货周转率</td><td>销售收入/存货</td></tr>
<tr><td>流动资产周转率</td><td>销售收入/流动资产</td></tr>
<tr><td>总资产周转率</td><td>销售收入/总资产</td></tr>
<tr><td rowspan="6">偿债能力</td><td>流动比率</td><td>流动资产/流动负债</td></tr>
<tr><td>速动比率</td><td>速动资产/流动负债</td></tr>
<tr><td>资产负债率</td><td>总负债/总资产</td></tr>
<tr><td>产权比率</td><td>总负债/股东权益</td></tr>
<tr><td>权益乘数</td><td>总资产/股东权益</td></tr>
<tr><td>利息保障倍数</td><td>（利润总额+利息支出）/利息支出</td></tr>
<tr><td rowspan="4">发展能力</td><td>销售增长率</td><td>销售增长额/期初销售收入</td></tr>
<tr><td>资本保值增值率</td><td>扣除客观因素后的期末所有者权益总额/期初所有者权益总额</td></tr>
<tr><td>资本积累率</td><td>股东权益增加额/期初股东权益</td></tr>
<tr><td>技术投入比率</td><td>本年科技支出合计/本年营业收入</td></tr>
</table>

续表

评价维度		具体指标	指标的说明
社会效益指标体系	服务规模	地区覆盖范围	根据覆盖区域信息打分
		出版语种	根据语种数量打分
		主体学科类型	根据覆盖的学科类型信息打分
		发行网点	根据发行渠道信息打分
		市场份额	主营业务收入/当年中国出版印刷发行收入
		版权输出	根据版权输出的信息打分
	服务水平	出版工程入选项目	根据出版工程的信息打分
		获奖图书数量	出版企业三大国家级奖项获奖情况
		再版率	根据比率打分
	社会满意度	政府投入经费	根据年报中的“政府补贴”打分
		员工学历构成	根据比率打分
		顾客满意度	根据顾客网评打分
		公益捐赠	根据公益捐赠占营业收入的比率打分

（四）评价指标权重的分配及评分标准

无论是内部控制评价指标体系还是业绩评价指标体系，都是一个多层次、全方位的复杂指标体系，如何合理地确定各级指标的权重，以持续有效地反映企业的经营管理水平，是一个重要且困难的问题。

目前学术界普遍运用的确定指标权重的方法有德尔菲法（张福玲，2013）、层次分析法（高德山，郑少锋，廖正华，2006）。考虑到本文涉及的评价指标较为复杂，且具有突出的行业特殊性，因此主要采用德尔菲法确定指标权重，即通过行业内专家组的多次打分，确定最终的指标权重。张福玲（2013）在《企业内部控制评价指标体系的构建》一文中指出“依据德尔菲法、层次分析法等方法，由各位内部审计专家多次打分，最后求出算术平均数，确定各指标的权重。其中，第一级评价因素的权重之和为1，各级各个评价因素下属的下一级评价因素的权重之和为1。根据重要性原则，对指标体系进行评分时，重要地位的指标对内部控制的影响大，其权重也大；反之亦然”。

1. 内部控制评价体系的权重分配及评分标准

内部控制评价体系共有五个一级评价维度，每个评价维度缺一不可，共同反映了内部控制评价体系的方方面面，地位也基本同等重要，因此每个一级评价维度均赋权重20分，即内控环境（20分），风险评估（20分）、控制活动（20分）、信息与沟通（20分）以及内部监督（20分）。

内控环境下的二级评价维度赋权重如下：发展战略3分，企业文化3分，董事会与审计委员会4分，管理层3分，人力资源3分以及社会责任4分。

风险评估下的二级评价维度赋权重如下：目标设定5分，目标保证5分，风险识别5分以及风险应对5分。

控制活动下的二级评价维度赋权重如下：活动控制10分，业绩控制10分。

信息与沟通下的二级评价维度赋权重如下：信息10分，沟通10分。

内部监督下的二级评价维度赋权重如下：监督主体6分，监督组织6分，监督活动8分。

在评分标准的设计中，评分标准共分为三个档，良好档的分值范围为0.8~1，一般档的分值范围为0.5~0.8，较差档的分值范围为0~0.5。如果某指标完成较好，其评价得分=良好档最高分×权重。如果该指标只是简单提到，评价得分=良好档最低分×权重。如果该具体指标未找到资料，但根据该前后相关指标的完成情况不错，分值为一般档最低分乘以权重。如果具体指标没有设立，或未找到资料且前后相关指标也差强人意，分值为较差档0分。在对内部控制进行评价时，根据具体情况和分值临界值标准，给出合理恰当的得分。

2. 以结果为导向的企业业绩评价体系的权重分配及评分标准

出版企业的业绩评价体系共分为两大体系，分别是经济效益指标体系和社会效益指标体系，考虑到出版业行业的特殊性，需要把社会效益放在足够重要的位置，且社会效益指标也在一定程度上反映了企业的经济效益。所以在对企业业绩评价体系的权重设计中，经济效益指标体系赋权重40分，社会效益指标体系赋权重60分。

在经济效益指标体系中，4个评价维度各赋权重10分。在盈利能力的权重分配中，销售净利率赋权重3分，总资产净利率赋权重4分，权益净利率赋权重3分。在营运能力的权重分配中，应收账款周转率赋权重3分，存货周转率赋权重2分，流动资产周转率赋权重2分，总资产周转率赋权重3分。在偿债能力的权重分配中，流动比率和利息保障倍数赋权重各1分，速动比率、资产负债率、产权比率和权益乘数各赋权重2分。在发展能力的权重分配中，销售增长率和技术投入比率赋权重各2分，资本保值增值率和资本积累率赋权重各3分。

在社会效益指标体系中，3个评价维度各赋权重20分。在服务规模的权重分配中，主体学科类型和版权输出赋权重各4分，地区覆盖范围、出版语种、发行网点、市场份额赋权重各3分。在服务水平的权重分配中，出版工程入选项目赋权重6分，获奖图书数量和再版率赋权重各7分。在社会满意度的权重分配中，政府投入经费和员工学历构成赋权重各4分，顾客满意度和公益捐赠赋权重各6分。

在评分标准的设计中，同样将评分标准分为良好档，一般档和较差档。良好档分值是0.8~1，一般档是0.5~0.8，较差档是0~0.5。根据行业标准和企业的实际情况，用相应档乘以对应的权重，最终给出合理恰当的得分。

（五）引入内部控制的出版企业业绩评价指标评分与得分的计算

在出版企业内部控制评价体系和业绩评价体系设计完成的基础上，构建引入内部控制的出版企业业绩评价体系就比较简单了。内部控制是否有效是反映企业经营管理水平的重要标准，内部控制是内置于企业日常经营管理的一个有效机制，是构成日常经营管理过程的一部分。基于这个基本的理念，将内部控制评价结果以过程因素融入出版企业业绩评价指标体系。

具体而言，首先，对内部控制的有效性进行评价，评价结果是百分制的数值（记作A），将评价结果转化成百分数（记作B=A/100×100%），这个百分数B称作内控调整系数。其次，对出版企业的业绩进行评价，评价结果是百分制的数值（记作C）。最后，由于内部控制是一个过程因素，因此内控调整系数应作为乘数，乘以业绩评价结果，融入业绩评价体系中，对业绩评价结果进行修正。基于内控的出版企业业绩评价结果就等于B×C，这样企业的业绩评价结果就直接反映了企业内部控制的有效性，完善后的业绩评价体系不仅关注当前发展，而且关注未来发展，有利于促进出版企业的可持续发展。具体公式如下：

某出版企业业绩的最终评价得分=该企业的内部控制评价得分/100×100%×业绩评价得分

三、基于内控的出版企业业绩评价体系的实证检验

（一）实证检验对象的选择

随着文化体制改革的深入，中国出版业发展迅速，竞争日益激烈，出版企业纷纷兼并重组上市，借助上市融集更多资金，谋求更多发展机会来做大做强。截至2012年上半年，中国出版业已有32家上市公司，其中在内地有26家上市，在中国香港有5家上市，在美国有1家。在中国内地上市的出版业集团有12家，分别是博瑞传播（600880）、辽宁出版传媒（601999）、华闻传媒（000793）、时代出版（600551）、天舟文化（300148）、皖新传媒（601801）、新华传媒（600825）、粤传媒（002181）、中南传媒（601098）、中文传媒（600373）、新华传媒（600825）和ST传媒（000504）。上市之后的出版企业虽然资产规模快速壮大，但很大一部分并未将出版印刷发行作为主业，引起了行业内的争议。例如，本文剔除了ST传媒和主业并不是出版业的企业集团，最终选取了5家出版业集团作为实证检验的对象，分别是时代出版（600551）、天舟文化（300148）、出版传媒（601999）、皖新传媒（601801）和中南传媒（601098）。通过实证检验，更直观地体现内部控制评价结果对出

版企业绩效评价体系的修正调整作用。

（二）实证检验结果

根据上文交代的指标评分方法，本文首先计算得到各评价对象的内部控制评价得分与排名，以及单纯的业绩评价得分与排名，然后用内控调整系数对内控评价结果进行调整，从而最终得到引入内部控制的出版企业业绩评价结果（具体过程略）。最终的评价结果具体见表3。

表3　**引入内部控制的出版企业绩效评价结果**

项　目 \ 出版集团		出版传媒	时代出版	天舟文化	皖新传媒	中南传媒
基于结果的绩效评价（A）	得分	73.85	78.5	76.15	73.45	83.15
	排名	4	2	3	5	1
基于过程的绩效评价（B）	得分	75.1	83.575	84.55	80.85	74.1
	排名	4	2	1	3	5
内控调整系数（C=B÷100）	–	0.75	0.84	0.85	0.81	0.74
引入内控的绩效评价D（=A×C）	得分	55.46	65.61	64.38	59.38	61.61
	排名	5	1	2	4	3

从表3中不难看出，内控调整系数对绩效评价结果进行了修正调整，直接影响了企业的绩效评价最终评价得分与排名，其中以中南传媒最为典型。在未引入内部控制进行调整之前，中南传媒的经济效益、社会效益综合得分为83.15，名列5家被评价公司之首。然而受其内部控制表现不佳的牵累（得分仅为74.1，名列最后一名），其最终绩效得分为61.61，排名也从最初的第1名滑落至第3名。相反，天舟文化的经济效益、社会效益评价虽弱于中南传媒，但其有效的内部控制不仅弥补了这一不足，而且帮助其成功逆转，在最终排名中排在第2位。可见，引入内部控制的绩效评价体系能够有效引导企业重视过程管理和内部控制，从而促进企业实现长远可持续发展。

四、推动出版企业绩效提升的政策建议

推动文化大发展大繁荣，建设文化强国，需要建设一批品牌卓著、实力雄厚、具有国际竞争力的骨干出版传媒企业。

（一）以效益增长为核心，着力提升企业经济效益

1. 开源与节流并举，提高盈利能力

首先，应继续贯彻执行“走出去”国际化战略，并采取有力措施，在加快和推进重点投资项目建设、形成新的效益增长点的同时，有效利用展会平台促进销售增长，提升企业经营绩效。

其次，应强化选题管理，控制选题规模，加强动态监控，提升选题效益质量。应以重点图书项目为核心，调整图书结构，配置优势资源，构建重点产品

结构体系，使重点图书出版常态化，从而提升图书出版整体质量，提高主业竞争实力。

再次，应及时关注、认真研究国家有关政策，准确把握产业发展新态势，加大项目开发力度，做好项目策划、论证及实施，最大限度利用政策，争取更好的发展。

最后，应通过与下属子公司、分公司合作而实现的集约经营、规模发展、资源互惠、互利共赢，以及加强生产资料集中采购等，降低生产成本。

2. 加强财务管理，提升企业偿债能力

首先，应关注和有效应对财务风险及其变化。随着财务环境的变迁，出版企业所承担的风险会随之发生变化。出版传媒公司必须强化风险意识及时捕捉外部环境变化所带来的风险变动，并采取有效措施予以应对。例如，强化外汇风险管理，科学预测汇率变化及其对企业现金流量的影响；加强应收账款管理，避免坏账发生等。

其次，应正确把握负债经营的度。企业的偿债能力是随着企业自身发展及外部环境的变化而不同的，因此要及时计算出符合企业实际情况的负债临界点，并在达到临界点之前加大负债的额度，这样才会使企业获得更多的财务杠杆效益，提高经济效益。同时，应合理设计、严格控制企业的负债比重与债务期限结构，避免因无法支付到期债务而引发财务危机甚至破产的情况发生。

最后，合理安排筹资活动，保证债务及时清偿。在日常的经营过程中，出版传媒应注意建立并保持良好的信用记录，及时清偿到期债务，提高企业信誉度。同时，应科学管理并使用前期已筹集的股权与债务资金，并在企业遇到偿债危机时加强与债权人的沟通协商，避免因债权人讨债而把企业逼向破产边缘的情况发生。

3. 以出版数字化为契机，加快科技进步和自主创新，提升发展潜力

首先，企业应提高对出版数字化的认识与投入。推进出版数字化，是出版产业适应文化与科技融合的大趋势，加快转型升级，实现可持续发展的必然要求。近年来，紧跟数字出版发展态势，积极打造数字出版新业态，探索转型升级新途径，有了良好的起步。但总体来看，目前出版企业推进转型升级的力度还不够大，步伐还不够快，还没有取得根本性的突破。为此，企业应进一步提高对出版数字化的认识，加大对出版数字化的资金与技术人才投入，推动数字出版的健康发展和企业的战略升级。

其次，政府有关部门应进一步研究出台更具指导性、引领性的产业规划和产业政策，推动出版传媒企业向数字化转型。应制定统一的行业标准，推动数字出版产业的健康有序发展；研究改进著作权保护的政策法规，解决好著作权人版权保护与出版企业纸质版权和数字版权运营脱节的问题；加大国家财政资金扶持，重点支持骨干出版传媒企业的数字化项目建设和产品

研发。

最后，依托科技进步，加大内容创新。应广泛吸纳和有效利用高科技技术与人才，并以此为支撑，调整充实十二五规划，优化选题计划，多出好书、精品书，带动整体质量的全面提升，奠定企业健康发展的坚实基础。

（二）突出重点，提高企业内部控制有效性

1. 建立健全各项控制活动，提高控制活动有效性

公司应以全面贯彻落实修订后的内部控制制度为契机，进一步转变作风，强化管理，严肃流程，提高内部控制活动的有效性。应为企业采购、生产、销售、管理等各项活动建立规范的内部控制制度，为各具体事项设计并实施规范的操作程序。同时，公司高管应重视企业绩效评价，并设计和实施切实可行的绩效评价体系，能够针对具体事项设计并使用全面可量、能够有效激励和约束员工行为的业绩评价计量指标与评分方法。

2. 加强风险评估，有效识别和应对风险

首先，应有效控制选题风险。应通过科学设计、有效实施内部控制制度与流程等，最大限度地保证选题的定位准确、具有鲜明时代性和重大价值、容易被市场接受和认可。

其次，应严格执行风险控制政策，有效防范和应对经营风险。应加大应收账款管理，压缩应收账款总量；应通过严格图书选题、控制生产规模和再版数量等，降低退货率，避免存货积压与浪费。

最后，加强人才管理，防止人才短缺与人才流失风险。针对出版业知识和智力密集的行业特点，以及未来业务规模扩大与出版发行业务多元化发展所产生的巨大的人才需求，出版传媒应通过进一步完善制度建设、严格经营管控、鼓励科技进步、深化用工制度改革等，防范和降低人才短缺与人才流失风险。

3. 完善信息系统建设与维护，加强沟通与交流

首先，应加强出版传媒信息系统的建设与维护。应建立完善的内部控制信息系统，并设立专门的机构或个人负责信息系统的建设、维护与管理工作；应设有完善的信息系统维护和安全维护措施，并聘请专门人员准确辨识所获信息。同时，应时刻保持企业内部信息的传递渠道畅通无阻。

其次，应注重加强信息在企业内部的沟通与交流。应以信息系统为平台和媒介，将信息迅速、准确和真实的传递到企业内部各级人员，确保各级员工都清楚自己的工作职责。应有开放的上下级沟通渠道，避免信息传递的延迟或失真。同时，当沟通出现偏差时，各级员工都能做到以大局为重。

五、结语

（一）指标体系构建后会起到的积极作用

引入内部控制的企业业绩评价体系，体现了出版业的行业特点，经济效益和社会效益并重、财务指标和非财务指标并重，比较全面有针对性地反映了出版业的经营管理水平。内部控制融入企业业绩评价体系，完善后的企业业绩评价体系能够直接反映企业内部控制是否有效，将内部控制对于经营管理的作用融入企业业绩评价过程中，减少了企业经营管理人员只注重短期利益的行为，更有利于促进管理人员注重企业的可持续发展，对提高出版企业的竞争能力，促进整个文化产业的做强、做大有着积极作用。

（二）对该指标体系可能有的局限和注意事项的说明

引入内部控制的出版企业业绩评价体系，虽然一定程度上体现了出版企业的行业经营特点，但并不全面，考虑到数据的可得性，有些指标并未纳入，所以该指标体系有待于进一步调整。本文在将内部控制作为过程因素融入企业业绩评价体系的环节中，采用的是将内部控制评价结果作为一个单一的内控调整系数一次性地融入，对企业业绩的各个方面做了同样程度的调整，这样内控评价对企业业绩的修正作用并不是最大的，是本指标体系的局限性所在，需要进一步研究内部控制每个方面是如何影响企业业绩的，以便利用内控的不同方面有针对性地调整企业业绩评价结果。

参考文献

[1]梅艳晓．绩效评价体系内部控制纳入的过程观[J]．商业时代,2009(22):35-36.

[2]马丽英．内部控制评价指标及其与企业绩效评价指标体系的融合[J]．廊坊师范学院学报:社会科学版,2011(6):100-103.

[3]周红燕．内部控制评价指标在企业业绩评价体系中的应用[J]．商业会计,2011(29):61-62.

[4]谭文浩,饶庆林．基于绩效考核的内部控制体系构建[J]．财务与会计:理财版,2010(10):27-29.

[5]陈鹰,张蕊．面向绩效管理的企业业绩评价发展研究综述[J]．经济问题探索,2013(2):178-181.

[6]马英华,胡国强．我国企业业绩评价体系的回顾与展望[J]．会计之友,2009(2):61-63.

[7]李绮,张静玲．企业内部控制与绩效管理[J]．财会通讯:综合版,2010(10):98-99.

[8]周小燕．我国企业内部控制有效性评价指标体系[J]．财经科学,2012(5):

117-124.

[9]高德山,郑少锋,廖正华．业绩评价体系各层次指标权重的确定[J]．中国管理信息化,2006(8):24-26.

[10] BAND W. Performance Metrics Keep Customer Satisfaction Programs on Track [J]. Marketing News,1990,12(5).

[11] MASKELL B. Performance Measurement for World Class Manufacturing [J]. Corporate Controller,1992,11(12):44-48.

[12] JAMES Q,HOFFMAN J. A Case Study Approach for Developing a Project Performance Evaluation System [J]. International Journal of Project Management,2011,2(2):155-164.

[13] JASMIJN C. The Determinants and Performance Effects of Managers' Performance Evaluation Biases[J]. The Accounting Review: 2011,(86):1549-1575.

Study on the Performance Evaluation System of Publishing Companies by Introducing Internal Control—Empirical Test Based on Publication Media Limited Companies

Abstract As the release of the last publishing company to be restructured in 2011,the restructuring of Chinese publishing houses has finally been finished. The have been being the main body of modern market economy,publishing companies are faced with unprecedented opportunities and challenges. In this context,it's urgent to build a performance evaluation system which is scientific,reasonable and adaptive to publishing companies. This paper firstly introduces the related indexes of internal control. Then it builds a new performance evaluation system on the basis of the traditional performance evaluation systems and combined with the economical and social benefits. Lastly,it empirically examines this new system.

Key Words Performance Evaluation　Internal Control　Publishing Companies